Mary A. Green
4801 S. Milnor Dr.
Memphis, TN 38128

BETTER THAN GOLD

Edited by
CLINTON T. HOWELL

Illustrated with woodcuts by
THOMAS BEWICK & HIS SCHOOL

publishers since 1798

THOMAS NELSON PUBLISHERS
Nashville

✦ACKNOWLEDGMENTS✦

The editor has made diligent effort to trace the ownership of all copyrighted poems. It is his belief that the necessary permissions from authors or their authorized agents have been obtained. In the event of any question arising as to the use of any selection, the editor, while expressing regret for any error he has unconsciously made, will be pleased to make the necessary arrangement and correction in future editions of this book.

The editor has also made every effort to trace the authorship of all selections. When no name appears the authorship is unknown.

Acknowledgment is made to the following for granting permission to reprint copyrighted selections:

ABINGDON PRESS for "Alive Forever" from *Hilltop Verses* by Ralph S. Cushman; "In Thankfulness" from *Halfway Up The Sky* by Jane Merchant, copyright 1955 assigned to Abingdon Press. Used by permission.

CHRISTY & MOORE, LTD. for "Little Roads To Happiness" by Wilhelmina Stitch.

DODD, MEAD & COMPANY, INC. for "Comfort" by Robert Service from *The Collected Poems of Robert Service.* "Death Is A Door" from *A Star In A Well* by Nancy Byrd Turner.

DAVID HIGHAM ASSOCIATES, LTD. for "The Quarrel" by Eleanor Farjeon from *Silver And Snow.*

DOUBLEDAY & COMPANY, INC. for selection from "Midstream" by Helen Keller, copyright 1929 by Helen Keller. Copyright 1929 by Crowell Publishing Company. Reprinted by permission of Doubleday & Company, Inc.; "When She Must Go" from *Dark Cavalier* by Margaret Widdemer. Copyright 1958 by Margaret Widdemer. Reprinted by permission of Doubleday & Company, Inc.

E. P. DUTTON & COMPANY, INC. for "Dusk" from *Shining Rain* by Helen Welshimer, copyright 1943. "Little Roads To Happiness"

from *Silken Threads* by Wilhelmina Stitch, copyright 1930 by Wilhelmina Stitch.

FIRST CHURCH OF CHRIST, SCIENTIST, Maywood, Illinois, for "Easter," "Faith For Tomorrow," "God Give Me Joy" and "Take Time To Live" by Thomas Curtis Clark.

HARPER AND ROW, INC. for "I Think That God Is Proud" from *Poems Of Inspiration And Courage* by Grace Noll Crowell, copyright 1938 by Harper & Brothers; renewed 1966 by Grace Noll Crowell. "This Too Will Pass", copyright 1936 by Harper & Brothers; renewed 1964 by Grace Noll Crowell. "In My Need" from *Bright Harvest* by Grace Noll Crowell, copyright 1952 by Harper and Row Publishers, Inc.

J. B. LIPPINCOTT COMPANY for "The Quarrel" by Eleanor Farjeon, copyright 1933, renewed 1961 by Eleanor Farjeon. From the book *Poems For Children,* copyright 1951. Reprinted by permission of J. B. Lippincott Company.

KING FEATURES SYNDICATE for "Pain" by Elsie Robinson.

THE MACMILLAN COMPANY for "On Growing Old" by John Masefield. Copyright 1920 and renewed 1948 John Masefield. Reprinted by permission of The Macmillan Company; "Alchemy," "The Lamps," "The Song" by Sara Teasdale from *Collected Poems,* copyright 1917 by The Macmillan Company, renewed 1945 by Mamie T. Wheless. Used by permission of The Macmillan Company.

VIRGIL MARKHAM for "Rules For The Road" by Edwin Markham.

JOHN G. NIEHARDT for "Let Me Live Out My Years" from *Lyric And Dramatic Poems* published by the University of Nebraska Press.

MISS THEODORA OXENHAM for poems by her father, John Oxenham.

ALFRED GRANT WALTON for "First Impressions" and "The Sincere Man."

Tenth printing

Copyright © 1970 by Clinton T. Howell

ISBN 0-8407-5224-5

Library of Congress Catalog Card Number: 70-131117

❈CONTENTS❈

BETTER THAN GOLD

Better than grandeur, better than gold,
Than rank and titles a thousandfold,
Is a healthy body and a mind at ease,
And simple pleasures that always please.
A heart that can feel for another's woe,
And share his joys with a genial glow;
With sympathies large enough to enfold
All men as brothers, is better than gold.

Better than gold is a conscience clear,
Though toiling for bread in an humble sphere,
Doubly blessed with content and health,
Untried by the lusts and cares of wealth,
Lowly living and lofty thought
Adorn and ennoble a poor man's cot;
For mind and morals in nature's plan
Are the genuine tests of an earnest man.

Better than gold is a peaceful home
Where all the fireside characters come,
The shrine of love, the heaven of life,
Hallowed by mother, or sister, or wife.
However humble the home may be,
Or tried with sorrow by heaven's decree,
The blessings that never were bought or sold,
And center there, are better than gold.

—Abram Joseph Ryan

DEDICATION

To my wife
Peggy Lou Huffman Howell

PREFACE

One of the purposes of poetry is to show the dimensions of man that are "mid-way in scale between the atom and the stars"—and to make all the days of our life, each moment of our life, holy to us.

In these days when both the atom and the star are within the reach of man, it is more important than ever that the great thoughts of the past continue to lift him above the petty, the humdrum and the disappointing and to bring forth "divine feelings kindred with the skies."

It is that purpose to which this volume addresses itself—to enrich, ennoble, and encourage.

These inspiring selections have guided hosts of our people—young and old—to a fuller life and they can do the same for you, your family and your friends.

The thirty-five sections cover every facet of everyday living.

The masterful Old English woodcuts were collected from many sources and selected for their intrinsic beauty to implement the effective value of the text. We feel that you will appreciate this heritage of superb craftsmanship as you benefit from the blessing of their loveliness.

Clinton T. Howell

ADVICE

Stand straight;
Step firmly, throw your weight:
The heaven is high above your head
And the good gray road is faithful to your tread.

Be strong:
Sing to your heart a battle song:
Though hidden foemen lie in wait,
Something is in you that can smile at Fate.

Press through:
Nothing can harm if you are true.
And when the night comes, rest:
The earth is friendly as a mother's breast.

—EDWIN MARKHAM

This time, like all other times, is a very good one, if we but know what to do with it.

—RALPH W. EMERSON

This above all: to thine own self be true,
And it must follow, as the night the day,
Thou canst not then be false to any man.

—SHAKESPEARE

Never esteem anything as of advantage to thee that shall make thee break thy word or lose thy self-respect.

—MARCUS AURELIUS

To cancel wrong it ever was required
The wrong should be forgiven, and forgot:
Ah, see, how well have thou and I conspired,
Since I forgive, and thou rememberest not!

—EDITH M. THOMAS

Oh, my dear friends, you who are letting miserable misunderstandings run on from year to year, meaning to clear them up some day; you who are keeping wretched quarrels alive because you cannot quite make up your mind that now is the day to sacrifice your pride and kill them; you who are passing men sullenly upon the street, not speaking to them out of some silly spite, and yet knowing that it would fill you with shame and remorse if you heard that one of these men were dead to-morrow morning; you who are letting your neighbor starve, till you hear that he is dying of starvation; or letting your friend's heart ache for a word of appreciation or sympathy, which you mean to give him some day,—if you only could know and see and feel, all of a sudden, that "the time is short," how it would break the spell! How you would go instantly and do the thing which you might never have another chance to do.

—PHILLIPS BROOKS

Do your best loyally and cheerfully, and suffer yourself to feel no anxiety nor fear. Your times are in God's hands. He has assigned you your place; He will direct your paths; He will accept your efforts, if they be faithful.

—CANON FARRAR

THE MOST VITAL THING

When you feel like saying something
That you know you will regret,
Or keenly feel an insult
Not quite easy to forget,
That's the time to curb resentment
And maintain a mental peace,
For when your mind is tranquil
All your ill-thoughts simply cease.

It is easy to be angry
When defrauded or defied,
To be peeved and disappointed
If your wishes are denied;
But to win a worthwhile battle
Over selfishness and spite,
You must learn to keep strict silence
Though you know you're in the right.

So keep your mental balance
When confronted by a foe,
Be it enemy in ambush,
Or some danger that you know.
If you are poised and tranquil
When all around is strife,
Be assured that you have mastered
The most vital thing in life.

—GRENVILLE KLEISER

We are spinning our own fates, good or evil, never to be undone. Every smallest stroke of virtue or vice leaves its never-so-little scar. The drunken Rip Van Winkle, in Jefferson's play, excuses himself for every fresh dereliction by saying, "I won't count this time!" Well, he may not count it, and a kind Heaven may not count it; but it is being counted none the less. Down among his nerve-cells and fibers the molecules are counting it, registering and storing it up to be used against him when the next temptation comes. Nothing we ever do is, in strict scientific literalness, wiped out.

Of course, this has its good side as well as its bad one.

—WILLIAM JAMES

Be of good cheer, brave spirit; steadfastly serve that low whisper thou hast served; for know, God hath a select family of sons now scattered wide thro' earth, and each alone, who are thy spiritual kindred, and each one by constant service to that inward law, is weaving the sublime proportions of a true monarch's soul. Beauty and strength, the riches of a spotless memory, the eloquence of truth, the wisdom got by searching of a clear and loving eye that seeth as God seeth. These are their gifts, and Time, who keeps God's word, brings on the day to seal the marriage of these minds with thine, thine everlasting lovers. Ye shall be the salt of all the elements, world of the world.

—RALPH W. EMERSON

BEFORE IT IS TOO LATE

If you have a tender message,
Or a loving word to say,
Do not wait till you forget it,
But whisper it today;
The tender word unspoken,
The letter never sent,
The long forgotten messages,
The wealth of love unspent—
For these some hearts are breaking,
For these some loved ones wait;
So show them that you care for them
Before it is too late.

—FRANK HERBERT SWEET

ARE YOU FEELING BLUE?

If you wake in the morning and feel a bit blue
And wondering whatever's the matter
*   with you,*
Don't go on a grouch the rest of the day
And make other people the penalty pay,
Just try to suppress it, and put on a grin
And no one will know what has happened
*   within;*
Speak a kind word, yea! do a good deed,
And others your action will certainly heed.
'Twas long ago said, but today it is true,
As you measure to others, it's meted to you.

—JOHN DALE KEMPSTER

For those who seek Truth and would follow her; for those who recognize Justice and would stand for her, success is not the only thing. Success! Why, Falsehood has often that to give; and Injustice often has that to give. Must not Truth and Justice have something to give that is their own by proper right—theirs in essence, and not by accident? That they have, and not here and now, every one who has felt their exaltation knows.

—HENRY GEORGE

WHAT IS GLORY? WHAT IS FAME?

What is Glory? What is Fame?
The echo of a long-lost name;
A breath, an idle hour's brief talk;
The shadow of an arrant naught;
A flower that blossoms for a day,
*   Dying next morrow;*
A stream that hurries on its way,
*   Singing of sorrow;*
The last drop of a bootless shower,
Shed on a sere and leafless bower;
A rose, stuck in a dead man's breast,
This is the World's fame at the best!

—WILLIAM MOTHERWELL

If the day and the night are such that you greet them with joy, and life emits a fragrance like flowers and sweet-scented herbs, is more elastic, more starry, more immortal,— that is your success.

—HENRY DAVID THOREAU

"Laffing iz the sensation ov pheeling good all over, and showing it principally in one spot."

—JOSH BILLINGS

AN INSPIRATION

However the battle is ended,
Though proudly the victor comes
With fluttering flags and prancing nags
And echoing roll of drums,
Still truth proclaims this motto,
In letters of living light,—
No question is ever settled,
Until it is settled right.

Though the heel of the strong oppressor
May grind the weak to dust,
And the voices of fame with one acclaim
May call him great and just,
Let those who applaud take warning,
And keep this motto in sight,—
No question is ever settled
Until it is settled right.

Let those who have failed take courage;
Tho' the enemy seems to have won,
Tho' his ranks are strong, if he be in the
wrong
The battle is not yet done;
For, as sure as the morning follows
The darkest hour of the night,
No question is ever settled
Until it is settled right.

O man bowed down with labor!
O woman, young, yet old!
O heart oppressed in the toiler's breast
And crushed by the power of gold!
Keep on with your weary battle
Against triumphant might;
No question is ever settled
Until it is settled right.

—ELLA WHEELER WILCOX

There's not much practical Christianity in the man who lives on better terms with angels and seraphs, than with his children, servants and neighbors.

—HENRY WARD BEECHER

LIVING

If through the years we're not to do
Much finer deeds than we have done;
If we must merely wander through
Time's garden, idling in the sun;
If there is nothing big ahead,
Why do we fear to join the dead?

Unless to-morrow means that we
Shall do some needed service here;
That tasks are waiting you and me
That will be lost, save we appear;
Then why this dreadful thought of sorrow
That we may never see to-morrow?

If all our finest deeds are done,
And all our splendor's in the past;
If there's no battle to be won,
What matter if to-day's our last?
Is life so sweet that we would live
Though nothing back to life we give?

It is not greatness to have clung
To life through eighty fruitless years;
The man who dies in action, young,
Deserves our praises and our cheers,
Who ventures all for one great deed
And gives his life to serve life's need.

—EDGAR A. GUEST

O, that men should put an enemy in their mouths to steal away their brains!

—SHAKESPEARE

A great man is he who has not lost the heart of a child.

—MENCIUS

Find the work you love and do it in spite of thunder. Be moderate in everything: food, drink, work, rest, and all bodily desires. Serve yourself by serving others. Get money, but don't let money get you. Let no man say of you that you mistreated any living creature. Let your constant aim be to bring a bit of sunshine into the life of every being you meet. Don't worry, laugh often—you will be happy.

To, put your creed into your deed, Nor speak
with double tongue.

—RALPH W. EMERSON

SPEAK GENTLY

Speak gently; it is better far
  To rule by love than fear;
Speak gently; let no harsh word mar
  The good we may do here.

Speak gently to the little child;
  Its love be sure to gain;
Teach it in accents soft and mild;
  It may not long remain.

Speak gently to the young; for they
  Will have enough to bear;
Pass through this life as best they may,
  'Tis full of anxious care.

Speak gently to the aged one.
  Grieve not the careworn heart;
Whose sands of life are nearly run,
  Let such in peace depart.

Speak gently, kindly to the poor,
  Let no harsh tone be heard;
They have enough they must endure,
  Without an unkind word.

Speak gently to the erring; know
  They must have toiled in vain;
Perchance unkindness made them so;
  Oh, win them back again.

Speak gently; Love doth whisper low
  The hearts that true hearts bind.
And gently Friendship's accents flow;
  Affection's voice is kind.

Speak gently; 'tis a little thing
  Dropped in the heart's deep well;
The good, the joy that it may bring,
  Eternity shall tell.

—G. W. LANGFORD

Love the truth but pardon error.

—VOLTAIRE

WILL

There is no chance, no destiny, no fate,
Can circumvent or hinder or control
The firm resolve of a determined soul.
Gifts count for nothing; will alone is great;
All things give way before it, soon or late.
What obstacle can stay the mighty force
Of the sea-seeking river in its course,
Or cause the ascending orb of day to wait?
Each wellborn soul must win what it
  deserves.
Let the fool prate of luck. The fortunate
Is he whose earnest purpose never swerves,
Whose slightest action or inaction serves
The one great aim. Why, even Death stands
  still,
And waits an hour sometimes for such a will.

—ELLA WHEELER WILCOX

When you have closed your doors, and
darkened your room, remember never to
say that you are alone, for you are not alone;
God is within, and your genius is within,—and
what need have they of light to see what you
are doing?

—EPICTETUS

THE POWER OF LITTLE THINGS

The memory of a kindly word
For long gone by,
The fragrance of a fading flower
Sent lovingly,
The gleaming of a sudden smile
Or sudden tear,
The warm pressure of the hand,
The tone of cheer.
The note that only bears a verse
From God's own Word:—
Such tiny things we hardly count
As ministry,
The givers deeming they have shown
Scant sympathy;
But when the heart is overwrought,
Oh, who can tell
The power of such tiny things
To make it well!

—FRANCIS RIDLEY HAVERGAL

That man, I think, has a liberal education whose body has been so trained in youth that it is the ready servant of his will, and does with ease and pleasure all that, as a mechanism, it is capable of; whose intellect is a clear, cold, logic engine, with all its parts of equal strength and in smooth running order, ready, like a steam-engine, to be turned to any kind of work and to spin the gossamers as well as forge the anchors of the mind; whose mind is stored with the knowledge of the great fundamental truths of Nature and the laws of her operations; one who, no stunted ascetic, is full of life and fire, but whose passions have been trained to come to heel by a vigorous will, the servant of a tender conscience; one who has learned to love all beauty, whether of Nature or of art, to hate all vileness, and to esteem others as himself.

—THOMAS HENRY HUXLEY

The most important thought I ever had was that of my individual responsibility to God.

—DANIEL WEBSTER

Use well the moment; what the hour
Brings for thy use is in thy power;
And what thou best canst understand
Is just the thing lies nearest to thy hand.

—GOETHE

Endeavor to be patient in bearing the defects and infirmities of others, of what sort soever they be; for thou thyself also hast many failings which must be borne with by others.

—THOMAS À KEMPIS

Let mystery have its place in you; do not be always turning up your whole soil with the ploughshare of self-examination, but leave a little fallow corner in your heart ready for any seed the winds may bring, and reserve a nook of shadow for the passing bird; keep a place in your heart for the unexpected guest, an altar for the unknown God.

—HENRI FREDERIC AMIEL

TAKE TIME TO LIVE

Take time to live;
The world has much to give,
Of faith and hope and love:
Of faith that life is good,
That human brotherhood
Shall no illusion prove;
Of hope that future years
Shall bring the best, in spite
Of those whose darkened sight
Would stir our doubts and fears;
Of love, that makes of life,
With all its griefs, a song;
A friend, of conquered wrong;
A symphony, of strife.
Take time to live,
Nor to vain mammon give
Your fruitful years.

Take time to live;
The world has much to give
Of sweet content; of joy
At duty bravely done;
Of hope, that every sun
Shall bring more fair employ.
Take time to live,
For life has much to give
Despite the cynic's sneer
That all's forever wrong;
There's much that calls for song.
To fate lend not your ear.
Take time to live;
The world has much to give.

—THOMAS CURTIS CLARK

SIMPLICITY

Be simple, unaffected; be honest in your speaking and writing. Never use a long word when a short one will do. Do not call a spade a well-known oblong instrument of manual industry; let a house be a house, not a residence; a place a place, not a locality, and so of the rest. Where a short word will do, you always lose by using a long one. You lose in clearness, you lose in honest expression of your meaning; and in the estimation of all men who are competent to judge, you lose in reputation for ability.

—WILLIAM CULLEN BRYANT

Envy assails the noblest; the wind howls round the highest peaks.

—OVID

Conquer a man who never gives by gifts;
    Subdue untruthful men by truthfulness;
Vanquish an angry man by gentleness; And
overcome the evil man by goodness.

—THE MAHA-BHARATA

THE TONE OF VOICE

*It's not so much what you say
As the manner in which you say it;
It's not so much the language you use
As the tone in which you convey it;
"Come here!" I sharply said,
And the child cowered and wept.
"Come here," I said—
He looked and smiled
And straight to my lap he crept.
Words may be mild and fair
And the tone may pierce like a dart;
Words may be soft as the summer air
But the tone may break my heart;
For words come from the mind
Grow by study and art—
But tone leaps from the inner self
Revealing the state of the heart.
Whether you know it or not,
Whether you mean or care,
Gentleness, kindness, love, and hate,
Envy, anger, are there.
Then, would you quarrels avoid
And peace and love rejoice?
Keep anger not only out of your words—
Keep it out of your voice.*

True sincerity sends for no witnesses.

Every one should consider his body as a priceless gift from one whom he loves above all, a marvelous work of art, of indescribable beauty, and mastery beyond human conception, and so delicate that a word, a breath, a look, nay, a thought may injure it.

—NIKOLA TESLA

When a man of genius is in full swing, never contradict him, set him straight or try to reason with him. Give him a free field. A listener is sure to get a greater quantity of good, no matter how mixed, than if the man is thwarted. Let Pegasus bolt—he will bring you up in a place you know nothing about!

—LINNAEUS

ON FILE

*If an unkind word appears,
    File the thing away.
If some novelty it jeers,
    File the thing away.
If some clever little bit
Of a sharp and pointed wit,
Carrying a sting with it—
    File the thing away.*

*If some bit of gossip come,
    File the thing away.
Scandalously spicy crumb,
    File the thing away.
If suspicion comes to you
That your neighbor isn't true
Let me tell you what to do—
    File the thing away.*

*Do this for a little while,
Then go out and burn the file.*

—JOHN KENDRICK BANGS

Probably he who never made a mistake never made a discovery.

—SMILES

There is genius and power in persistence. It conquers all opposers; it gives confidence; it annihilates obstacles. Everybody believes in the determined man. People know that when he undertakes a thing, the battle is half won, for his rule is to accomplish whatever he sets out to do.

—ORISON SWEET MARDEN

Truth is God's daughter.

—SPANISH PROVERB

An ounce of loyalty is worth a pound of cleverness.

SEASONABLE LIVING

The wisest men you ever knew
Have never dreamed it treason
To rest a bit—and jest a bit,
And balance up their reason;
To laugh a bit—and chaff a bit,
And joke a bit in season.

MAKING LIFE COUNT FOR GOD

In his letter to the Philippians, Paul writes: "For his sake I have lost everything." This is not the sigh of a sad soul. It is the slogan of victory. It is not an announcement of failure, but a declaration of success. Paul is not posting a notice of bankruptcy. He is advertising an investment that will pay increasing dividends forever. He is not plunged into regret, but thrilled with the ecstasy of joy. He is not asking for sympathy. He is inviting congratulations.

—JAMES I. VANCE

I will speak ill of no man, not even in matter of truth; but rather excuse the faults I hear charged upon others, and upon proper occasion speak all the good I know of everybody.

—BENJAMIN FRANKLIN

He who loves best his fellow-man
Is loving God the holiest way he can.

—ALICE CARY

TRUE BROTHERHOOD

God, what a world, if men in street and mart
Felt that same kinship of the human heart
Which makes them, in the face of fire and
flood,
Rise to the meaning of True Brotherhood.

—ELLA WHEELER WILCOX

A hedge between, keeps friendship green.

Goodness is the only investment that never fails.

—HENRY D. THOREAU

Anxiety is the poison of human life.

—BLAIR

There are some who want to get rid of their past, who, if they could, would begin all over again, . . . but you must learn, you must let God teach you, that the only way to get rid of your past is to get a future out of it.

—PHILLIPS BROOKS

Charms strike the sight, but merit wins the soul.

—ALEXANDER POPE

I'll not willingly offend,
Nor be easily offended;
What's amiss I'll strive to mend,
And endure what can't be mended.

—ISAAC WATTS

Do not let the good things of life rob you of the best things.

—MALTBIE D. BABCOCK

Take yesterday's worries and sort them all
out
And you'll wonder whatever you worried
about.
Look back, at the cares that once furrowed
your brow,
I fancy you'll smile at most of them now.
They seemed terrible then, but they really
were not,
For once out of the woods, all the fears are
forgot.

AGE

Ah nothing is too late till the tired heart shall cease to palpitate.
Cato learned Greek at eighty; Sophocles wrote his grand
　　　　Oedipus, and Simonides
Bore off the prize of verse from his compeers
When each had numbered more than fourscore years.

Chaucer, at Woodstock with the nightingales,
At sixty wrote the Canterbury Tales;
Goethe at Weimar, toiling to the last
Completed Faust *when eighty years were past.*

For age is opportunity no less
Than youth itself, though in another dress,
And as the evening twilight fades away
The sky is filled with stars, invisible by day.

—HENRY WADSWORTH LONGFELLOW

TO AGE

Welcome, old friend! These many years
Have we lived door by door;
The Fates have laid aside their shears
Perhaps for some few more.

I was indocile at an age
When better boys were taught,
But thou at length hast made me sage,
If I am sage in aught.

Little I know from other men,
Too little they from me,
But thou hast pointed well the pen
That writes these lines to thee.

Thanks for expelling Fear and Hope,
One vile, the other vain;
One's scourge, the other's telescope,
I shall not see again;

Rather what lies before my feet
My notice shall engage—
He who hath braved Youth's dizzy heat
Dreads not the frost of Age.

—Walter Savage Landor

As for old age, embrace and love it. It abounds with pleasure, if you know how to use it. The gradually (I do not say rapidly) declining years are amongst the sweetest in a man's life; and, I maintain, that even where they have reached the extreme limit, they have their pleasure still.

—Seneca

SONNET

Sad is our youth, for it is ever going,
Crumbling away beneath our very feet;
Sad is our life, for onward it is flowing
In currents unperceived, because so fleet;
Sad are our hopes, for they were sweet in
sowing—
But tares, self-sown, have overtopped the
wheat;
Sad are our joys, for they were sweet in
blowing—
And still, oh still, their dying breath is
sweet;
And sweet is youth, although it hath bereft us
Of that which made our childhood sweeter
still;
And sweet is middle life, for it hath left us
A nearer good to cure an older ill;
And sweet are all things, when we learn to
prize them
Not for their sake, but His who grants them,
or denies them!

—Aubrey De Vere

There is a peculiar beauty about godly old age—the beauty of holiness. Husband and wife who have fought the world side by side, who have made common stock of joy or sorrow, and become aged together, are not unfrequently found curiously alike in personal appearance, in pitch and tone of voice, just as twin pebbles on the beach, exposed to the same tidal influences, are each other's alter ego.

—Alexander Smith

Age is a quality of mind;
If you've left your
Dreams behind,
If hope is cold,
If you no longer look ahead,
If your ambitious fires
Are dead,
Then, you are old!

Great it is to believe the dream
When we stand in youth by the starry stream;
But a greater thing is to fight life thru
And say at the end, "The dream is true!"

Yes, I am old;—my strength declines,
   And wrinkles tell the touch of time,
Yet might I fancy these the signs
   Not of decay, but manhood's prime;
For all within is young and glowing,
Spite of old age's outward showing.

Yes, I am old;—the ball, the song,
   The turf, the gun, no more allure;
I shun the gay and gilded throng;
   Yet, ah! how far more sweet the pure
Home's tranquil joys, and mental treasures,
Than dissipation's proudest pleasures!

Yes, I am old;—Ambition's call,—
   Fame, wealth, distinction's keen pursuit,
That once could charm and cheat me—all
   Are now detected, passive, mute.
Thank God! the passions and their riot
Are barter'd for content and quiet.

Yes, I am old;—but as I press
   The vale of years with willing feet,
Still do I find life's sorrows less,
   And all its hallow'd joys more sweet;
Since Time, for every rose he snatches,
Takes fifty thorns with all their scratches.

My wife—God bless her! is as dear
   As when I plighted first my troth;
I feel, in every child's career,
   The joys of renovated youth:
And as to Nature—I behold her
With fresh delight as I grow older.

Yes, I am old;—and death hath ta'en
   Full many a friend, to memory dear;
Yet, when I die, 'twill soothe the pain
   Of quitting my survivors here,
To think how all will be delighted,
When in the skies again united!

Yes, I am old;—experience now,
   That best of guides, hath made me sage,
And thus instructed, I avow
   My firm conviction, that old age,
Of all our various terms of living,
Deserves the warmest, best thanksgiving!

It is not by the gray of the hair
that one knows the age of the heart.—

—BULWER

I used to think that growing old was reckoned
   just in years,
But who can name the very date when weariness appears?
I find no stated time when man, obedient to a
   law,
Must settle in an easy chair and from the
   world withdraw.
Old Age is rather curious, or so it seems to
   me.
I know old men at forty and young men at
   seventy-three.

I'm done with counting life by years or tem-
   ples turning gray.
No man is old who wakes with joy to greet
   another day.
What if the body cannot dance with youth's
   elastic spring?
There's many a vibrant interest to which the
   mind can cling.
'Tis in the spirit Age must dwell, or this
   would never be:
I know old men at forty and young men at
   seventy-three.

Some men keep all their friendships warm,
   and welcome friendships new,
They have no time to sit and mourn the
   things they used to do.
This changing world they greet with joy and
   never bow to fate;
On every fresh adventure they set out with
   hearts elate.
From chilling fear and bitter dread they keep
   their spirits free
While some seem old at forty they stay young
   at seventy-three.

So much to do, so much to learn, so much in
   which to share!
With twinkling eyes and minds alert some
   brave both time and care.
And this I've learned from other men, that
   only they are old
Who think with something that has passed
   the tale of life is told.
For Age is not alone of time, or we should
   never see
Men old and bent at forty and men young at
   seventy-three.

—EDGAR A. GUEST

STAYING YOUNG

To be young is not a matter of years. Youth lives forever in a love for the beauty that is in the world, in the mountains, the sea, and sky, and in lovely faces through which shines the kindliness of the inner mind.

It is the tuning into the orchestra of living sound, the soughing of the wind in the trees, the whisper and flow of the tide on wide beaches, the pounding of surf on the rocks, the chattering of brooks over the stones, the pattering of rain on leaves, the song of birds, and of peepers in the spring marshes, and the joyous lilt of sweet laughter.

Youth lives without counting the years in a fluid mind which is open to new theories, fresh opinions, changing impressions, and in the willingness to make new beginnings.

What is it to stay young? It is the ability to hold fast to old friends, and to make new ones, to keep forever our beloved in dear remembrance, and to open our hearts quickly to a light knock on the door.

—CORNELIA ROGERS

THE FLIGHT OF YOUTH

There are gains for all our losses,
  There are balms for all our pain,
But when Youth, the dream, departs,
It takes something from our hearts,
  And it never comes again.

We are stronger, we are better,
  Under Manhood's sterner reign,
Still we feel that something sweet
Followed Youth, with flying feet,
  And will never come again.

Something beautiful has vanished,
  And we sigh for it in vain;
We behold it everywhere,
In the earth and in the air,
  But it never comes again.

—RICHARD HENRY STODDARD

The ultimate evil is to leave the company of the living before you die.

—SENECA

As the bird trims her to the gale,
I trim myself to the storm of time,
I man the rudder, reef the sail,
Obey the voice at eve obeyed at prime:
"Lowly faithful, banish fear,
Right onward drive unharmed;
The port, well worth the cruise, is near,
And every wave is charmed."

—RALPH W. EMERSON

ON GROWING OLD

Be with me, Beauty, for the fire is dying,
My dog and I are old, too old for roving,
Man, whose young passion sets the spindrift
  flying,
Is soon too lame to march, too cold for loving.
I take the book and gather to the fire,
Turning old yellow leaves; minute by minute,
The clock ticks to my heart; a withered wire
Moves a thin ghost of music in the spinet.
I cannot sail your seas, I cannot wander,
Your cornland, nor your hill-land nor your
  valleys,
Ever again, nor share the battle yonder
Where the young knight the broken squadron
  rallies.
Only stay quiet while my mind remembers
The beauty of fire from the beauty of embers.

Beauty, have pity, for the strong have power,
The rich their wealth, the beautiful their
  grace,
Summer of man its sunlight and its flower,
Spring-time of man all April in a face.
Only, as in the jostling in the Strand,
Where the mob thrusts or loiters or is loud,
The beggar with the saucer in his hand
Asks only a penny from the passing crowd.
So, from this glittering world with all its
  fashion,
Its fire and play of men, its stir, its march,
Let me have wisdom, Beauty, wisdom and
  passion,
Bread to the soul, rain where the summers
  parch.
Give me but these, and though the darkness
  close
Even the night will blossom as the rose.

—JOHN MASEFIELD

✦ARTS✦

Raphael paints wisdom,
Handel sings it,
Phidias carves it,
Shakespeare writes it,
Christopher Wren builds it,
Luther preaches it,
Washington arms it,
Watts mechanizes it.

—Ralph Waldo Emerson

Art is more godlike than science. Science discovers; art creates.

—JOHN OPIE

*To me it seems that when God
conceived the world,
that was poetry;
He formed it,
and that was sculpture;
He varied and colored it,
and that was painting;
and then, crowning all,
He peopled it with living beings,
and that was the grand, divine,
eternal drama.*

—CHARLOTTE CUSHMAN

ART AND CULTURE

Art is one of the noblest forms of human culture. The artistic gift is one of the rarest of endowments. While many have the power of artistic appreciation only a minority have the artistic touch and skill. The culture of a nation is infallibly revealed in the quality of its art and in the nature of its artistic life.

The Editor of *The Hibbert Journal*, Principal L. P. Jacks, had a great passage on "The Significance of Art." He said: "Art is the name for the most complete and most intense form of expression of the inner life of man. Its exercise compels a combination of the highest human faculties of conscience, intellect, imagination, feeling, and skill, and becomes successful in proportion as these faculties, are, on the one hand, strong and versatile, and, on the other, charged with the personal life and force of their possessor. When these are present in the highest degree the result of the artist's efforts is the creation of great, lovely and immortal works. The successful pursuit of the Fine Arts demands, as its first condition, the concentration of faculties upon the matter in hand and the yielding up of the entire man to the artistic; and the more complete the self-surrender of the Artist, the nobler will be the result. In all great artistic work, therefore, we have a more perfect self-revelation of the worker's soul than in any other type of human expression."

—JOHN G. BOWRAN

All the arts are brothers; each one is a light to the others.

—VOLTAIRE

Great art is an instant arrested in eternity.

—JAMES G. HUNEKER

From FRA LIPPO LIPPI

*For, don't you mark, we're made so that we love
First when we see them painted, things we have passed
Perhaps a hundred times nor cared to see;
And so they are better, painted—better to us,
Which is the same thing. Art was given for that;
God uses us to help each other so,
Lending our minds out.*

—ROBERT BROWNING

Art comes to you proposing frankly to give nothing but the highest quality to your moments as they pass.

—WALTER HORATIO PATER

If people knew how hard I have had to work to gain my mastery, it wouldn't seem wonderful at all.

—MICHELANGELO

All works of taste must bear a price in proportion to the skill, taste, time, expense and risk attending their invention and manufacture.

Those things called dear are, when justly estimated, the cheapest: they are attended with much less profit to the Artist than those which everybody calls cheap.

Beautiful forms and compositions are not made by chance, nor can they ever, in any material, be made at small expense.

A composition for cheapness and not excellence of workmanship is the most frequent and certain cause of the rapid decay and entire destruction of arts and manufacturers.

—JOSIAH WEDGWOOD

I am happy in having learned to distinguish between ownership and possession. Books, pictures, and all the beauty of the world belong to those who love and understand them. All of these things that I am entitled to, I have—I own them by divine right. So I care not a bit who possesses them. I used to care very much and consequently was very unhappy.

—JAMES HOWARD KELLER

In landscape the painter should give the suggestion of a fairer creation than we know. The details, the prose of nature, he should omit and give only the spirit and splendor. In a portrait he must inscibe the character and not the features.

—RALPH W. EMERSON

ARCHITECTURE AND LITERATURE

Architecture is also symbolic of an epoch. Its relations with literature are of a most intimate character, and it will often be a correct guide in determining the spirit of an age or people. The variety and conflict of opinion in a representative author may render it difficult to catch the prevailing tone of society in which he moves, whereas the expression of a building is one, and therefore unmistakable. The same national genius inspires both the literature and the architecture, and, in consequence, both express the same spirit. Hegel says: "Nations have deposited the most holy, rich, and intense of their ideas in works of art, and art is the key to the philosophy and religion of a people."

Though Greece received her architecture from Egypt, as she did her alphabet from Phoenicia, still all her structures have a characteristic phase that marks them as Grecian. The grace and symmetry pervading column, frieze, and architrave—

"The whole so measured true, so lessen'd off
By fine proportion, that the marble pile
. . . light as fabrics looked,
That from the magic wand aerial rise"—
partake of the innate beauty of her language, and symbolize that harmony in her spiritual and physical development, which produces a corresponding harmony in her poetry and her sculpture, and made Greece supreme in the expression of physical beauty.

Architecture has been called "frozen music," and better still, "the poetry of repose," It were more correct, if not equally pointed, to consider it the stone embodiment of a people's genius—a grand hieroglyphic, which, when rightly deciphered, reveals the spirit in which a people thinks and works.

—BROTHER AZARIAS

Art is not a sermon, and the artist is not a preacher. Art accomplishes by indirection. The beautiful refines. The perfect in art suggests the perfect in conduct. The harmony in music teaches, without intention, the lesson of proportion in life. The bird in his song has no moral purpose, and yet the influence is humanizing. The beautiful in nature acts through appreciation and sympathy. It does not browbeat, neither does it humiliate. It is beautiful without regard to you.

Roses would be unbearable if in their red and perfumed hearts were mottoes to the effect that bears eat bad boys and that honesty is the best policy.

Art creates an atmosphere in which the proprieties, the amenities, and the virtues unconsciously grow. The rain does not lecture the seed. The light does not make rules for the vine and flower. The heart is softened by the pathos of the perfect.

—ROBERT G. INGERSOLL

A room hung with pictures is a room hung with thoughts.

—JOSHUA REYNOLDS

If you accept art, it must be part of your your daily lives, and the daily life of every man. It will be with us wherever we go, in the ancient city full of traditions of past time, in the newly cleared farm in America, or the colonies, where no man has dwelt for tradition to gather around him; in the quiet country-side, as in the busy town, no place shall be without it. You will have it with you in your sorrow as in your joy, in your work-a-day as in your leisure. It shall be no respecter of persons, but be shared by gentle and simple, learned and unlearned, and be as a language that all can understand. It will not hinder any work that is necessary to the life of man at the best, but it will destroy all degrading toil, all enervating luxury, all foppish frivolity. It will be the deadly foe of ignorance, dishonesty and tyranny, and will foster good-will, fair dealing and confidence between man and man. It will teach you to respect the highest intellect with a manly reverence but not to despise any man who does not pretend to be what he is not.

—WILLIAM MORRIS

Art is the gift of God, and must be used unto His glory. That in art is highest which aims at this.

—MICHELANGELO

What is the good of prescribing to art the the roads that it must follow?

To do so is to doubt art, which develops normally according to the laws of Nature, and must be exclusively occupied in responding to human needs. Art has always shown itself faithful to Nature, and has marched with social progress. The ideal of beauty can not perish in a healthy society; we must then give liberty to art, and leave her to herself. Have confidence in her; she will reach her end, and if she strays from the way she will soon reach it again; society itself will be the guide. No single artist, not Shakespeare himself, can prescibe to art her roads and aims.

—DOSTOEVSKI

We ought to acquaint ourselves with the beautiful; we ought to contemplate it with rapture, and attempt to raise ourselves up to its height. And in order to gain strength for that, we must keep ourselves thoroughly unselfish—we must not make it our own, but rather seek to communicate it; indeed, to make a sacrifice of it to those who are dear and precious to us.

—GOETHE

So Art has become foolishly counfounded with education—that all should be equally qualified.

Whereas, while polish, refinement, culture and breeding are in no way arguments for artistic results, it is also no reproach to the most finished scholar or greatest gentleman in the land that he be absolutely without eye for painting or ear for music—that in his heart he prefer the popular print to the scratch of Rembrandt's needle, or the songs of the hall to Beethoven's C minor symphony. Let him have but the wit to say so, and not feel the admission a proof of inferiority.

Art happens—no hovel is safe from it, no Prince may depend upon it, the vastest intelligence can not bring it about, and puny efforts to make it universal end in quaint comedy, and coarse farce.

This is as it should be—and all attempts to make it otherwise are due to the eloquence of the ignorant, the zeal of the conceited.

—JAMES M. WHISTLER

ASPIRATION

Far away there in the sunshine are my highest aspirations. I may not reach them, but I can look up and see their beauty, believe in them, and try to follow where they lead.

—Louisa May Alcott

The true worth of a man is to be measured by the objects he pursues.

—MARCUS AURELIUS

Some men see things as they are
and say, 'Why?'
I dream things that never were
and say, 'Why not?' "

—ROBERT F. KENNEDY

Yet after brick and steel
and stone are gone,
And flesh and blood are dust,
the dream lives on.

—ANDERSON M. SCRUGGS

DREAM-PEDLARY

If there were dreams to sell,
What would you buy?
Some cost a passing bell;
Some a light sigh,
That shakes from Life's fresh crown
Only a rose-leaf down.
If there were dreams to sell,
Merry and sad to tell,
And if ... rier rang the bell,
Wha would you buy?

A cottage lone and still,
With bowers nigh,
Shadowy, my woes to still,
Until I die.

Such pearl from Life's fresh crown
Fain would I shake me down.
Were dreams to have at will,
This would best heal my ill,
This would I buy.

—THOMAS LOVELL BEDDOES

It is not what man does which exalts him, but what man would do!

—ROBERT BROWNING

It seems to me we can never give up longing and wishing while we are thoroughly alive. There are certain things we feel to be beautiful and good, and we must hunger after them.

—GEORGE ELIOT

To live in the presence of great truths and eternal laws, to be led by permanent ideals —that is what keeps a man patient when the world ignores him, and calm and unspoiled when the world praises him.

—A. PEABODY

If a man constantly aspires, is he not elevated?

—HENRY DAVID THOREAU

THE DREAMS AHEAD

What would we do in this world of ours
Were it not for the dreams ahead?
For thorns are mixed with the blooming
flowers
No matter which path we tread.

And each of us has his golden goal,
Stretching far into the years;
And ever he climbs with a hopeful soul,
With alternate smiles and tears.

That dream ahead is what holds him up
Through the storms of a ceaseless fight;
When his lips are pressed to the wormwood's
cup
And clouds shut out the light.

To some it's a dream of high estate;
To some it's a dream of wealth;
To some it's a dream of a truce with Fate
In a constant search for health.

To some it's a dream of home and wife;
To some it's a crown above;
The dreams ahead are what make each life—
The dreams—and faith—and love!

—EDWIN CARLILE LITSEY

MY GOALS

A little braver when the skies are gray,
A little stronger when the road seems long,
A little more of patience through the day,
And not so quick to magnify a wrong.

A little kinder, both of thought and deed,
A little gentler with the old and weak,
Swifter to sense another's pressing need
And not so fast the hurtful phrase to
speak.

These are my goals—not flung beyond my
power,
Not dreams of glory, beautiful but vain,
Not the great heights where buds of genius
flower,
But simple splendors which I ought to
gain.

These I can do and be from day to day
Along the humble pathway where I plod,
So that at last when I am called away
I need not make apologies to God.

—EDGAR A. GUEST

A PRAYER

Lord make me a channel of Thy peace,
That where there is hatred I may bring love,
That where there is wrong I may bring the
spirit of forgiveness.
That where there is discord I may bring
harmony,
That where there is error I may bring truth,
That where there is doubt I may bring faith,
That where there is despair I may bring
hope

That where there are shadows I may bring
Thy light,
That where there is sadness I may bring joy.
Lord, grant that I may seek rather to comfort
than to be comforted;
To understand than to be understood;
To love than to be loved;
For it is by giving that one receives;
It is by self-forgetting that one finds;
It is by forgiving that one is forgiven;
It is by dying that one awakens to eternal
life.

—ST. FRANCIS OF ASSISI

MY CASTLE

Fast within the walls of Somewhere,
On the stream of Bye and Bye,
I can see its turrets rising,
Close against the distant sky;
Through its lofty halls I wander,
While the moonlight sheds its beams
On each treasured thing of beauty,
In the castle of my dreams.

Could I take you to my stronghold,
You would ask that you might stay,
Where the birds in joyful chorus,
Chant the songs of yesterday;
Where the golden light of fancy,
Like some distant beacon gleams,
Guiding on to scenes of rapture,
In the castle of my dreams.

—FLORENCE BORNER

Your old men shall dream dreams, and your young men shall see visions.

—JOEL 3:1

Go confidently in the direction of your dreams! Live the life you've imagined! As you simplify your life, the laws of the universe will be simpler, solitude will not be solitude, poverty will not be poverty, nor weakness weakness.

—HENRY DAVID THOREAU

SO FAITH IS STRONG

So faith is strong
Only when we are strong, shrinks when we
 shrink.
It comes when music stirs us, and the chords,
Moving on some grand climax, shake our
 souls
With influx new that makes new energies.
It comes in swellings of the heart and tears
That rise at noble and at gentle deeds.
It comes in moments of heroic love,
Unjealous joy in joy not made for us;
In conscious triumph of the good within,
Making us worship goodness that rebukes.
Even our failures are a prophecy,
Even our yearnings and our bitter tears
After that fair and true we cannot grasp.
Presentiment of better things on earth
Sweeps in with every force that stirs our
 souls
To admiration, self-renouncing love.

—GEORGE ELIOT

THE LONELY WAY

I'll hide my heart where the white stars burn
 And the clean winds sweep the sky,
That none may seek it out or learn
 Of the dreams that whisper by.

For the great souls choose the lonely way,
 Though tears are dew mist there,
And the fierce white light of the searching
  day
 Lays the scars of the seared heart bare.

Oh, lone and stark the white way streams
 Like the lash of a scourging rod;
But the stars are there, and those whispering
  dreams—
 Aye, and the heart of God.

ASPIRATION

The planted seed, consigned to common
  earth,
 Disdains to moulder with the baser clay
 But rises up to meet the light of day,
Spreads all its leaves and flowers and tendrils
  forth
 And, bathed and ripened in the genial ray,
Pours out its perfume on the wandering gales

Till on the fragrant breath its life exhiles.

So this immortal gem within my breast
 Would strive to pierce the dull, dark clod
  of sense,
 With aspirations winged and intense,
Would so stretch upward, in its tireless
  quest,
To meet the Central Soul, its source, its rest:
So in the fragrance of the immortal flower,
High thoughts and noble deeds, its life it
  would outpour.

—ANNE CHARLOTTE LYNCH

THE CRY OF THE DREAMER

I am tired of planning and toiling
 In the crowded hives of men;
Heart-weary of building and spoiling,
 And spoiling and building again,
And I long for the dear old river,
 Where I dreamed my youth away;
For a dreamer lives forever
 And a toiler dies in a day.

I am sick of the showy seeming
 Of a life that is half a lie:
Of the faces lined with scheming
 In the throng that hurries by.
From the sleepless thoughts' endeavor
 I would go where the children play;
For a dreamer lives forever,
 And a thinker dies in a day.
I can feel no pride, but pity
 For the burdens the rich endure:
There is nothing sweet in the city
 But the patient lives of the poor.
Oh! the little hands too skillful,
 And the child mind choked with weeds!
The daughter's heart grown willful,
 And the father's heart that bleeds!

No, no! From the street's rude bustle,
 From trophies of mart and stage,
I would fly to the wood's low rustle
 And the meadow's kindly page.
Let me dream as of old by the river,
 And be loved for the dream alway;
For a dreamer lives forever,
 And a toiler dies in a day.

—JOHN BOYLE O'REILLY

THE BIBLE

Within this ample volume lies
The mystery of mysteries.
Happiest they of human race
To whom their God has given grace
To read, to fear, to hope, to pray,
To lift the latch, to force the way;
But better had they ne'er been born
That read to doubt or read to scorn.

—WALTER SCOTT

The Bible is God's chart for you to steer by, to keep you from the bottom of the sea, and to show you where the harbor is, and how to reach it without running on rocks and bars.

—HENRY WARD BEECHER

Another fascinating way to study the Bible is to get two or three different translations and read a passage in each of them. This will often open up new meanings. Remember, the Bible is God's book, His revelation to man, and when we go to it with an open mind we will find blessings untold.

—BILLY GRAHAM

Dr. Joseph Sizoo, one of the great ministers of America for a number of years, tells us that when he was discouraged and in despair, one day he turned to the New Testament almost in desperation. He opened it, and his eyes picked up the words, ". . . he that hath sent me is with me: the Father hath not left me alone; . . ." He took those words and said them over, and put them in his heart. He said, "My life has been different every hour since that day. Those words have become the Golden Text of my life—never a day has passed that I haven't said them over." " . . . he that hath sent me is with me: the Father hath not left me alone; . . ."

—T. F. ADAMS

God's gifts put man's best dreams to shame.

—ELIZABETH BARRETT BROWNING

THE UNIVERSAL BOOK

How many ages and generations
Have brooded and wept and agonized
Over this Book!
What untellable joys and ecstasies,
What support to martyrs at the stake!
To what myriads has it been
The shore and rock of safety—
The refuge from the driving tempest
*   and wreck.*
Translated into all languages,
How it has united this diverse world!
Of its thousands there is not a verse,
Not a word but is thick-studded
With human emotion.

GOD'S UNCHANGING WORD

For feelings come and feelings go,
And feelings are deceiving;
My warrant is the word of God,
Naught else is worth believing.
Though all my heart should feel condemned
For want of some sweet token,
There is One greater than my heart
Whose word cannot be broken.
I'll trust in God's unchanging word
Till soul and body sever;
For, though all things shall pass away,
His word shall stand forever.

—MARTIN LUTHER

The whole Bible was given to us by inspiration from God and is useful to teach us what is true and to make us realize what is wrong in our lives; it straightens us out and helps us do what is right. It is God's way of making us well-prepared at every point, fully equipped to do good to everyone.

—II TIM. 3:16, 17

THE WORD OF GOD

The Word of God which ne'er shall cease,
Proclaims free pardon, grace and peace,

Salvation shows in Christ alone,
The perfect will of God makes known.

This holy Word exposes sin,
Convinces us that we're unclean,
Points out the wretched, ruined state
Of all mankind, both small and great.

It then reveals God's boundless grace,
Which justifies our sinful race,
And gives eternal life to all
Who will accept the gospel call.

It gently heals the broken heart,
And heavenly riches doth impart,
Unfolds redemption's wondrous plan,
Thro' Christ's atoning death for man.

O God, in Whom our trust we place,
We thank Thee for Thy Word of grace;
Help us its precepts to obey,
Till we shall live in endless day.

—JOHN HUSS

BIBLE VISTAS

The Bible is not only many books, it is a literature. History, poetry, prophecy, philosophy, theology, oratory, humor, sarcasm, irony, music, drama, tragedy, strategy, love tales, war tales, travelogues, laws, jurisprudence, songs, sermons, warning, prayers, all are here. Was there ever such a literature? The Bible begins with a garden and ends with a city. It starts with a morning followed by a night and ends with a day that shall know no night. It breaks the silence with: "In the beginning God," and it hushes the universe to sleep with: "The grace of our Lord Jesus Christ be with you all." It finds man at the shut gates of the lost Eden, and leaves him before the open door at the top of the road. It begins with: "Thou art cursed," and it ends with: "Whosoever will may come." On its first page is condemnation. On its last page is invitation. At the shut gate stands an angel with drawn sword, and at the open door the Spirit and the bride wait to welcome all who would enter the door which no man can shut.

The Bible breaks at dawn with God's voice saying: "Let there be light." It sets at dusk with God's truth proclaiming: "Let there be life." Between the two speak all voices that can breathe a prayer, plead a need, confess a sin, utter a warning, sob a sorrow, or sigh a penitent's tear. Between the two are the tragedies of hate, the follies of fear, the stain and shame of sin, the paralysis of doubt, the torment of despair, and the choke of the fog that ends it all. Between the two are the stories of nations, the acclaim of heroes, the fall of empires, the rise of kingdoms, the decline of dynasties, the tramp of armies, the crack and crash of civilizations, and the coming of him who is "the bright and morning star."

—JAMES I. VANCE

The twenty-third psalm is the nightingale of the psalms. It is small, of a homely feather, singing shyly out of obscurity; but, oh, it has filled the air of the whole world with melodious joy, greater than the heart can conceive. Blessed be the day on which that psalm was born.

—HENRY WARD BEECHER

My mother's influence in molding my character was conspicuous. She forced me to learn daily long chapters of the Bible by heart. To that discipline and patient, accurate resolve I owe not only much of my general power of taking pains, but the best of my taste for literature.

—JOHN RUSKIN

No sciences are better attested than the religion of the Bible.

—ISAAC NEWTON

DELIGHT IN GOD'S WORD

There is no book like the Bible. It is a miracle of literature, a perennial spring of wisdom, a wonder-book of surprises, a revelation of mystery, an infallible guide of conduct, and an unspeakable source of comfort. Give no heed to people who discredit it, for they speak without knowledge. It is the Word of God in the inspired speech of humanity.

Read it for yourself. Read it through. Study it according to directions. Live by its principles. Believe its messages. Follow its precepts. No man is uneducated who knows the Bible, and no man is wise who is ignorant of its teachings. Every day is begun at its open page. It lies close at hand in all my work. I never go anywhere without it, and in it is my chief joy.

—SAMUEL CHADWICK

The Bible has been the Magna Charta of the poor and of the oppressed. Down to modern times, no state has had a constitution in which the interests of the people are so largely taken into account; in which the duties, so much more than the privileges, of rulers are insisted upon, as that drawn up for Israel in Deuteronomy and Leviticus. Nowhere is the fundamental truth, that the welfare of the state, in the long run, depends upon the righteousness of the citizen, so strongly laid down. The Bible is the most democratic book in the world.

—THOMAS HUXLEY

THE BEST SELLING BOOK

The largest and most important influence of the Bible in literature lies beyond all these visible effects upon language and style and imagery and form. It comes from the strange power of the book to nourish and inspire, to mould and guide, the inner life of man. "It finds me," said Coleridge; and the word of the philosopher is one that the plain man can understand and repeat.

The hunger for happiness which lies in every human heart can never be satisfied without righteousness; and the reason why the Bible reaches down so deep into the breast of man is because it brings news of a kingdom which *is* righteousness and peace and joy in the Holy Spirit. It brings this news not in the form of a dogma, a definition, a scientific statement, but in the form of literature, a living picture of experiences, a perfect ideal embodied in a Character and a Life. And because it does this, it has inspiration for those who write in the service of truth and humanity.

The Bible has been the favorite book of those who were troubled and downtrodden, and of those who bore the great burden of a great task. New light has broken forth from it to lead the upward struggle of mankind from age to age. Men have come back to it because they could not do without it. Nor will its influence wane, its radiance be darkened, unless literature ceases to express the noblest of human longings, the highest of human hopes, and mankind forgets all that is now incarnate in the central figure of the Bible,— the Divine Deliverer.

—HENRY VAN DYKE

Thy Word is like a garden, Lord,
With flowers bright and fair;
And every one who seeks may pluck
A lovely cluster there.

—EDWIN HODDER

He knew the book from A to Z;
His mind had mastered every part;
A fine achievement, but alas!
It never got into his heart.

—C. W. VANDENBERGH

THE BIBLE

Study it carefully,
Think of it prayerfully,
Till in thy heart its precepts dwell.
Slight not its history,
Ponder its mystery;
None can e'er prize it too fondly or well.

Accept the glad tidings,
The warnings and chidings
Found in this volume of heavenly lore.
With faith that's unfailing
And love all-prevailing,
Trust in its promises of life evermore.

May this message of love
From the Father above
Unto all nations and kindreds be given;
Till the ransomed shall raise
Joyous anthems of praise,
Hallelujahs in earth and in heaven.

BOOKS

There is no frigate like a book
To take us lands away,
Nor any coursers like a page
Of prancing poetry.

This traverse may the poorest take
Without oppress of toll;
How frugal is the chariot
That bears a human soul!

—EMILY DICKINSON

The true University of these days is a Collection of Books.

—THOMAS CARLYLE

The main thing about a book is not in what it says, but in what it asks and suggests. The interrogation-point is the accusing finger of orthodoxy, which would rather be denounced than questioned.

—HORACE TRAUBEL

What a place to be in is an old library! It seems as if all the souls of all the writers that had bequeathed their labors to these Bodleians were reposing here as in some dormitory, or middle state. I do not want to handle, to profane the leaves, their winding-sheets. I could as soon dislodge a shade. I seem to inhale learning, walking amid their foliage; and the odor of their moth-scented coverings is fragrant as the first bloom of these sciential apples which grew amid the happy orchard.

—CHARLES LAMB

Literature is the immortality of speech.

—AUGUST WILHELM VON SCHLEGEL

Reading maketh a full man; conference a ready man; and writing an exact man; and, therefore, if a man write little, he had need have a great memory; if he confer little, he had need have a present wit; and if he read little, he had need have much cunning, to seem to know that he doth not.

—FRANCIS BACON

When I consider what some books have done for the world, and what they are doing, how they keep up our hope, awaken new courage and faith, soothe pain, give an ideal life to those whose hours are cold and hard, bind together distant ages and foreign lands, create new worlds of beauty, bring down truth from heaven; I give eternal blessings for this gift, and thank God for books.

—JAMES FREEMAN CLARKE

Book love, my friends, is your pass to the greatest, the purest, and the most perfect pleasure that God has prepared for His creatures. It lasts when all other pleasures fade. It will support you when all other recreations are gone. It will last you until your death. It will make your hours pleasant to you as long as you live.

—ANTHONY TROLLOPE

A house without books is like a room without windows.

—HORACE MANN

Books, like proverbs, receive their chief value from the stamp and esteem of ages through which they passed.

—WILLIAM TEMPLE

When I am attacked by gloomy thoughts, nothing helps me so much as running to my books. They quickly absorb me and banish the clouds from my mind.

—MICHEL DE MONTAIGNE

The books which help you most are those which make you think the most. The hardest way of learning is by easy reading: but a great book that comes from a great thinker,—it is a ship of thought, deep freighted with truth and with beauty.

—THEODORE PARKER

Books are the true levelers. They give to all who faithfully use them the society, the spiritual presence, of the best and greatest of our race.

—W. E. CHANNING

The Love of Books, the Golden Key
That opens the Enchanted Door.

—ANDREW LANG

MY BOOKS AND I

My books and I are good old pals:
  My laughing books are gay,
Just suited for my merry moods
  When I am wont to play.
Bill Nye comes down to joke with me
  And, Oh, the joy he spreads.
Just like two fools we sit and laugh
  And shake our merry heads.

When I am in a thoughtful mood,
  With Stevenson I sit,
Who seems to know I've had enough
  Of Bill Nye and his wit.
And so, more thoughtful than I am,
  He talks of lofty things,
And thus an evening hour we spend
  Sedate and grave as kings.

And should my soul be torn with grief
  Upon my shelf I find
A little volume, torn and thumbed,
  For comfort just designed.
I take my little Bible down
  And read its pages o'er,
And when I part from it I find
  I'm stronger than before.

—EDGAR A. GUEST

BOOKS ARE YOURS

Within whose silent chambers treasure lies
Preserved from age to age; more precious far
Than that accumulated store of gold
And orient gems which, for a day of need,
The Sultan hides deep in ancestral tombs.
These hoards of truth you can unlock at will.

—WILLIAM WORDSWORTH

THE OLD LIBRARIAN

I watched him one day fingering a shelf
Caressingly, forgetful of himself
And all around him. Very well I knew
He could not see the titles, but he threw
A touch of ownership into his hand
As if he still were privileged to command
Their journeyings. I paused to read his face.
In all that sunny, quiet, crowded place
There was not one who wore so proud a look
As if he knew he was with friends, and took
Sweet pleasure in the knowledge.
  Row by row
His fingers greeted them in gentle, slow,
And measured salutation. Long years moved
In memory past those volumes that he loved;
Season of service, outgrown now and gone
Like old books over-read, dog-eared and torn,
Thrown to the dustheap!
  And I turned away
Lest my quick tears should cause him
  some dismay!

—ANNA HAMILTON WOOD

Books are the food of youth, the delight of old age; the ornament of prosperity, the refuge and comfort of adversity; a delight at home, and no hindrance abroad; companions by night, in travelling, in the country.

—MARCUS TULLIUS CICERO

The best of a book is not the thought which it contains, but the thought which it suggests; just as the charm of music dwells not in the tones but in the echoes of our hearts.

—OLIVER WENDELL HOLMES

THE GIFT

Once, long ago, a friend gave me a book
  Of poems—gems, the fruit of many minds;
I read them, thoughtless of the toil they
    took—
  The words moved softly as a stream that
    winds.

But now I know the lines I glibly read
  Perhaps were born of pain—
    a broken heart;
Regret that followed with its stealthy tread—
  The arrow of remorse with searching dart.

For wisdom comes with time's stern
    tutelage;
  The years are keys, unlocking many a door;
And sometimes as I read mist blurs the page,
  Here soul meets soul, a precious golden
    store.

—MARGARET E. BRUNER

I conceive that a knowledge of books is the basis on which all other knowledge rests.

—GEORGE WASHINGTON

When a book raises your spirit and inspires you with noble and manly thoughts, seek for no other test of its excellence. It is good and made by a good workman.

—JEAN DE LA BRUYERÈ

The first time I read an excellent book, it is to me as if I had gained a new friend. When I read over a book I have perused before, it resembles a meeting with an old one.

—OLIVER GOLDSMITH

Books never pall on me. They discourse with us, they take counsel with us, and are united to us by a certain living chatty familiarity. And not only does each book inspire the sense that it belongs to its readers, but it also suggests the name of others, and one begets the desire of the other.

—FRANCESCO PETRARCH

THE LIBRARY A GLORIOUS COURT

That place, that does contain
My books, the best companions, is to me
A glorious court, where hourly I converse
With the old sages and philosophers.
And sometimes, for variety, I confer
With kings and emperors,
  and weigh their counsels;
Calling their victories, if unjustly got,
Unto a strict account: and in my fancy,
Deface their ill-planned statues. Can I then
Part with such constant pleasures, to embrace
Uncertain vanities? No: be it your care
To augment your heap of wealth;
  it shall be mine
To increase in knowledge.
  Lights there for my study!

—J. FLETCHER

Printing is a good business. It is clean, honorable, respectable. It is celebrated as a trainer of men for higher stations in life. It has many inspiring traditions and legends. It combines the need for knowledge of everything under the sun: mathematics, mechanics, language, spelling, grammar, color, composition, salesmanship; there is indeed no limit to the accomplishments that are required of the printer. The printer is brought into contact with all other vocations and professions. No vocation or profession can really exist without the printing-press. From text-books to novels, from pamphlets to newspapers, from tickets to tax-bills, no man can evade the printed word.

—HENRY P. PORTER

The cloak that I left at Troas with Carpus, when thou comest bring with thee, and the books, but especially the parchments.

—ST. PAUL (II Timothy 4:13)

That is a good book which is opened with expectation and closed with profit.

—LOUISA MAY ALCOTT

❧ BROTHERHOOD ❧

The crest and crowning of all good,
Life's final star, is Brotherhood;
For it will bring again to earth
Her long-lost Poesy and Mirth:
Will send new light on every face,
A kingly power upon the race.
And till it comes, we men are slaves,
And travel downward to the dust of graves.

Come, clear the way, then, clear the way:
Blind creeds and kings have had their day.
Break the dead branches from the path:
Our hope is in the aftermath—
Our hope is in heroic men,
Star-led to build the world again.
To this event the ages ran:
Make way for Brotherhood—make way for Man!

—Edwin Markham

A word—a look—has crushed to earth,
Full many a budding flower,
Which had a smile but owned its birth,
Would bless life's darkest hour.

Then deem it not an idle thing,
A pleasant word to speak;
The face you wear, the thoughts you bring,
A heart may heal or break.

What do we live for, if it is not to make life less difficult to each other?

—GEORGE ELIOT

Let us walk joyfully over this earth answering to that of God in every man.

—GEORGE FOX

To be needed in other human lives—is there anything greater or more beautiful in this world!

—DAVID GRAYSON

THE NEW TRINITY

Three things must a man possess if his soul
   would live,
   And know life's perfect good—
Three things would the all-supplying Father
   give—
Bread, Beauty and Brotherhood.

—EDWIN MARKHAM

The equal right of all men to the use of land is as clear as their equal right to breathe the air—it is a right proclaimed by the fact of their existence. For we can not suppose that some men have a right to be in this world, and others no right.

—HENRY GEORGE

WE ARE ALL KIN

We are all kin—oh, make us kin indeed!
Spirit of Christ, we answer to thy call
Our Father makes of us one family
One Infinite Great Love doth claim us all,—
   All one in him!

We are all kin, though wide our various
   ways.
Spirit of Christ, that lives within all life,
Break down the barriers that time has reared,
Heal every wound and end the fruitless
   strife!

—JOHN OXENHAM

A LITTLE WORD

A little word in kindness spoken,
   A motion or a tear,
Has often healed the heart that's broken!
   And made a friend sincere.

THY NEIGHBOR

Who is thy neighbor? He whom thou
   Hast power to aid or bless,
Whose aching heart or burning brow
   Thy soothing hand may press.

Thy neighbor? 'Tis the fainting poor
   Whose eye with want is dim.
Oh, enter thou his humble door
   With aid and peace for him.

Thy neighbor? He who drinks the cup
   When sorrow drowns the brim;
With words of high sustaining hope
   Go thou and comfort him.

Thy neighbor? 'Tis the weary slave,
Fettered in mind and limb;
He hath no hope this side the grave.
Go thou and ransom him.

Thy neighbor? Pass no mourner by.
Perhaps thou canst redeem
A breaking heart from misery.
Go share thy lot with him.

Bigotry has no head and can not think, no heart and can not feel. When she moves it is in wrath; when she pauses it is amid ruin. Her prayers are curses, her God is a demon, her communion is death, her vengeance is eternity, her decalogue written in the blood of her victims, and if she stops for a moment in her infernal flight it is upon a kindred rock to whet her vulture fang for a more sanguinary desolation.

—DANIEL O'CONNELL

And man, whose heaven-erected face
The smiles of love adorn,
Man's inhumanity to man,
Makes countless thousands mourn.

—ROBERT BURNS

"HULLO!"

W'en you see a man in woe,
Walk right up and say "hullo!"
Say "hullo," and' "how d'ye do!"
"How's the world a usin' you?"
Slap the fellow on his back,
Bring your han' down with a whack;
Waltz right up, an' don't go slow,
Grin an' shake an' say "hullo!"

Is he clothed in rags? O sho!
Walk right up an' say "hullo!"
Rags is but a cotton roll
Jest for wrappin' up a soul;
An' a soul is worth a true
Hale an' hearty "how d'ye do!"
Don't wait for the crowd to go,
Walk right up and say "hullo!"

W'en big vessels meet, they say,
They saloot an' sail away.

Jest the same are you an' me,
Lonesome ships upon a sea:
Each one sailing his own jog
For a port beyond the fog.
Let your speakin' trumpet blow,
Lift your horn an' cry "hullo!"

Say "hullo," an' "how d'ye do!"
Other folks are good as you.
W'en you leave your house of clay,
Wanderin' in the Far-Away,
W'en you travel through the strange
Country t'other side the range,
Then the souls you've cheered will know
Who you be, an' say "hullo!"

—SAM WALTER FOSS

The joys and sorrows of others are ours as much as theirs, and in proper time as we feel this and learn to live so that the whole world shares the life that flows through us, do our minds learn the Secret of Peace.

—ANNIE BESANT

Try to care about something in this vast world besides the gratification of small selfish desires. Try to care for what is best in thought and action—something that is good apart from the accidents of your own lot. Look on other lives besides your own. See what their troubles are, and how they are borne.

—GEORGE ELIOT

The responsibility of tolerance lies with those who have the wider vision.

—GEORGE ELIOT

GIVING

God gives us joy that we may give;
He gives us joy that we may share;
Sometimes He gives us loads to lift
That we may learn to bear.
For life is gladder when we give,
And love is sweeter when we share,
And heavy loads rest lightly too
When we have learned to bear.

We have committed the Golden Rule to memory; let us now commit it to life.

We have preached Brotherhood for centuries; we now need to find a material basis for brotherhood. Government must be made the organ of Fraternity—a working-form for comrade-love.

Think on this—work on this.

—EDWIN MARKHAM

BROTHERS ALL

We're brothers all, whate'er the place,
Brothers whether in rags or lace,
Brothers all, by the good Lord's grace.

Some may sit in a royal hall,
Some may dwell where the rooms are small,
But under the skin we are brothers all.

Some may toil 'neath the burning sun,
Some may dream where the waters run,
But we're brothers all when the day is done.

By the sun that shines and the rains that fall,
By the shadows flung on the garden wall,
By the good Lord's grace, we are brothers all.

By the hurt that comes and the falling tear,
By the common grief at the silent bier,
And the grave that awaits,
    we are brothers here.

—EDGAR A. GUEST

There is one place of refuge in this planet for any man—that is in another man's heart. To live is to make of one's heart a swinging door.

—HOWARD THURMAN

It is not enough to say: "Be brotherly." It does not suffice to long for such comradeship, or even to predict it. We may sing with Robert Burns:

"It's coming yet for a' that,
That man to man the warl' o'er
Shall brithers be, and a' that."

But the song will not work the miracle. It is not enough to call to a barren bed of desert sand: "Be flushed with a living stream," but if you can open a spring in the hills, you may have a river that will not run dry. If we are to have brotherhood, we must have people who are brotherly, who have the fountain of brotherhood in their hearts, who have discovered that they are brothers because they have found that God is their Father. Then when you tell them to be brotherly, they will not stare at you and go on tearing at each others' throats. Then when you preach the Golden Rule, you will find that in the redeemed life resides the power to translate the rule from a stagy motto into a transforming experience.

—JAMES I. VANCE

We are all of us fellow-passengers on the same planet and we are all of us equally responsible for the happiness and the well-being of the world in which we happen to live.

—HENDRIK WILLEM VAN LOON

Behave toward every one as if receiving a great guest.

—CONFUCIUS

BROTHERHOOD OF MAN

In ages past, by act of God,
A world for man was made.
Great treasures He bestowed on us,
And a master plan He laid.

He gave us brothers, one and all,
Our blessings for to share.
He thought of you, He thought of me
He asked us but to care.

This upward look and will to give,
With no thought of reward,
Is gratitude for love received,
From a kind and gracious Lord.

So give us strength and will to do
And a heart brimful for others.
And when we pray and ask for aid,
May it be for all our brothers.

—RAYMOND CHEETHAM

❖ CHALLENGE ❖

We men of earth have here the stuff
Of Paradise—we have enough!
We need no other thing to build
The stairs unto the unfulfilled . . .
Here on the paths of every day—
Here on the common human way—
Is all the busy gods would take
To build a heaven, to mould and make
New Edens. Ours is the stuff sublime
To build Eternity in time.

—Edwin Markham

Honest good humor is the oil and wine of a merry meeting, and there is no jovial companionship equal to that where the jokes are rather small and the laughter abundant.

—WASHINGTON IRVING

CALL TO JOY

Away with pouting and with pining,
So long as youth and springtime bloom!
Why, when life's morning sun is shining,
Why should the brow be clothed in
gloom?

On every road the Pleasures greet us,
As through life's pilgrimage we roam;
With wreaths of flowers they come to meet
us,
And lead us onward to our home.

The rivulet purls and plays as lightly
As when it danced to Eden's breeze;
The lovely moon still beams as brightly
As when she shone through Adam's trees.

—LUDWIG H. C. HÖLTY

DO NOT LET YOURSELF

WORRY *when you are doing your best.*
HURRY *when success depends upon*
accuracy.
THINK *evil of a friend until you have*
the facts.
BELIEVE *a thing is impossible without*
trying it.
WASTE *time on peevish and peeving*
matters.
IMAGINE *that good intentions are a*
satisfying excuse.
HARBOR *bitterness in your soul toward*
God and man.

Five great enemies to peace inhabit with us, namely, avarice, ambition, envy, anger, and pride. If these enemies were to be banished, we should infallibly enjoy perpetual peace.

—PETRARCH

PHILOSOPHY

Laugh a little—love a little
As you go your way!
Work a little—play a little,
Do this every day!

Give a little—take a little,
Never mind a frown—
Make your smile a welcomed thing
All around the town!

Laugh a little—love a little
Skies are always blue!
Every cloud has silver linings—
But it's up to you!

—PHILLIPS

THE LAST FIVE MINUTES

If we discovered," the late Christopher Morley observed, "that we had only five minutes left to say all we wanted to say, every telephone booth would be occupied by people calling other people to stammer that they loved them."

Why wait until the last five minutes?

I am only one,
But still I am one.
I cannot do everything,
But still I can do something;
And because I cannot do everything
I will not refuse to do the something
that I can do.

—EDWARD EVERETT HALE

ENCOURAGEMENT

I hold him dearest who aspires
To kindle in my heart the fires
Of best desires.

I hold the man of all most dear
Who, when I stumble, draweth near
With word of cheer.

I hold that man of best interests
Who giveth me not paltry pence,
But confidence.

For there are men who quick caress
Will give to laurel-crowned success—
To nothing less.

But, oh, how dearer far are they
Who help me on the upward way
When skies are gray.

If so it be that I attain
The mountain peak, and leave the plain
And paths of pain,
My prayers shall first be upward sent
For those dear frieds of mine who lent
Encouragement.

—DOUGLAS MALLOCH

If we wish to be just judges of all things, let us first persuade ourselves of this: that there is not one of us without fault; no man is found who can acquit himself; and he who calls himself innocent does so with reference to a witness, and not to his conscience.

—SENECA

Judge not thy friend until thou standest in his place.

—RABBI HILLEL

Nothing to live for? Soul, that cannot be,
Though when hearts break, the world seems
  emptiness;
But unto thee I bring in thy distress
A message, born of love and sympathy,
And it may prove, O soul, the golden key
To all things beautiful and good, and bless

Thy life which looks to thee so comfortless!
This is the word: "Some one hath need of
  thee."

—EMMA C. DOWD

WHAT IS A MAN

What is a man
If his chief good and market of his time
Be but to sleep and feed? a beast, no more.
Sure, he that made us with such large
  discourse
Looking before and after, gave us not
That capability and god-like reason
To fust in us unused.

—SHAKESPEARE

Born in an age and country in which knowledge and opportunity abound as never before, how can you sit with folded hands, asking God's aid in work for which He has already given you the necessary faculties and strength? Even when the Chosen People supposed their progress checked by the Red Sea, and their leader paused for Divine help, the Lord said, "Wherefore criest thou unto me? Speak unto the children of Israel, *that they go forward.*"

—O. S. MARDEN

Do not let the good things of life rob you of the best things.

—MALTBIE D. BABCOCK

The greater man, the greater courtesy.

—ALFRED TENNYSON

Wouldst shape a noble life? Then cast
No backward glances toward the past,
And though somewhat be lost and gone,
Yet do thou act as one new-born;
What each day needs, that shalt thou ask,
Each day will set its proper task.

—GOETHE

SEE IT THROUGH

When you're up against a trouble,
Meet it squarely, face to face;
Lift your chin and set your shoulders,
Plant your feet and take a brace.
When it's vain to try to dodge it,
Do the best that you can do;
You may fail, but you may conquer,
See it through!

Black may be the clouds about you
And your future may seem grim,
But don't let your nerve desert you;
Keep yourself in fighting trim.
If the worst is bound to happen,
Spite of all that you can do,
Running from it will not save you,
See it through!

Even hope may seem but futile,
When with troubles you're beset,
But remember you are facing
Just what other men have met.
You may fail, but fall still fighting;
Don't give up, whate'er you do;
Eyes front, head high to the finish.
See it through!

—EDGAR A. GUEST

N othing is impossible to a willing heart.

—THOMAS HEYWOOD

AT THE DOOR

Children are at the door.
Shall I let them in?
If I let them in, I can do no more the
work I love;
If I bid them go, I then can work no more
For thinking that I should have let them
in
And worked no more.

Duty is at the door.
Shall I let her in?
If I let her in, my life must change its
course;
If I bid her go, my life will change itself
For thinking that I should have let her in
And followed her.

Love is at the door.
Shall I let him in?
If I let him in, my heart's content may cease;
If I bid him go, I may weap bitter tears
For thinking that I should have to let him in
to wound me
With an arrow from his sheath.

—LILLIE FULLER MERRIAM

THE GOSPEL ACCORDING TO YOU

There's a sweet old story translated for men,
But writ in the long, long ago—
The Gospel according to Mark, Luke, and
and John—
Of Christ and His mission below.
You are writing a gospel, a chapter each day,
By deeds that you do, by words that you
say.
Men read what you write, whether faithless
or true.
Say, what is the gospel according to you?

Men read and admire the gospel of Christ,
With its love so unfailing and true;
But what do they say, and what do they
think
Of the gospel according to you?

'Tis a wonderful story, that gospel of love,
As it shines in the Christ-life divine,
And oh, that its truth might be told again
In the story of your life and mine!

Unselfish mirrors in every scene,
Love blossoms on every sod,
And back from its vision the heart comes to
tell
The wonderful goodness of God.

You are writing each day a letter to men;
Take care that the writing is true.
'Tis the only gospel some men will read,
That gospel according to you.

T he wise and active conquer difficulties by daring to attempt them. Slothfulness and folly shiver and shrink at the sight of toil and hazard, and make the impossibility they fear.

—NICHOLAS ROWE

HEROES

They dared beyond their strength, hazarded beyond their judgment, and in extremities were of excellent hope.

—THUCYDIDES

The ideal man bears the accidents of life with dignity and grace, making the best of circumstances.

—ARISTOTLE

So to conduct one's life as to realize oneself —this seems to me the highest attainment possible to a human being. It is the task of one and all of us, but most of us bungle it.

—HENRIK IBSEN

No man ever sank under the burden of the day. It is when tomorrow's burden is added to the burden of today, that the weight is more than a man can bear.

—GEORGE MACDONALD

Climb far, your goal the sky, your aim the star.

To believe in something not yet proved and to underwrite it with our lives; it is the only way we can leave the future open.

—LILLIAN SMITH

Objects which are usually the motives of our travels by land and by sea are often overlooked and neglected if they lie under our eye. . . . We put off from time to time going and seeing what we know we have an opportunity of seeing when we please.

—PLINY THE YOUNGER

Go to your bosom;
Knock there, and ask your heart what it doth
know . . .

SHAKESPEARE

My share of the work of the world may be limited, but the fact that it is work makes it precious. Darwin could work only half an hour at a time; yet in many digilent half-hours he laid anew the foundations of philosophy.

Green, the historian, tells us that the world is moved not only by the mighty shoves of the heroes, but also by the aggregate of the tiny pushes of each honest worker.

—HELEN KELLER

TEAM WORK

It's all very well to have courage and skill
And it's fine to be counted a star,
But the single deed with its touch of thrill
Doesn't tell the man you are;
For there's no lone hand in the game we
play,
We must work to a bigger scheme,
And the thing that counts in the world
to-day
Is, How do you pull with the team?

They may sound your praise and call you
great,
They may single you out for fame,
But you must work with your running mate
Or you'll never win the game;
Oh, never the work of life is done
By the man with a selfish dream,
For the battle is lost or the battle is won
By the spirit of the team.

You may think it fine to be praised for skill,
But a greater thing to do
Is to set your mind and set your will
On the goal that's just in view;
It's helping your fellowman to score
When his chances hopeless seem;
Its forgetting self till the game is o'er
And fighting for the team.

—EDGAR A. GUEST

I'll not willingly offend,
Nor be easily offended;
What's amiss I'll strive to mend,
And endure what can't be mended.

—ISAAC WATTS

THE CRITIC

A little seed lay on the ground,
And soon began to sprout;
"Now, which of all the flowers around,"
It mused, "shall I come out?
The lily's face is fair and proud,
But just a trifle cold;
The rose, I think, is rather loud,
And then, its fashion's old.
The violet is all very well,
But not a flower I'd choose;
Nor yet the Canterbury bell—
I never cared for blues."
And so it critized each flower,
This supercilious seed,
Until it woke one summer morn,
And found itself—a weed.

DAY BY DAY

Charge not thyself with the weight of a year,
Child of the Master, faithful and dear:
Choose not the cross for the coming week,
For that is more than He bids thee seek.

Bend not thine arms for tommorrow's load;
Thou mayest leave that to thy gracious God.
"Daily," only He saith to thee,
"Take up thy cross and follow Me."

IT CAN BE DONE

The man who misses all the fun
Is he who says, "It can't be done."
In solemn pride he stands aloof
And greets each venture with reproof.
Had he the power he'd efface
The history of the human race;
We'd have no radio or motor cars,
No streets lit by electric stars;
No telegraph nor telephone,
We'd linger in the age of stone.
The world would sleep if things were run
By men who say "It can't be done."

Intelligence and courtesy not always are
    combined;
Often in a wooden house, a golden room we
    find.

—HENRY WADSWORTH LONGFELLOW

YOU NEVER CAN TELL

You never can tell when you send a word
    Like an arrow shot from a bow
By an archer blind, be it cruel or kind,
    Just where it may chance to go.
It may pierce the breast of your dearest
        friend,
    Tipped with its poison or balm,
To a stranger's heart in life's great mart
    It may carry its pain or its calm.

You never can tell when you do an act
    Just what the result will be,
But with every deed you are sowing a seed,
    Though the harvest you may not see.
Each kindly act is an acorn dropped
    In God's productive soil;
You may not know, but the tree shall grow
    With shelter for those who toil.

You never can tell what your thoughts will do
    In bringing you hate or love,
For thoughts are things, and their airy wings
    Are swifter than carrier doves.
They follow the law of the universe—
    Each thing must create its kind,
And they speed o'er the track to bring you
        back
    Whatever went out from your mind.

—ELLA WHEELER WILCOX

SMALL SOUL

The woodchuck told it all about.
    "I'm going to build a dwelling
Six stories high, up to the sky!"
    He never tired of telling.

He dug the cellar smooth and well
    But made no more advances;
That lovely hole so pleased his soul
    And satisfied his fancies.

—L. J. BRIDGMAN

K nowledge is essential to conquest; only
    according to our ignorance are we helpless.
Thought creates character. Character can
dominate conditions. Will creates circumstances and environment.

—ANNIE BESANT

CHARACTER

$\mathfrak{C}$ ivilization can only revive when there shall come into being in a number of individuals a new tone of mind, independent of the prevalent one among the crowd, and in opposition to it—a tone of mind which will gradually win influence over the collective one, and in the end determine its character. Only an ethical movement can rescue us from barbarism, and the ethical comes into existence only in individuals.

—ALBERT SCHWEITZER

others beg their way upward; bear the pain of disappointed hopes, while others gain the accomplishment of theirs by flattery; forego the gracious pressure of the hand for which others cringe and crawl. Wrap yourself in your own virtue, and seek a friend and your daily bread. If you have in such a course grown gray with unblenched honor, bless God, and die.

—HEINZELMANN

Take care that the divinity within you has a creditable charge to preside over.

—MARCUS AURELIUS

THE TRUE MAN

This is the sort of a man was he:
True when it hurt him a lot to be;
Tight in a corner an' knowin' a lie
Would have helped him out, but he wouldn't
　　buy
His freedom there in so cheap a way—
He told the truth though he had to pay.

Honest! Not in the easy sense,
When he needn't worry about expense—
We'll all play square when it doesn't count
And the sum at stake's not a large amount—
But he was square when the times were bad,
An' keepin' his word took all he had.

Honor is something we all profess,
But most of us cheat—some more,
　　some less—
An' the real test isn't the way we do
When there isn't a pinch in either shoe;
It's whether we're true to our best or not
When the right thing's certain to hurt a lot.

That is the sort of a man was he:
Straight when it hurt him a lot to be;
Times when a lie would have paid him well,
No matter the cost, the truth he'd tell;
An' he'd rather go down to a drab defeat
Than save himself if he had to cheat.

—EDGAR A. GUEST

Be and continue poor, young man, while others around you grow rich by fraud and disloyalty; be without place or power, while

MORE PRECIOUS

Truth, be more precious to me than eyes
Of happy love; burn hotter in my throat
Than passion, and possess me like my pride;
More sweet than freedom, more desired than
　　joy,
More sacred than the pleasing of a friend.

—MAX EASTMAN

The measure of a man's real character is what he would do if he knew he would never be found out.

—THOMAS MACAULEY

ARISTOCRACY

The pedigree of honey
Does not concern the bee;
A clover, any time, to him
　　Is aristocracy.

—EMILY DICKINSON

I think, therefore I am.

—RENÉ DESCARTES

DEMETRIUS

It was a saying of his that to friends in prosperity we should go when invited, but to those in misfortune unbidden.

When told that the Athenians had thrown

down his statues, he answered, "But not my character, for which they erected them."

PEOPLE LIKED HIM

People liked him, not because
 He was rich or known to fame;
He had never won applause
 As a star in any game.
His was not a brilliant style,
 His was not a forceful way,
But he had a gentle smile
 And a kindly word to say.

Never arrogant or proud,
 On he went with manner mild;
Never quarrelsome or loud,
 Just as simple as a child;
Honest, patient, brave and true:
 Thus he lived from day to day,
Doing what he found to do
 In a cheerful sort of way.

Wasn't one to boast of gold
 Or belittle it with sneers,
Didn't change from hot to cold,
 Kept his friends throughout the years,
Sort of man you like to meet
 Any time or any place.
There was always something sweet
 And refreshing in his face.

Sort of man you'd like to be:
 Balanced well and truly square;
Patient in adversity,
 Generous when his skies were fair.
Never lied to friend or foe,
 Never rash in word or deed,
Quick to come and slow to go
 In a neighbor's time of need.

Never rose to wealth or fame,
 Simply lived, and simply died,
But the passing of his name
 Left a sorrow, far and wide.
Not for glory he'd attained,
 Nor for what he had of pelf,
Were the friends that he had gained,
 But for what he was himself.

—EDGAR A. GUEST

I would compromise war. I would compromise glory. I would compromise every-
thing at that point where hate comes in, where misery comes in, where love ceases to be love, and life begins its descent into the valley of the shadow of death. But I would not compromise Truth. I would not compromise the right.

—HENRY WATTERSON

TRIBUTE ON THE PASSING OF A VERY REAL PERSON

People are of two kinds, and he
Was the kind I'd like to be.
Some preach their virtues, and a few
Express their lives by what they do;
That sort was he. No flowery phrase
Or glibly spoken word of praise
Won friends for him. He wasn't cheap
Or shallow, but his course ran deep,
And it was pure. You know the kind.
Not many in life you find
Whose deeds outrun their words so far
That more than what they seem, they are.

A GOOD NAME

Iago. Good name in man and woman,
 dear my lord,
Is the immediate jewel of their souls:
Who steals my purse steals trash;
 'tis something, nothing;
'Twas mine, 'tis his, and has been slave to
 thousands.
But he that filches from me my good name
Robs me of that which not enriches him
And makes me poor indeed.

—SHAKESPEARE

CONVERSATION

For good or ill, your conversation is your advertisement. Every time you open your mouth, you let men look into your mind.

—BRUCE BARTON

Self love, my liege, is not so vile a sin
As self neglecting.

—SHAKESPEARE

Some day, in years to come, you will be wrestling with the great temptation, or trembling under the great sorrow of your life. But the real struggle is here, now, in these quiet weeks. Now it is being decided whether, in the day of your supreme sorrow or temptation, you shall miserably fail or gloriously conquer. Character cannot be made except by a steady, long-continued process.

—PHILLIPS BROOKS

PROFIT AND LOSS

I counted dollars while God counted crosses;
I counted gains while He counted losses!
I counted my worth by the things gained in
    store,
But He sized me up by the scars that I bore;
I coveted honors and sought for degrees;
He wept as He counted the hours on
    my knees.
And I never knew till one day by a grave
How vain are the things that we spend
    life to save.
I did not yet know until Jim went above
That richest is he who is rich in God's love!

THE SINCERE MAN

What gifts of speech a man may own,
   What grace of manners may appear,
Have little worth unless his heart
   Be honest, forthright and sincere.

The sincere man is like a rock,
   As true as time; with honest eye
He looks you squarely in the face
   Nor turns aside to make reply.

Nothing is hidden; there is no sham,
   No camouflage to caution care,
No ifs or buts to haunt the mind,
   Or secret doubts to linger there.

A crystal candor marks his speech,
   With conscience clear he goes his way,
He does the thing he thinks is right
   Nor cares a whit what others say.

Give me a man that is sincere,
   And though a wealth of faults attend,
I shall clasp his hand in mine
   And claim him as a trusted friend!

—ALFRED GRANT WALTON

THE PURE IN HEART

Blessed are the pure in heart:
They have loved the better part,
When life's journey they have trod,
They shall go to see their God.

Till in glory they appear,
They shall often see Him here,
And His grace shall learn to know
In His glorious works below.

When the sun begins to rise,
Spreading brightness through the skies.
They will love to praise and bless
Christ, the Sun of Righteousness.

In the watches of the night,
When the stars are clear and bright,
"Thus the just shall shine," they say,
"In the Resurrection Day."

God in everything they see;
First in all their thoughts is He.
They have loved the better part,
Blessed are the pure in heart!

—JOHN MASON NEALE

WHAT YOU ARE

Men took everything that Jesus had, His liberty, His legal rights, His physical beauty, His reputation, His life—but they could not take away what He was . . . So the real values of life are internal, not external; and what counts with God—and sooner or later with men—is, not what a man has, but what he is.

—MALTBIE D. BABCOCK

Abraham Lincoln . . . was at home and welcome with the humblest, and with a spirit and a practical vein in the times of terror that commanded the admiration of the wisest. His heart was as great as the world, but there was no room in it to hold the memory of a wrong.

—RALPH W. EMERSON

❧ THE CHURCH ❧

Beautiful is the large church,
With stately arch and steeple;
Neighborly is the small church,
With groups of friendly people;
Reverent is the old church,
With centuries of grace;
And a wooden church or a stone church
Can hold an altar place.
And whether it be a rich church
Or a poor church anywhere,
Truly it is a great church
If God is worshiped there.

Not forsaking the assembling of ourselves together, as the manner of some is.

—HEB. 10:25

A Christian church is a body or collection of persons, voluntarily associated together, professing to believe what Christ teaches, to do what Christ enjoins, to imitate his example, cherish his spirit, and make known his gospel to others.

—R. F. SAMPLE

A world without a *Sabbath* would be like a man without a smile, like a summer without flowers, and like a homestead without a garden. It is the joyous day of the whole week.

—HENRY WARD BEECHER

IN HIS STEPS

It is the personal element that Christian discipleship needs to emphasize. The gift, without the giver, is bare. The Christianity that attempts to suffer by proxy is not the Christianity of Christ. Each individual Christian, business man, citizen, needs to follow in His steps along the path of personal sacrifice for Him. There is not a different path to-day from that of Jesus' own times. It is the same path. The call of this century ... is a call for a discipleship, a new following of Jesus, more like the early, simple, apostolic Christianity when the disciples left all and literally followed the Master. Nothing but a discipleship of this kind can face the destructive selfishness of the age, with any hope of overcoming it. There is a great quantity of nominal Christianity to-day. There is a need of more of the real kind. We need a revival of the Christianity of Christ.

—CHARLES M. SHELDON

PRAYER ON ENTERING CHURCH

Heat and burden of the day
Help us, Lord, to put away.
Let no crowding, fretting cares
Keep earth-bound our spirit's prayers.
Carping criticism take
From our hearts for Jesus' sake.

Thy will be done on earth,
On bended knee we pray,
Then leave our prayer before the throne
And rise and go our way.

And earth is filled with woe,
And war, and evil, still,
For lack of men whose prayer is, Lo
I come to do thy will.

Thy will be done on the earth,
Lord, grant me grace to see
That if Thy will is to be done,
It must be done by me.

—MERRILL

A HOUSE NOT MADE WITH HANDS

O where are kings and empires now,
Of old that went and came?
But, Lord, Thy church is praying yet,
A thousand years the same.

We mark her goodly battlements,
And her foundations strong;
We hear within the solemn voice
Of her unending song.

Unshaken as eternal hills,

Immovable she stands,
A mountain that shall fill the earth,
A house not made with hands.

—A. CLEVELAND COXE

TO THE PREACHER

Preach about yesterday, Preacher!
The time so far away:
When the hand of Deity smote and slew,
And the heathen plagued the stiff-necked
Jew;
Or when the Man of Sorrow came,
And blessed the people who cursed His
name—
Preach about yesterday, Preacher,
Not about today!

Preach about tomorrow, Preacher!
Beyond this world's decay:
Of the sheepfold Paradise we priced
When we pinned our faith to
Jesus Christ;
Of those hot depths that shall receive
The goats who would not so believe—
Preach about tomorrow, Preacher,
Not about today!

Preach about the old sins, Preacher!
And the old virtues, too:
You must not steal nor take man's life,
You must not covet your neighbor's wife,
And woman must cling at every cost
To her one virtue, or she is lost—
Preach about the old sins, Preacher!
Not about the new!

Preach about the other man, Preacher!
The man we all can see!
The man of oaths, the man of strife,
The man who drinks and beats his wife,
Who helps his mates to fret and shirk
When all they need is to keep at work—
Preach about the other man, Preacher!
Not about me!

—CHARLOTTE PERKINS GILMAN

WHERE WERE YOU?

"I came to your church last Sunday,
I walked up and down the aisle,
I noticed your seat was vacant,"
Said the Master, with kindly smile.

"Yes, I was at home," I answered,
"Some folks from up Salem way
Drove down for a week-end visit,
So we stayed in the house all day."

Or, "I had an awful headache,"
"I had a roast in the pan,"
Or, "We overslept this morning,
But I go whenever I can."

The Master gazed at me sadly,
As He was about to speak,
"My child," He replied, "Are there not
Six other days in the week?"

I saw I had grieved my Master,
As slowly He turned away,
And I vowed He'd not find me absent
Again on His holy day!

ON CHURCH BUILDING

God builds no churches! By His plan,
That labor has been left to man.
No spires miraculously rise,
No little mission from the skies
Falls on a bleak and barren place
To be a source of strength and grace.
The humblest church demands its price
In human toil and sacrifice.

Men call the church the House of God,
Towards which the toil stained pilgrims plod
In search of strength and rest and hope,
As blindly through life's mists they grope,
And there God dwells, but it is man
Who builds that house and draws its plan;
Pays for the mortar and the stone
That none need seek for God alone.

There is no church but what proclaims
The gifts of countless generous names.
Ages before us spires were raised
'Neath which Almighty God was praised
As proof that He was then, as now.
Those sacred altars, where men bow
Their heads in prayer and sorrow lifts
Its heavy weight, are Christian gifts!

The humblest spire in mortal ken,
Where God abides, was built by men.
And if the church is still to grow,
Is still the light of hope to throw
Across the valleys of despair,
Men still must build God's house of prayer.
God sends no churches from the skies,
Out of our hearts must they arise!

—EDGAR A. GUEST

Who builds a church to God, and not to
    fame,
Will never mark the marble with his name.

—ALEXANDER POPE

RELIGION

Walking with God is keeping step with him, never running before Him, never lagging behind. Not the songs I sing about Him, not even the prayers I offer to Him, not even the donations I make towards His work; but the love that waits his command, and marches the moment the command is heard, that is religion.

—G. CAMPBELL MORGAN

AN OLD QUESTION

Question: Can I be a Christian without joining a church?

Answer: Yes, it is possible. It is something like being:

    A Student who will not go to school;
    A Soldier who will not join the army;
    A Citizen who does not pay taxes or vote;
    A Salesman with no customers;
    An Explorer with no base camp;
    A Seaman on a ship without a crew;
    A Business Man on a deserted island;
    An Author without readers;
    A Tuba Player without an orchestra;
    A Parent without a family;
    A Football Player without a team;
    A Politician who is a hermit;
    A Scientist who does not share his
      findings;
    A Bee without a hive.

MY CHURCH AND I

I am part of the Church, one among many, but I am one.

I need the Church for the development of the buried life within me; the Church in turn needs me.

The Church may be human in its organization, but it is divine in its purpose. That purpose is to point me to God.

Participating in the privileges of the Church, I shall also share in its responsibilities taking it upon myself to carry my fair share of the load, not grudgingly but joyfully.

To the extent that I fail in my responsibility, the Church fails; to the extent that I succeed, the Church succeeds.

I shall not wait to be drafted for service to my Church; I shall volunteer, saying, "Here am I, send me!"

I shall be loyal in my attendance, generous in my gifts, kind in my criticisms, creative in my suggestions, loving in my attitudes.

I shall give to the Church my interests, my enthusiasm, my devotion—most of all, MYSELF!

—HAROLD W. ROUPP

A SUN-DAY HYMN

Lord of all being! throned afar,
Thy glory flames from sun and star;
Centre and soul of every sphere,
Yet to each loving heart how near!

Sun of our life, thy quickening ray
Sheds on our path the glow of day;
Star of our hope, thy softened light
Cheers the long watches of the night.

Our midnight is thy smile withdrawn;
Our noontide is thy gracious dawn;
Our rainbow arch thy mercy's sign;
All, save the clouds of sin, are thine!

Lord of all life, below, above,
Whose light is truth, whose warmth is love,
Before thy ever-blazing throne
We ask no lustre of our own.

—OLIVER WENDELL HOLMES

CONTENTMENT

Contentment lies not in the enjoyment of ease—
a life of luxury—
but comes only to him that labors and
*   overcomes—*
to him that performs the task in hand and reaps
the satisfaction of work well done.

—Oscar Wilde

When we cannot find contentment in ourselves, it is useless to seek it elsewhere.

—FRANCOIS DE LA ROCHEFOUCAULD

NEEDS

I want a little house
  Upon a little hill,
With lilacs laughing at the door
  When afternoons are still.

I want an apple tree
  Laden with drifts of bloom;
I want blue china all about
  In every room.

I want a little path
  Bordered with brilliant phlox,
And on each windowsill I want
  A painted flower box.

And then—I want you there
  In sun, and frost, and rain,
To smile when I come trudging home
  Through a dim, scented lane.

For what's a little house
  Upon a little hill,
Unless you light the fire for me
  When nights are strangely still?

—CHARLES HANSON TOWNE

Fortify yourself with contentment, for this is an impregnable fortress.

—EPICTETUS

I never hesitate about scraping out the work of days, and beginning afresh, so as to satisfy myself, and try to do better. Ah! that "better" which one feels in one's soul, and without which no true artist is ever content!

Others may approve and admire; but that counts for nothing, compared with one's own feeling of what ought to be.

—JEAN LOUIS MEISSONIER

CONTENTMENT

Sweet are the thoughts that savour of
    content,
  The quiet mind is richer than a crown.
A mind content both crown and kingdom is.

—ROBERT GREENE

The wise man looks inside his heart and finds eternal peace.

—HINDU PROVERB

With a few flowers in my garden, half a dozen pictures and some books, I live without envy.

—LOPE DE VEGA

We shall be made truly wise if we be made content; content, too, not only with what we can understand, but content with what we do not understand—the habit of mind which theologians call, and rightly, faith in God.

—CHARLES KINGSLEY

When I would beget content and increase confidence in the power and wisdom and providence of Almighty God, I will walk the meadows by some gliding stream, and there contemplate the lilies that take no care, and those very many other little living creatures that are not only created, but fed (man knows not how) by the goodness of the God of Nature, and therefore trust in Him.

—IZAAK WALTON

COMPENSATION

Who never wept knows laughter but a jest;
Who never failed, no victory has sought;
Who never suffered, never lived his best;
Who never doubted, never really thought;

Who never feared, real courage has not
*   shown;*
Who never faltered, lacks a real intent;
Whose soul was never troubled has not
*   known*
The sweetness and the peace of real content.

—E. M. BRAINARD

FOR A CONTENTED LIFE

Health enough to make work a pleasure.
Wealth enough to support your needs.
Strength to battle with difficulties and
*   overcome them.*
Grace enough to confess your sins and
*   forsake them.*
Patience enough to toil until some good is
*   accomplished.*
Charity enough to see some good in your
*   neighbor.*
Love enough to move you to be useful and
*   helpful to others.*
Faith enough to make real the things of God.
Hope enough to remove all anxious fears
*   concerning the future.*

—GOETHE

HE THAT HAS LIGHT WITHIN

He that has light within his own clear breast
May sit i' the centre, and enjoy bright day:
But he that hides a dark soul and foul
*   thoughts*
Benighted walks under the mid-day sun;
Himself is his own dungeon.

—JOHN MILTON

I AM CONTENT

The longer I live the more my mind dwells upon the beauty and wonder of the world....

I have loved the feel of the grass under my feet, and the sound of the running streams by my side. The hum of the wind in the tree-tops has always been good music to me, and the face of the fields has often comforted me more than the faces of men.

I am in love with this world; by my constitution I have nestled lovingly in it. It has been home. It has been my point of outlook into the universe. I have not bruised myself against it, nor tried to use it ignobly.

I have tilled its soil, I have gathered its harvests, I have waited upon its seasons, and always have I reaped what I have sown.

While I delved I did not lose sight of the sky overhead. While I gathered its bread and meat for my body, I did not neglect to gather its bread and meat for my soul.

I have climbed its mountains, roamed its forests, sailed its waters, crossed its deserts, felt the sting of its frosts, the oppression of its heats, the drench of its rains, the fury of its winds, and always have beauty and joy waited upon my goings and comings.

—JOHN BURROUGHS

You will succeed best when you put the restless, anxious side of affairs out of mind, and allow the restful side to live in your thoughts.

—MARGARET STOWE

CHOOSE BOTH

There are two ways of being happy: We may either diminish our wants or augment our means—either will do—the result is the same; and it is for each man to decide for himself, and do that which happens to be the easiest.

If you are idle or sick or poor, however hard it may be to diminish your wants, it will be harder to augment your means.

If you are active and prosperous or young or in good health, it may be easier for you to augment your means than to diminish your wants.

But if you are wise, you will do both at the same time, young or old, rich or poor, sick or well; and if you are very wise you will do both in such a way as to augment the general happiness of society.

—BENJAMIN FRANKLIN

FOR THIS

I do not count the hours I spend
In wandering by the sea;
The forest is my loyal friend,
Like God it useth me:

Or on the mountain-crest sublime,
Or down the oaken glade,
O what have I to do with Time?
For this the day was made.

—RALPH WALDO EMERSON

Of the blessings set before you, make your choice and be content.

—SAMUEL JOHNSON

CHEERFULNESS TAUGHT BY REASON

I think we are too ready with complaint
   In this fair world of God's. Had we no
       hope
   Indeed beyond the zenith and the slope
Of yon gray blank of sky, we might be faint
To muse upon eternity's constraint
   Round our aspirant souls. But since the
       scope
   Must widen early, is it well to droop
For a few days consumed in loss and taint?
O pusillanimous Heart, be comforted,—
   And like a cheerful traveler, take the road,
Singing beside the hedge. What if the bread
   Be bitter in thine inn, and thou unshod
To meet the flints?—At least it may be said,
   "Because the way is short,
       I thank thee, God!"*

ELIZABETH BARRETT BROWNING

I love to be alone. I never found the companion that was so companionable as solitude.

—HENRY D. THOREAU

TRUST

Give us great dreams, O God, while Thou
   art giving,
   And keep the end; it is enough if we
Live by the hope, nor falter in the living,
   That lures us on from dust to dignity.

Give us the courage of the soul's high vision,
   Though its fulfillment here we never see:
The heart to make and keep the brave
   decision,
   And faith to leave the ultimate with Thee.

—MARIE LE NART

PRAYER

I do not ask to walk smooth paths
Nor bear an easy load.
I pray for strength and fortitude
To climb the rock strewn road.

Give me such courage I can scale
The hardest peaks alone
And transform every stumbling block
Into a stepping stone.

—GAIL BROOK BURKET

Gently loosens He thy hold
Of the treasured FORMER things—
Loves and joys that were of old,
Shapes to which the spirit clings,
And alone, above He stands,
Stretching forth beseeching Hands.

—TEERSTEGAN

PRAYER FOR A BUSY AGE

In the name of Jesus Christ, who was never in a hurry, we pray, O God, that Thou wilt slow us down, for we know that we live too fast. With all of eternity before us, make us take time to live—time to get acquainted with Thee, time to enjoy Thy blessings, and time to know each other.

—PETER MARSHALL

COURAGE

You gain strength, courage and confidence by every experience in which you really stop to look fear in the face. You are able to say to yourself, "I lived through this horror. I can take the next thing that comes along." . . . You must do the thing you think you cannot do.

—ELEANOR ROOSEVELT

COURAGE

"We met by chance—I do not know his
　　name,
Whither he went his way or whence he came
　　again.
He said no word but 'Courage': then again
'Courage,' he said, and gripped me by the
　　hands.
A moment—he was vanished in the throng
That hurried homeward in the drizzling rain.
I wonder if he knows and understands
How suddenly the world was full of song;
Laughter and hope had burst their
　　prison bars,
And life had lost its loneliness and pain.
My fears were underfoot. I saw the stars
The blinding mists had hid this many a day,
And clear before me gleamed a great
　　highway,
Where yesterday I sought a path in vain."

　　　　　　　　　　—E. WILLIAMS DAVID

RESURGENCE

Out of the earth, the rose,
　　Out of the night, the dawn:
Out of my heart, with all its woes,
　　High courage to press on.

　　　　　　　—LAURA LEE RANDALL

Happy he who dares courageously to defend
what he loves.

　　　　　　　　　　　　—OVID

EVENTIDE

At cool of day, with God I walk
　　My garden's grateful shade;
I hear His voice among the trees,
　　And I am not afraid.

He speaks to me in every wind,
　　He smiles from every star;
He is not deaf to me, nor blind,
　　Nor absent, nor afar.

His hand that shuts the flowers to sleep,
　　Each in its dewy fold,
Is strong my feeble life to keep,
　　And competent to hold.

The powers below and powers above,
　　Are subject to His care—
I cannot wander from His love
　　Who loves me everywhere.

Thus dowered, and guarded thus, with Him
　　I walk this peaceful shade;
I hear His voice among the trees,
　　And I am not afraid.

　　　　　—CAROLINE ATHERTON MASON

A crowd of troubles passed him by
　　As he with courage waited;
He said, "Where do you troubles fly
　　When you are thus belated?"
"We go," they say, "to those who mope,
　　Who look on life dejected,
Who weakly say 'good-bye' to hope,
　　We go where we're expected."

　　　　　　　—FRANCIS J. ALLISON

Love contains no fear—indeed fully de-
veloped love expels every particle of fear,
for fear always contains some of the torture
of feeling guilty.

　　　　　　　　　　—I JOHN 4:18

From ALUMNUS FOOTBALL

You'll find the road is long and rough,
　　with soft spots far apart,
Where only those can make the grade who
　　have the Uphill Heart,

And when they stop you with a thud or
    jolt you with a crack,
Let Courage call the signals as you keep on
    coming back.
Keep coming back, and though the world
    may romp across your spine,
Let every game's end find you still upon the
    battling line:
For when the One Great Scorer comes to
    mark against your name,
He writes—not that you won or lost—
    but how you played the game.

—GRANTLAND RICE

COURAGE

The courage that my mother had
    Went with her, and is with her still:
Rock from New England quarried;
    Now granite in a granite hill.

The golden brooch my mother wore
    She left behind for me to wear;
I have no thing I treasure more:
    Yet, it is something I could spare.

Oh, if instead she'd left to me
    The thing she took into the grave!—
That courage like a rock, which she
    Has no more need of, and I have.

—EDNA ST. VINCENT MILLAY

To live with fear and not be afraid is the final test of maturity.

—EDWARD WEEKS

FEAR AND LOVE

    I do not fear
To walk the lonely road
Which leads far out into
The sullen night. Nor do
I fear the rebel, wind-tossed
Sea that stretches onward, far,
Beyond the might of human hands
Or human loves. It is the
Brooding, sharp-thorned discontent
I fear, the nagging days without
A sound of song; the sunlit

Noon of ease; the burden of
Delight and—flattery. It is
The hate-touched soul I dread,
The joyless heart; the unhappy
Faces in the streets; the
Smouldering fires of unforgiven
Slights. These do I fear. Not
Night, nor surging seas, nor
Rebel winds. But hearts unlovely,
and unloved.

—JAMES A. FRASER

COURAGEOUS DEFENDER

No one can bar the road to truth, and to advance its cause I'm ready to accept even death.

—ALEXANDER SOLZHENITSYN

UNAFRAID

Afraid? Of what?
To feel the spirit's glad release?
To pass from pain to perfect peace,
The strife and strain of life to cease?
    Afraid—of that?

Afraid? Of what?
Afraid to see the Saviour's face,
To hear His welcome, and to trace
The glory gleam from wounds of grace?
    Afraid—of that?

Afraid? Of what?
A flash—a crash—a pierced heart;
Darkness—light—O heaven's art!
A wound of His a counterpart!
    Afraid—of that?

Afraid? Of what?
To enter into Heaven's rest,
And yet to serve the Master blest,
From service good to service best?
    Afraid—of that?

Afraid? Of what?
To do by death what life could not—
Baptize with death a stony plot,
Till souls shall blossom from that spot?
    Afraid—of that?

—E. H. HAMILTON

THE SOUL'S DEFIANCE

I said to Sorrow's awful storm,
    That beat against my breast,
Rage on—thou mayst destroy this form,
    And lay it low at rest;
But still the spirit that now brooks
    Thy tempest, raging high,
Undaunted on its fury looks,
    With steadfast eye.

I said to Penury's meagre train,
    Come on—your threats I brave;
My last poor life-drop you may drain,
    And crush me to the grave;
Yet still the spirit that endures
    Shall mock your force the while,
And meet each cold, cold grasp of yours
    With bitter smile.

I said to cold Neglect and Scorn,
    Pass on—I heed you not;
Ye may pursue me till my form
    And being are forgot;
Yet still the spirit, which ye see
    Undaunted by your wiles,
Draws from its own nobility
    Its highborn smiles.

I said to Friendship's menaced blow,
    Strike deep—my heart shall bear;
Thou canst but add one bitter woe
    To those already there;
Yet still the spirit that sustains
    This last severe distress,
Shall smile upon its keenest pains,
    And scorn redress.

I said to Death's uplifted dart,
    Aim sure—oh, why delay?
Thou wilt not find a fearful heart—
    A weak, reluctant prey;
For still the spirit firm and free,
    Unruffled by this last dismay,
Wrapt in its own eternity,
    Shall pass away.

—Lavinia Stoddard

"NO!"

Learn to speak this little word
In its proper place—
Let no timid doubt be heard,
Clothed with sceptic grace;
Let thy lips, without disguise,
Boldly pour it out;
Though a thousand dulcet lies
Keep hovering about.
For be sure our lives would lose
Future years of woe;
If our courage could refuse
The present hour with "No."

—Eliza Cook

QUO VADIS?

Peter, outworn
And menaced by the sword,
Shook off the dust of Rome;
And, as he fled,
Met one with eager face,
Hastening cityward,
And, to his vast amaze,
It was the Lord.

"Lord, whither goest Thou?"
He cried, importunate;
And Christ replied,
    "Peter I suffer loss,
    I go to take thy place,
    To bear thy cross."

Then Peter bowed his head,
Discomforted;
Then at the Master's feet,
Found grace complete,
And courage, and new faith,
And turned, with Him
To death.

—John Oxenham

Heroism is the brilliant triumph of the soul over the flesh, that is to say over fear: fear of poverty, of suffering, of calumny, of illness, of loneliness and of death. There is no real piety without heroism. It is the glorious concentration of courage.

—Henri Frederic Amiel

He that loses wealth loses much:
But he that loses courage loses all.

—Cervantes

❈DEATH❈

Death stands above me, whispering low
I know not what into my ear;
Of his strange language all I know
Is, there is not a word of fear.

—WALTER SAVAGE LANDOR

What is so universal as death must be benefit.

—SCHILLER

MY LAST DAY

*If this were my last day I'm almost sure
I'd spend it working in my garden. I
Would dig about my little plants, and try
To make them happy, so they would endure
Long after me. Then I would hide secure
Where my green arbor shades me from
   the sky,
And watch how bird and bee and butterfly
Came hovering to every flowery lure.
Then, as I rested, perhaps a friend or two,
Lovers of flowers would come, and we
   would walk
About my little garden paths and talk
Of peaceful times when all the world
   seemed true.
This may be my last day, for all I know;
What a temptation just to spend it so!*

—SPICER

*This world's a city, full of straying streets;
And death's the market-place, where each
   one meets.*

—SHAKESPEARE

THE SHADOW

*Shapeless and grim,
A Shadow dim
O'erhung the ways,
And darkened all my days.
And all who saw,
With bated breath,
Said, "It is Death!"*

*And I, in weakness
Slipping towards the Night,
In sore affright
Looked up. And lo!—
No Spectre grim,
But just a dim
Sweet face,
A sweet high mother-face,
A face like Christ's Own Mother's face,
Alight with tenderness
And grace.*

*"Thou art not Death!" I cried;—
For Life's supremest fantasy
Had never thus envisaged Death to me;—
"Thou are not Death, the End!"*

*In accents winning,
Came the answer,—"Friend,
   There is no Death!
   I am the Beginning,
   —Not the End!'*

—JOHN OXENHAM

God's finger touched him, and he slept.

—ALFRED TENNYSON

I know of but one remedy against the fear of death that is effectual and that will stand the test either of a sick-bed or of a sound mind—that is, a good life, a clear conscience, an honest heart, and a well-ordered conversation; to carry the thoughts of dying men about us, and so to live before we die as we shall wish we had when we come to it.

*For Death
Now I know, is that first breath
Which our souls draw when we enter
Life, which is of all life center.*

—EDWIN ARNOLD

DEATH IS A DOOR

Death is only an old door
Set in a garden wall.
On quiet hinges it gives at dusk,
When the thrushes call.

Along the lintel are green leaves,
Beyond, the light lies still;
Very weary and willing feet
Go over that sill.

There is nothing to trouble any heart,
Nothing to hurt at all.
Death is only an old door
In a garden wall.

—NANCY BYRD TURNER

O HAPPY SOUL

O happy soul, be thankful now, and rest!
Heaven is a goodly land;
And God is love; and those he loves are
blest;
Now thou dost understand
The least thou hast is better than the best
That thou didst hope for; now upon thine
eyes
The new life opens fair;
Before thy feet the blessed journey lies
Through homelands everywhere;
And heaven to thee is all a sweet surprise.

—WASHINGTON GLADDEN

THE DYING CHRISTIAN TO HIS SOUL

Vital spark of heav'nly flame!
Quit, O quit this mortal frame:
Trembling, hoping, ling'ring, flying,
O the pain, the bliss of dying!
Cease, fond Nature, cease thy strife,
And let me languish into life.

Hark! they whisper; angels say,
Sister Spirit, come away!
What is this absorbs me quite?
Steals my senses, shuts my sight,
Drowns my spirits, draws my breath?
Tell me, my soul, can this be death?

The world recedes; it disappears!
Heav'n opens on my eyes! my ears
With sounds seraphic ring!

Lend, lend your wings! I mount! I fly!
O Grave! where is thy victory?
O Death! where is thy sting?

—ALEXANDER POPE

We are spirits. That bodies should be lent us, while they can afford us pleasure, assist us in acquiring knowledge, or in doing good to our fellow creatures, is a kind and benevolent act of God. When they become unfit for these purposes, and afford us pain instead of pleasure, instead of an aid become an incumbrance, and answer none of the intentions for which they were given, it is equally kind and benevolent, that a way is provided by which we may get rid of them. Death is that way. Our friend and we were invited abroad on a party of pleasure, which is to last forever. His chair was ready first and he has gone before us. We could not all conveniently start together; and why should you and I be grieved at this, since we are soon to follow, and know where to find him.

—BENJAMIN FRANKLIN

BEYOND DEATH

When she who was the source of all my sighs
Fled from the world, herself, my straining
sight,
Nature, who gave us that unique delight,
Was sunk in shame, and we had weeping
eyes.
Yet shall not vauntful death enjoy the prize,
This sun of suns which then he veiled
in night;
For Love hath triumphed, lifting up her
light
On earth, and 'mid the saints in Paradise.

What though remorseless and impiteous
doom
Deemed that the music of her deeds would
die,
And that her splendour would be sunk in
gloom?
The poet's page exalts her to the sky
With life more living in the lifeless tomb,
And Death translates her soul to reign
on high.

—MICHELANGELO

The wisest men are glad to die; no fear
Of death can touch a true philosopher.
Death sets the soul at liberty to fly.

—THOMAS MAY

Why be afraid of death,
    as though your life were breath?
Death but anoints your eyes with clay.
    O glad surprise!

Why should ye be forlorn?
    Death only husks the corn.
Why should you fear to meet the thresher
    of the wheat?

Is sleep a thing to dread?
    Yet sleeping you are dead
Till you awake and rise,
    here, or beyond the skies.

Why should it be a wrench to leave
    your wooden bench!
Why not, with happy shout,
    run home when school is out!
The dear ones left behind?
    Oh, foolish one and blind!
A day and you will meet—a night and
    you will greet.

This is the death of death,
    to breathe away a breath
And know the end of strife,
    and taste the deathless life,

And joy without a fear,
    and smile without a tear;
And work, nor care to rest,
    and find the last the best.

—MALTBIE D. BABCOCK

IMMORTALITY

What matters it to us who are immortal
Which side of the grave we stand on,
    when we know
That what the world calls death is but the
    portal
Leading to life again? 'Tis but to go
Across the gurgling river in the dark
Hanging on God; and but a moment so
Till we are over, and we disembark

And enter life afresh. 'Tis basely wrong
We should so meanly understrike the mark
As measures life by years; and all along
Busy ourselves arranging little schemes
That death will dash to pieces,
    when we might
Be building, far above those earthly dreams,
Houses that stand forever in God's sight.

OUT OF THIS LIFE

Out of this life I shall never take
Things of silver and gold I make.
All that I cherish and hoard away,
After I leave, on earth must stay.

Though I call it mine and I boast its worth,
I must give it up when I quit the earth.
All that I gather and all that I keep
I must leave behind when I fall asleep.

And I wonder often, just what I shall own,
In that other life when I pass alone,
What shall He find and what shall He see,
In the soul that answers the call for me?

Shall the great Judge learn when my task is
    through
That my soul had gathered some riches too?
Or shall at the last, it be mine to find,
That all I had worked for, I had left behind?

The milestones into headstones turn,
    And under each a friend.

—MARCUS TULLIUS CICERO

What is excellent,
As God lives, is permanent;
Hearts are dust, hearts' loves remain;
Hearts' love will meet again.

—RALPH WALDO EMERSON

There in the twilight cold and gray,
Lifeless, but beautiful, he lay,
And from the sky, serene and far,
A voice fell, like a falling star,
    Excelsior!

—HENRY WADSWORTH LONGFELLOW

FAILURE

What is a failure? It's only a spur
  To a man who receives it right,
And makes the spirit within him stir
  To go in once more and fight.
If you never have failed it's an even guess,
You never have won a high success.

—EDMUND VANCE COOKE

There are songs enough for the lovers
   Who share love's tender pain,
I sing for the one whose passion
   Is given all in vain.

And I know the solar system
   Must somewhere keep in space
A prize for that spent runner
   Who barely lost the race.

For the plan would be imperfect
   Unless it held some sphere
That paid for the toil and talent
   And love that are wasted here.

          —ELLA WHEELER WILCOX

No good thing is failure and no evil thing success.

It is hard to fail, but it is worse never to have tried to succeed. In this life we get nothing save by effort.

          —THEODORE ROOSEVELT

Self-distrust is the cause of most of our failures. In the assurance of strength there is strength, and they are the weakest, however strong, who have no faith in themselves or their powers.

          —BOVEE

Remorse is the form that failure takes when it has made a grab and got nothing.

LINES FOR DOUBTERS

I write these lines for doubting men:
   Of self-timidity beware.
One never knows the moment when
   A flash of pluck will banish care.
Hold fast and give no heed to fear;
   Battle the stream until you sink;
Failure is never quite so near
   As frightened people seem to think.

If now disaster sweeps away
   The little grain you thought to hold,
While still in health and strength you stay
   Your history's only partly told.
There still are left new goals to gain;
   'Tis only those who cease to strive
For whom no future hopes remain.
   Don't die while you are yet alive.

Grieve if you must a little while
   Oe'r what has happened, but return
Head high and brave and with a smile
   The lesson of your loss to learn.
Forget the past and face today
   With courage and with mind alert.
Who comes a victor from the fray
   Remembers not that he was hurt.
Before you lies another year
   And somewhere is your chance to win.

          —EDGAR A. GUEST

THE DISAPPOINTED

There are songs enough for the hero
   Who dwells on the heights of fame;
I sing of the disappointed—
   For those who have missed their aim.

I sing for the breathless runner,
   The eager, anxious soul,
Who falls with his strength exhausted,
   Almost in sight of the goal;

For the hearts that break in silence,
   With a sorow all unknown,
For those who need companions,
   Yet walk their ways alone.

FAITH

God knows, not I, the reason why
His winds of storm drive through
my door;
I am content to live or die
Just knowing this, nor knowing
more.
My Father's hand appointing me
My days and ways, so I am free.

—Margaret E. Sangster

dignity of a son of God. What Christ asks is that we shall try it out. He actually dares us to follow him. In that way, he says you shall win that prize in life, for which any man can with perfect reason afford to give everything else.

—WILFRED T. GRENFELL

Faith is the daring of the soul
to go farther than it can see.

—WILLIAM NEWTON CLARK

Fear knocked at the door. Faith answered. No one was there.

—OLD ENGLISH LEGEND

Howe'er it be, it seems to me,
'T is only noble to be good.
Kind hearts are more than coronets,
And simple faith than Norman blood.

—ALFRED TENNYSON

Faith is to believe what we do not see, and the reward of this faith is to see what we believe.

—ST. AUGUSTINE

The best definition of faith that I know is that it is reason grown courageous. Moreover, that is all that Christ ever asked us for, and the reason that he asked us for that was because he wants to use us. He needs our help. It is almost impossible to believe it, but God Almighty wants our help, so Christ tells us. Theoretically or mathematically this is unintelligible, that God should want human help. But this is the bottom of all Christ's teaching. The faith he asks for is not to understand him but to follow him. By that and that alone can man convert the tragedy of human life, full of disappointments, disillusionments, and with so-called death ever looming ahead, into the most glorious field of honor, worthy of the

CREDO

Not what, but Whom, I do believe,
That, in my darkest hour of need,
Hath comfort that no mortal creed
To mortal man may give;—
Not what, but Whom!
For Christ is more than all the creeds,
And His full life of gentle deeds
Shall all the creeds outlive.

Not what I do believe, but Whom!
Who walks beside me in the gloom?
Who shares the burden wearisome?
Who all the dim way doth illume,
And bids me look beyond the tomb
The larger life to live?—
Not what I do believe,
But Whom!
Not what
But Whom!

—JOHN OXENHAM

FROM FEAR INTO FAITH

Father, do Thou this day free me—
From fear of the future;
From anxiety for the morrow;
From bitterness toward anyone;
From cowardice in face of danger;
From laziness in face of work;
From failure before opportunity;
From weakness when Thy power is
at hand.

But fill me, I beseech Thee, with—
Love that knows no barriers;

Courage that cannot be shaken;
Faith strong enough for the darkness;
Strength sufficient for my tasks;
Loyalty to Thy kingdom's goal;
Wisdom to meet life's complexities;
Grace to meet life's perplexities;
Power to lift men unto Thee.

SOME DAY

Still we study, always failing!
God can read it, we must wait;
Wait, until He teach the mystery,
Then the wisdom-woven history
Faith shall read and love translate.

Leaflets now unpaged and scattered
Time's great library recieves;
When Eternity shall bind them,
Golden volumes we shall find them,
God's light falling on the leaves.

NOW

Now is the time to know my full salvation,
Now is the time to welcome Love's control;
Now is the time for deeper consecration
To serve our God with mind and heart and
soul.

I have no anxious thought about tomorrow;
No fear of ill; no need to wonder how
It will be freed of trouble, pain, or sorrow;
For when tomorrow comes, it will be now.

—LAURA LEE RANDALL

FAITH ENOUGH

God, if this were faith?
To go on forever and fail and go on again,
And be mauled to the earth and arise,
And contend for the shade of a word,
and a thing not seen with the eyes,
With half of a broken hope for a pillow at
night
That somehow the right is the right,
And the smooth shall bloom from the rough:
Lord, if that were enough.

—ROBERT LOUIS STEVENSON

A faith is not acquired by reasoning. One does not fall in love with a woman, or enter the womb of a church, as a result of logical persuasion. Reason may defend an act of faith—but only after the act has been committed, and the man committed to the act. Persuasion may play a part in a man's conversion; but only the part of bringing to its full and conscious climax a process which has been maturing in regions where no persuasion can penetrate. A faith is not acquired; it grows like a tree. Its crown points to the sky; its roots grow downward into the past and are nourished by the dark sap of the ancestral humus.

—ARTHUR KOESTLER

FAITH

Faith is not merely praying
Upon your knees at night;
Faith is not merely straying
Through darkness to the light.

Faith is not merely waiting
For glory that may be.
Faith is not merely hating
The sinful ecstasy.

Faith is the brave endeavor,
The splendid enterprise,
The strength to serve, whatever
Conditions may arise.

—S. E. KISER

Through the dark and stormy night
Faith beholds a feeble light
Up the blackness streaking;
Knowing God's own time is best,
In a patient hope I rest
For the full day-breaking!

—JOHN GREENLEAF WHITTIER

Christian faith is a grand cathedral, with divinely pictured windows.—Standing without, you can see no glory, nor can imagine any, but standing within every ray of light reveals a harmony of unspeakable splendors.

—NATHANIEL HAWTHORNE

WHICHEVER WAY THE WIND DOTH BLOW

Whichever way the wind doth blow
Some heart is glad to have it so;
Then blow it east or blow it west,
The wind that blows, that wind is best.

My little craft sails not alone;
A thousand fleets from every zone
Are out upon a thousand seas;
And what for me were favoring breeze
Might dash another, with the shock
Of doom upon some hidden rock.
And so I do not dare to pray
For winds to waft me on my way,
But leave it to a Higher Will
To stay or speed me; trusting still
That all is well, and sure that He
Who launched my bark, will sail with me
Through storm and calm, and will not fail
Whatever breezes may prevail
To land me, every peril past,
Within His sheltering Heaven at last.

Then whatsoever wind doth blow,
My heart is glad to have it so;
And blow it east or blow it west,
The wind that blows, that wind is best.

—Caroline A. Mason

FAITH

The strength of a man is the faith he holds
And the courage that his faith gives;
It makes him true to himself, and moulds
The shape of the life he lives.
It keeps him steadfast and of good cheer,
And the road of his life is straight.
He moves with a splendid lack of fear,
As he laughs at the stings of fate.

He faces the future with calm clear eyes
And a purpose that naught can dim.
It seems that the distant starlit skies
Are near to the heart of him.
Though the rest be blind, yet he can see
By a faith that can never fail,
And patience will his watch word be
To the end of his earthly trail.

He fills his mission and will not swerve
Though a legion bar the way.
He marches on, and will take no curve
Just because of what others say.
So give me that man whose faith declines
To be hostage to any fears.
For he sees that a radiant beauty shines
Down the slope of the changing years.

—Lyda Smathers Holtzclaw

Faith looks across the storm—
It does not doubt
Or stop to look at clouds
And things without.

Faith does not question why
When all his ways
Are hard to understand,
But trusts and prays.

It seeks the greatest gift
And asks not sight;
It does not need to see—
He is its light.

Above the tempest's roar
It hears his voice;
And, with its hands in his,
Faith can rejoice.

It fears no cloud, or wind
That it can bring;
Faith looks across the storm
And still can sing.

A PARABLE FROM LIEBIG

The church bells were ringing, the Devil sat
singing
On the stump of a rotting old tree;
"Oh, faith, it grows cold, and the creeds they
grow old,
And the world is nigh ready for me."

The bells went on ringing, a spirit came
singing,
And smiled as he crumbled the tree;
'Yon wood does but perish new seedlings to
cherish,
And the world is too live yet for thee."

—Charles Kingsley

FRIENDSHIP

Art thou lonely, O my brother?
Share thy little with another!
Stretch a hand to one unfriended,
And thy loneliness is ended.

—JOHN OXENHAM

Of tender glance and gentle tone,
   Of thoughts that cheer and bless!

If sorrow comes to me I know
That friends will walk the way I go,
   And, as the shadows fall,
I know that I will raise my eyes
And see—ah, hope that never dies!—
   The dearest Friend of All.

      —MARGARET E. SANGSTER

God never loved me in so sweet a way before
'Tis He alone who can such blessings send,
And when His love would new expressions
   find,
He brought thee to me, and He said,
   'Behold a friend.'

THE THINGS I PRIZE

These are the things I prize
   And hold of dearest worth:
Light of the sapphire skies,
Peace of the silent hills,
Shelter of the forests, comfort of the grass,
Music of birds, murmur of little rills,
Shadows of cloud that swiftly pass,
   And, after showers,
   The smell of flowers
And of the good brown earth—
And best of all, along the way, friendship
   and mirth.

      —HENRY VAN DYKE

Friendship throws a greater lustre on prosperity, while it lightens adversity by sharing in its griefs and anxieties.

      —MARCUS TULLIUS CICERO

Friendship—one soul in two bodies.

      —PYTHAGORAS

GRATITUDE

I thank You, God in Heaven, for
   friends.
When morning wakes, when daytime
   ends,
   I have the consciousness
Of loving hands that touch my own,

Do not keep the alabaster box of your love and tenderness sealed up until your friends are dead. Fill their lives with sweetness. Speak approving, cheering words while their ears hear them, and while their hearts can be thrilled and made happier. The kind things you mean to say when they are gone, say before they go. The flowers you mean to send for their coffin, send to brighten and sweeten their homes before they leave them. If my friends have alabaster boxes laid away, full of fragrant perfumes of sympathy and affection, which they intend to break over my body, I would rather they would bring them out in my weary and troubled hours and open them, that I may be refreshed and cheered while I need them. I would rather have a plain coffin without flowers, a funeral without a eulogy, than a life without the sweetness and love emanating from sympathy. Let us learn to anoint our friends while they are yet among the living. Post-mortem kindness does not cheer the burdened heart; flowers on the coffin cast no fragrance backward over the weary way.

      —GEORGE W. CHILDS

Friends are like the sturdy oaks that rustle in the breeze when the summer suns are gone . . . Like the boughs of spicy evergreens pressed against our lives to shelter from the wintry blast. . . . Friends are like low blooming flowers that break at spring to light our path . . . Like the perfumed roses dropping petals of happiness around our door. . . . Friends are like green mosses clinging close to running brooks . . . Like the flowing streams spreading their moisture along the fields and asking no reward or pay. . . . Friends are like the shady nooks giving sweet release at evening's hush . . . Like the broad expanse of softest green and copper bronze to delight the eye. . . . Friends are like the gentle whisperings of a love divine . . . Forgiving and forgetting without a tinge of blame.

—BERTHA KEININGHAM

If a man does not make new acquaintances as he advances through life, he will soon find himself alone. A man, sir, must keep his friendships in constant repair.

—JOHNSON

Friends are necessary to a happy life. When friendship deserts us we are as lonely and helpless as a ship, left by the tide high upon the shore. When friendship returns to us, it is as though the tide came back, gave us buoyancy and freedom, and opened to us the wide places of the world.

—HARRY EMERSON FOSDICK

Now may the warming love of friends
Surround you as you go
Down path of light and laughter
Where the happy memories grow.

—HELEN LOWRIE MARSHALL

Blessed are they who have the gift of making friends, for it is one of God's best gifts. It involves many things, but above all, the power of going out of one's self and appreciating whatever is noble and loving in another.

—THOMAS HUGHES

What is the secret of making friends? There is no secret. Friends, like all good things in this life, can be had by anyone who wants them. There is only one simple rule to follow; it is this: To have a friend, be one yourself.

To be trusted is a greater compliment than to be loved.

—GEORGE MACDONALD

The best help is not to bear the troubles of others for them, but to inspire them with courage and energy to bear their burdens for themselves and meet the difficulties of life bravely.

—JOHN LUBBOCK

Every man should keep a fair-sized cemetery in which to bury the faults of his friends.

—HENRY WARD BEECHER

A friend is one who needs us and one whom we need. Around us may be many whose companionship we enjoy, but were they suddenly to drop out of their places there would be no soreness, no sense of deprivation, no lack of comfort. We do not need them; neither do they need us. A friend is one to whom we cling, though many leagues of space separate us. Though days pass with no sight of his face or word from his pen, we know our friend loves us and that when we meet again we will be on the same old terms: we shall begin where we left off. A friend is one in whom we can confide. The secret chambers of our soul open to his touch on the latch.

—JESSE DINGER

My dearest *meed* a friend's esteem and praise.

FRIENDS

Ain't it fine when things are going
　Topsy-turvy and askew
To discover someone showing
　Good old-fashioned faith in you?

Ain't it good when life seems dreary
　And your hopes about to end,
Just to feel the handclasp cheery
　Of a fine old loyal friend?

Gosh! one fellow to another
　Means a lot from day to day,
Seems we're living for each other
　In a friendly sort of way.

When a smile or cheerful greetin'
　Means so much to fellows sore,
Seems we ought to keep repeatin'
　Smiles an' praises more an' more.

　　　　　—EDGAR A. GUEST

In the hour of distress and misery the eye of every mortal turns to friendship; in the hour of gladness and conviviality, what is your want? It is friendship. When the heart overflows with gratitude, or with any other sweet and sacred sentiment, what is the word to which it would give utterance? A friend.

　　　　　—WALTER SAVAGE LANDOR

Rejoice in all the honors which come to those you know. That you know them makes you, in a sense, a partner in their fame; that you rejoice with them brings you their friendship.

　　　　　—HENRY WORTHINGTON

SEEDS OF KINDNESS

If you have a friend worth loving,
　Love him. Yes, and let him know
That you love him, ere life's evening
　Tinge his brow with sunset glow.
Why should good words ne'er be said
Of a friend—till he is dead?

If you hear a song that thrills you,
　Sung by any child of song,
Praise it. Do not let the singer
Wait deserved praises long.
Why should one who thrills your heart
Lack the joy you may impart?

If you hear a prayer that moves you
　By its humble, pleading tone,
Join it. Do not let the seeker
　Bow before his God alone.
Why should not your brother share
The strength of "two or three" in prayer?

Friendship hath the skill and observation of the best physician, the diligence and vigilance of the best nurse, and the tenderness and patience of the best mother.

　　　　　—EDWARD CLARENDON

I have loved my friend as I do virtue, my my soul, my God. From hence methinks I do conceive how God loves men, what happiness there is in the love of God. . . . There are wonders in true affection; . . . United souls are not satisfied with embraces, but desire to be truly each other; which being impossible, their desires are infinite, and must proceed without a possibility of satisfaction. Another misery there is in affection, that whom we truly love like our own, we forget their looks, nor can our memory retain the Idea of their faces; and it is no wonder, for they are our selves, and our affection makes their looks our own.

　　　　　—THOMAS BROWNE

We all belong to each other, but friendship is the especial accord of one life with a kindred life. We tremble at the threshold of any new friendship with awe and wonder and fear lest it should not be real or, believing that it is, lest we should prove ourselves unworthy of the solemn and holy contact of life with life, of soul with soul. We cannot live unworthy lives in the constant presence of noble beings to whom we belong and who believe that we are at least endeavoring after nobleness.

　　　　　—RALPH WALDO EMERSON

GRATITUDE

There are few things which bless and soothe the life of others more, or do them more good, than the giving of thanks. It makes men feel that they are some use in the world, and that is one of the finest impulses to a better life. It cheers many a wearied heart with pleasant hope and bids many a man who is sad in mood take courage.

—STOPFORD A. BROOKE

thought, that from our childhood God has been laying His fatherly hands upon us, and always in benediction; that even the strokes of His hands are blessings, and among the chiefest we have ever received. When this feeling is awakened, the heart beats with a pulse of thankfulness. Every gift has its return of praise. It awakens an uncreasing daily converse with our Father,—He speaking to us by the descent of blessing, we to Him by the ascent of thanksgiving. And all our whole life is thereby drawn under the light of His countenance, and is filled with a gladness, serenity, and peace which only thankful hearts can know.

—H. E. MANNING

FOR JOY

For each and every joyful thing,
For twilight swallows on the wing,
For all that nest and all that sing,—

For fountains cool that laugh and leap,
For rivers running to the deep,
For happy, care-forgetting sleep,—

For stars that pierce the sombre dark,
For morn, awaking with the lark,
For life new-stirring 'neath the bark,—

For sunshine and the blessed rain,
For budding grove and blossomy lane,
For the sweet silence of the plain,—

For bounty springing from the sod,
For every step by beauty trod,—
For each dear gift of joy, thank God!

—FLORENCE EARLE COATES

There is not a more pleasing exercise of the mind than gratitude.

—JOSEPH ADDISON

GRATITUDE

Gratitude consists in a watchful, minute attention to the particulars of our state, and to the multitude of God's gifts, taken one by one. It fills us with a consciousness that God loves and cares for us, even to the least event and the smallest need of life. It is a blessed

THANKS BE TO GOD

I do not thank Thee, Lord,
That I have bread to eat while others starve;
Nor yet for work to do
While empty hands solicit Heaven;
Nor for a body strong
While other bodies flatten beds of pain.
No, not for these do I give thanks!

But I am grateful, Lord,
Because my meager loaf I may divide;
For that my busy hands
May move to meet another's need;
Because my doubled strength
I may expend to steady one who faints.
Yes, for all these do I give thanks!

For heart to share, desire to bear
And will to lift,
Flamed into one by deathless Love—
Thanks be to God for this!
Unspeakable! His Gift!

—JANIE ALFORD

A PRAYER

Give me work to do;
Give me health;
Give me joy in simple things.
Give me an eye for beauty,
A tongue for truth,
A heart that loves,

A mind that reasons,
A sympathy that understands;
Give me neither malice nor envy,
But a true kindness
And a noble common sense.
At the close of each day
Give me a book,
And a friend with whom
I can be silent.

A MAN'S THANKSGIVING

God of commonsense, I give Thee thanks for the heavy blows of pain that drive me back from perilous ways into harmony with the laws of my being; for stinging whips of hunger and cold that urge to bitter strivings and glorious achievement; for steepness and roughness of the way and staunch virtues gained by climbing over jagged rocks of hardship and stumbling through dark and pathless sloughs of discouragement; for the acid blight of failure that has burned out of me all thought of easy victory and toughened my sinews for fiercer battles and greater triumphs; for mistakes I have made, and the priceless lessons I have learned from them; for disillusion and disappointment that have cleared my vision and spurred my desire; for strong appetites and passions and the power they give when under pressure and control; for my imperfections that give me the keen delight of striving toward perfection.

God of common good and human brotherhood, I give Thee thanks for siren songs of temptation that lure and entangle and the understanding of other men they reveal; for the weaknesses and failings of my neighbors and the joy of lending a helping hand; for my own shortcomings, sorrows and loneliness, that give me a deeper sympathy for others; for ingratitude and misunderstanding and the gladness of service without other reward than self-expression.

—ARTHUR W. NEWCOMB

DEAR LORD! KIND LORD!

Dear Lord! Kind Lord!
Gracious Lord! I pray

Thou wilt look on all I love
Tenderly today!

Weed their hearts of weariness,
Scatter every care
Down a wake of angel-wings
Winnowing the air.

And with all the needy
O divide, I pray,
This vast treasure of content
That is mine today.

—JAMES WHITCOMB RILEY

IN THANKFULNESS

As you well know, Lord, I forget Sometimes
The thanks I owe; sometimes gray niggling
worrries
Pile up and up, and seem so hugely tall
That I cannot see over them all.

And yet, though I complain instead of
praising,
You don't withdraw your constant
blessings, Lord.
You let me fret a little while—and then
You make me tall with gratitude again.

And for this, Lord, I thank you most of all,
For living moments when I stand erect
And see, beyond the drab molehills of care,
Mountains of blessings that are always there.

—JANE MERCHANT

PROFIT AND LOSS

I counted dollars while God counted crosses;
I counted gains while He counted losses!
I counted my worth by the things gained in
store,
But He sized me up by the scars that I bore;
I coveted honors and sought for degrees;
He wept as He counted the hours on
my knees.
And I never knew till one day by a grave
How vain are the things that we spend
life to save.
I did not yet know until Jim went above
That richest is he who is rich in God's love!

O Lord, that lends me life, lend me a heart
replete with thankfulness.

—SHAKESPEARE

For flowers that bloom about our feet;
For tender grass so fresh and sweet;
For song of bird and hum of bee;
For all things fair we hear and see,
Father in Heaven, we thank Thee!

—RALPH WALDO EMERSON

A THANKFUL HEART

Lord, Thou hast given me a cell
  Wherein to dwell,
A little house whose humble roof
  Is weatherproof....
Low is my porch as is my fate,
  Both void of state,
And yet the threshold of my door
  Is worn by the poor
Who hither come and freely get
  Good words or meat.
'Tis Thou that crown'st my glittering hearth
  With guileless mirth.
All these and better Thou dost send
   Me to this end,
  That I should render for my part
   A thankful heart.

—ROBERT HERRICK

THE LORD GIVETH

God lent him to me for my very own,
Let me become his father, me alone!
Gave him to me not for an hour—for years!
('Tis gratefulness gleams in my eyes,
  not tears.)
No joy that fathers know but it was mine,
And fathering that laddie strong and fine.

Time after time I said: ' 'Tis but a dream;
I shall wake to find things only seem
Grand as they are.' Yet still he lingered on
Till year on sweeter year had come and gone.
My heart is filled forever with a song,
Because God let me have my lad so long.

He was my own until I fully knew
And never could forget how deep and true
A father's love for his own son may be.
It drew me nearer God Himself; for He
Has loved His Son. (These are but
  grateful tears—
That he was with me all those happy years!)

—STRICKLAND GILLILAN

Gratitude is the fairest blossom which
springs from the soul.

—BALLOU

Into the well which supplies thee with water,
cast no stones.

—THE TALMUD

A thankful heart is not only the greatest virtue, but the parent of all the other virtues.

—CICERO

  Me to this end,
That I should render for my part
  A thankful heart.

—ROBERT HERRICK

CONSIDER WELL

Consider well that both by night and day
While we busily provide and care
For our disport, our revel and our play,
For pleasant melody and dainty fare,
Death stealeth on full slily; unaware
He lieth at hand and shall us all surprise,
We wot not when nor where nor in what
  wise.

When fierce temptations threat thy soul with
  loss
Think on His Passion and the bitter pain,
Think on the mortal anguish of the Cross,
Think on Christ's blood let out at every vein,
Think of His precious heart all rent in twain;
For thy redemption think all this was
  wrought,
Nor be that lost which He so dearly bought.

—THOMAS MORE

❧ HAPPINESS ❧

T he happiest people I know are people who know God. They have the biggest times, the heartiest laughs. There is real fun and joy and assurance that comes from knowing God, from having a strong faith in him.

—BILLY GRAHAM

The grand essentials to happiness in this life are something to do, something to love, and something to hope for.

—JOSEPH ADDISON

It was probably a mistake to pursue happiness; much better to create happiness; still better to create happiness for others. The more happiness you created for others the more would be yours—a solid satisfaction that no one could ever take away from you.

—LLOYD DOUGLAS

When we are collecting books, we are collecting happiness.

—VINCENT STARRETT

GOD GIVE ME JOY

God give me joy in the common things:
In the dawn that lures, the eve that sings.

In the new grass sparkling after rain,
In the late wind's wild and weird refrain;

In the springtime's spacious field of gold,
In the precious light by winter doled.

God give me joy in the love of friends,
In their dear home talk as summer ends;

In the songs of children, unrestrained;
In the sober wisdom age has gained.

God give me joy in the tasks that press,
In the memories that burn and bless;

In the thought that life has love to spend,
In the faith that God's at journey's end.

God give me hope for each day that springs,
God give me joy in the common things!

—THOMAS CURTIS CLARK

The longer I live the more I am convinced that the one thing worth living for and dying for is the privilege of making someone more happy and more useful. No man who ever does anything to lift his fellows ever makes a sacrifice.

—BOOKER T. WASHINGTON

It is undeniable that the great quest of humanity is happiness. But was the world created to be happy? How many are truly happy? I've studied people in all classes and conditions, and everywhere I have found, when you get below the surface, that it is mostly the insincere individual who says, "I am happy." Nearly everybody wants something he hasn't got, and as things are constructed, what he wants is money—more money than he has in his pocket.

But after all, money can buy only a few things. Why should any one envy the captains of industry? Their lives are made up of those vast, incessant worries from which the average individual is happily spared. Worry, worry, that is the evil of life.

What do I consider the nearest approximation to happiness of which the present human nature is capable? Why, living on a farm which is one's own, far from the hectic, artificial conditions of the city—a farm where one gets directly from one's own soil what one needs to sustain life, with a garden in front and a healthy, normal family to contribute those small domestic joys which relieve a man from business strain.

—THOMAS EDISON

I TASTE A LIQUOR NEVER BREWED

I taste a liquor never brewed,
From tankards scooped in pearl;
Not all the vats upon the Rhine
Yield such an alcohol!

Inebriate of air am I,
And debauchee of dew,
Reeling, through endless summer days,
From inns of molten blue.

When landlords turns the drunken bee
Out of the foxglove's door,
When butterflies renounce their drams,
I shall but drink the more!

Till seraphs swing their snowy hats,
And saints to windows run,
To see the little tippler
Leaning against the sun!

—EMILY DICKINSON

In nature there are no punishments and no rewards—just consequences.

—PIERCE HARRIS

The most evident sign of wisdom is continued cheerfulness.

—MICHEL DE MONTAIGNE

SUNSHINE AND MUSIC

A laugh is just like sunshine.
It freshens all the day,
It tips the peak of life with light,
And drives the clouds away.
The soul grows glad that hears it
And feels its courage strong.
A laugh is just like sunshine
For cheering folks along.

A laugh is just like music.
It lingers in the heart,
And where its melody is heard
The ills of life depart;
And happy thoughts come crowding
Its joyful notes to greet:
A laugh is just like music
For making living sweet.

The most unhappy man or woman on earth is the one who rises in the morning with nothing to do and wonders how he will pass off the day.

—LESLIE M. SHAW

It is only a poor sort of happiness that could ever come by caring very much about our own narrow pleasures. We can only have the highest happiness by having wide thoughts, and much feeling for the rest of the world, as well as ourselves; and this sort of happiness often brings so much pain with it that we can only tell it from pain by its being what we would choose before everything else, because our souls see it is good.

—GEORGE ELIOT

ONLY THE WISE MAN

Only the wise man draws from life, and from every stage of it, its true savour, because only he feels the beauty, the dignity, and the value of life. The flowers of youth may fade, but the summer, the autumn, and even the winter of human existence, have their majestic grandeur, which the wise man recognizes and glorifies. To see all things in God; to make of one's own life a journey towards the ideal; to live with gratitude, with devoutness, with gentleness and courage;—this was the splendid aim of Marcus Aurelius. And if you add to it the humility which kneels, and the charity which gives, you have the whole wisdom of the children of God, the immortal joy which is the heritage of the true Christian.

—HENRI FREDERIC AMIEL

The days that make us happy make us wise.

—JOHN MASEFIELD

Happiness follows simplicity.

—IRISH PROVERB

LITTLE ROADS TO HAPPINESS

The little roads to happiness,
   they are not hard to find;
They do not lead to great success—
   but to a quiet mind.
They do not lead to mighty power,
   nor to substantial wealth.
They bring one to a book, a flower,
   a song of cheer and health.
The little roads to happiness are free to
   everyone;
They lead one to the wind's caress,
   to kiss of friendly sun.
These little roads are shining white,
   for all the world to see;
Their sign-boards, pointing left and right,
   are love and sympathy.
The little roads of happiness have this
   most charming way;
No matter how they may digress throughout
   the busy day;
No matter where they twist and wind
   through fields of rich delight,
They're always of the self same mind to
   lead us home at night.

—WILHELMINA STITCH

THE JOY OF WORK

Give us, oh, give us, the man who sings at his work! He will do more in the same time,—he will do it better,—he will persevere longer. One is scarcely sensible of fatigue whilst he marches to music. The very stars are said to make harmony as they revolve in their spheres. Wondrous is the strength of cheerfulness, altogether past calculation in its powers of endurance. Efforts, to be permanently useful, must be uniformly joyous, a spirit all sunshine, graceful from very gladness, beautiful because bright.

—THOMAS CARLYLE

THE ROADS OF HAPPINESS

The roads of happiness are not
   The selfish roads of pleasure seeking,
Where cheeks are flushed with haste and hot
And none has time for kindly speaking.
But they're the roads where lovers stray,
   Where wives and husbands walk together
And children romp along the way
   Whenever it is pleasant weather.

The roads of happiness are trod
   By simple folks and tender-hearted,
By gentle folks that worship God
   And want to live their days unparted.
There kindly people stop and talk,
   Regardless of the chase for money,
There, arm in arm, the grown-ups walk
   And every eye you see is sunny.

The roads of happiness are lined,
   Not with the friends of royal splendor,
But with the loyal friends and kind
   That do the gentle deeds and tender.
There fame has never brought unrest
   Nor glory set men's hearts to aching;
There unabandoned is life's best
   For selfish love and money making.

The roads of happiness are those
   That do not lead to pomp and glory
But wind among the joys and woes
   That make the humble toiler's story.
The roads that oft we used to tread
   In early days when first we mated,
When hearts were light and cheeks were red,
   And days were not with burdens frieghted.

—EDGAR A. GUEST

THE HAPPY MAN

If you observe a really happy man you will find him building a boat, writing a symphony, educating his son, growing double dahlias in his garden, or looking for dinosaur eggs in the Gobi desert. He will not be searching for happiness as if it were a collar button that has rolled under the radiator. He will not be striving for it as if it were a goal in itself, nor will he be seeking for it among the nebulous wastes of metaphysics.

To find happiness we must seek for it in a focus outside ourselves.

—W. BERAN WOLFE

❖ THE HOME ❖

And where we love is home,
Home that our feet may leave, but not our
hearts.
The chain may lengthen, but it never parts.

—OLIVER WENDELL HOLMES

A COVENANT

We need to think of the home as the cradle into which the future is born.

We need to think of the family as the nursery in which the new social order is being reared.

The family is a covenant with posterity.

—SIDNEY GOLDSTEIN

DUSK

These are the things men seek at dusk:
*　Firelight across a room,*
Green splashing against dim roofs,
*　Gardens where flowers bloom.*
Lamplighted gold of a windowpane,
*　Trees with tall stars above,*
Women who watch a darkening street
*　For somebody they love.*
Faith of a small child's rhyming prayer,
*　Candle shine . . . tables spread*
With a blossom or two in a gay blue bowl,
*　Fragrance of crusted bread.*
For men may dream of a clipper ship,
*　A wharf or a gypsy camp,*
But their footsteps pattern a homing way
*　To a woman, a child, a lamp.*

—HELEN WELSHIMER

I would say to all: use your gentlest voice at home. Watch it day by day, as a pearl of great price; for it will be worth to you in days to come more than the best pearl hid in the sea. A kind voice is joy, like a lark's song, to a hearth at home. It is a light that sings as well as shines. Train it to sweet tones now, and it will keep in tune through life.

—ELIHU BURRITT

WHAT MAKES A HOME?

Love and sympathy and confidence,
The memories of childhood,
The kindness of parents,
The bright hopes of youth.
The sisters' pride,
The brothers' sympathy and help,
The mutual confidence,
The common hopes and interests and
*　sorrows—*
These create and sanctify the home.

—JOHN LUBBOCK

SEND HER A VALENTINE

Send her a valentine to say
You love her in the same old way.
Just drop the long familiar ways
And live again the old-time days
When love was new and youth was bright
And all was laughter and delight,
And treat her as you would if she
Were still the girl that used to be.

Pretend that all the years have passed
Without one cold and wintry blast;
That you are coming still to woo
Your sweetheart as you used to do;
Forget that you have walked along
The paths of life where right and wrong
And joy and grief in battle are,
And play the heart without a scar.

Be what you were when youth was fine
And send to her a valentine;
Forget the burdens and the woe
That have been given you to know
And to the wife, so fond and true,
The pledges of the past renew.
'Twill cure her life of every ill
To find that you're her sweetheart still.

—EDGAR A. GUEST

THE HOUSE YOU ARE BUILDING

Every spirit builds itself a house, and beyond its house a world, and beyond its world a heaven. Know then that the world exists for you. For you is the phenomenon perfect.

What we are, that only can we see.

All that Adam had, all that Caesar could, you have and can do. Adam called his house, heaven and earth. Caesar called his house, Rome.

You perhaps call yours a cobbler's trade; a scholar's garret. Yet line for line and point for point, your dominion is as great as theirs, though without fine names.

Build therefore your own world. As fast as you conform your life to the pure idea in your mind, that will unfold into great proportions.

—RALPH WALDO EMERSON

I AM YOUR WIFE

Oh, let me lay my head tonight upon your
*   breast*
And close my eyes against the light.
*   I fain would rest.*
I'm weary and the world looks sad.
*   This worldly strife*
Turns me to you! And, oh,
*   I'm glad to be your wife.*
Though friends may fail or turn aside,
*   yet I have you.*
And in your love I may abide for you
*   are true.*
My only solace in each grief, and in despair
Your tenderness is my relief.
*   It soothes each care.*
If joys of life could alienate this poor weak
*   heart*
From yours, then may no pleasure great
*   enough to part*
Our sympathies fall to my lot.
*   I'd ever remain*
Bereft of friends, though true or not,
*   just to retain*
Your true regard, your presence bright,
*   thru care and strife;*
And, oh, I thank my God tonight
*   I am your wife.*

JUST TO BE NEEDED

"She always seems so tied" is what
*   friends say;*
She never has a chance to get away.
Home, husband, children, duties great
*   or small,*
Keep her forever at their beck and call.
But she confides, with laughter in her eyes,
She never yet felt fretted by these ties.
"Just to be needed is more sweet," says she,
"Than any freedom in this world could be."

—MARY EVERSLEY

MARRIED LIFE

Getting married is easy. Staying married is more diffcult. Staying happily married for a lifetime should rank among the fine arts.

—FLACK

BEFORE AND AFTER MARRIAGE

We used to talk of so many things,
Roses and summer and golden rings,
Music and dances and books and plays,
Venice and moonlight and future days.

Now our chief subjects are food and bills,
Genevieve's measles and Johnny's ills;
New shoes for Betty, a hat for Jane,
Taxes, insurance, the mail and rain!

We used to say that Romance would stay.
We'd walk together a magic way!
Though we don't talk as in days of yore,
Strange, is it not, that I love you more?

—ANNE CAMPBELL

WE HAVE LIVED AND LOVED TOGETHER

We have lived and loved together
*   Through many changing years;*
We have shared each other's gladness
*   And wept each other's tears;*
I have known ne'er a sorrow
*   That was long unsoothed by thee;*
For thy smiles can make a summer
*   Where darkness else would be.*

Like the leaves that fall around us
　In autumn's fading hours,
Are the traitor's smiles, that darken
　When the cloud of sorrow lowers;
And though many such we've known, love,
　Too prone, alas, to range,
We both can speak of one love
　Which time can never change.

We have lived and loved together
　Through many changing years;
We have shared each other's gladness
　And wept each other's tears.
And let us hope the future
　As the past has been will be:
I will share with thee my sorrows,
　And thou thy joys with me.

—CHARLES JEFFERYS

ONE OF US TWO

The day will dawn, when one of us shall
　harken
　In vain to hear a voice that has grown
　dumb,
And morns will fade, noons pale,
　and shadows darken,
　While sad eyes watch for feet that
　never come.

One of us two must sometime face existence
　Alone with memories that but sharpen
　pain
And these sweet days shall shine back in
　the distance,
　Like dreams of summer dawns,
　in nights of rain.

One of us two, with tortured heart half
　broken,
　Shall read long-treasured letters through
　salt tears,
Shall kiss with anguished lips each
　cherished token,
　That speaks of these love-crowned,
　delicious years.

One of us two shall find all light, all beauty,
　All joy on earth, a tale forever done;
Shall know henceforth that life means only
　duty.
　Oh, God! Oh, God! have pity on that one.

—ELLA WHEELER WILCOX

WEDDING ANNIVERSARY

This is the anniversary of the day
　Of days, for us, when we with faith
　and hope
Fared forth together; solemn and yet gay
　We faced the future, for life's upward
　slope
Was joyous going, and we never thought
　Then, that there might be worries—
　hours of pain
And sleepless nights that left one
　overwrought—
　That loss would often come instead of
　gain.

But looking back, the time has not seemed
　long,
　Although the road, for us, was sometimes
　rough . . .
We have grown quiet and the buoyant song
　Once in our hearts sings low, and yet
　enough
Of loveliness still lives to make amend
　To us, for all the ills life chose to send.

—MARGARET E. BRUNER

WHAT MAKES A HOME

"What makes a home?"
I asked my little boy,
And this is what he said,
"You, mother,
And when father comes.
Our table set all shiny,
And my bed,
And mother, I think it's home,
Because we love each other."

You who are old and wise,
What would you say
If you were asked the question?
Tell me, pray.

And simply as a little child,
The old wise ones can answer nothing
　more—
A man, a woman and a child,
Their love,
Warm as the gold hearth fire along the floor.
A table, and a lamp for light.

And smooth white beds at night.
Only the old sweet fundamental things.

And long ago I learned—
Home may be near, home may be far
But it is anywhere
That love
And a few plain household treasures are.

BLIND LOVE

She knows her groceries, I guess;
She knows her onions, I confess;
She knows more than I can express.
I know you couldn't realize
How much she knows, she is so wise—
On any theme she can advise.
She knows the things that I do not
(And that is saying quite a lot);
When she speaks, all I say is, "What?"
I only wish that I could tell
The things she does one-half so well,
But I am just a plain dumbbell.
She is as wise as she can be,
But there's one thing she cannot see,
And that is—why she married me!

—Van H. Eshelman

HOUSE AND HOME

Anyone can build an altar; it requires God to provide the flame.

Anyone can build a house; we need the Lord for the creation of a home.

A house is an agglomeration of brick and stones, with an assorted collection of manufactured goods; a home is the abiding-place of ardent affection, of fervent hope, of genial trust.

There is many a homeless man who lives in a richly furnished house. There is many a fifteen-pound house in the crowded street which is an illuminated and beautiful home.

The sumptuously furnished house may only be an exquisitely sculptured tomb; the scantily furnished house may be the very hearthstone of the eternal God.

—John Henry Jowett

He is the half-part of a blessed man,
Left to be finished by such as she;
And she a fair divided excellence,
Whose fulness of perfection lies in him.

—Shakespeare

WHAT MAKES A HOME

A man can build a mansion
Anywhere this world about,
A man can build a palace
Richly furnish it throughout.

A man can build a mansion
Or a tiny cottage fair,
But it's not the hallowed place called
"Home"
'Til Mother's dwelling there.

A man can build a mansion
With a high and spacious dome,
But no man in this world can build
That precious thing called "Home."

A man can build a mansion
Carting treasures o'er the foam,
Yes, a man can build the building
But a woman makes it "Home."

HOME FOLKS

Home folks—love 'em, well I guess,
Hearts jest made of real kindness;
Miss 'em—I should say I do,
Don't find many folks as true.
Seems like now I jes' can hear
Home folks words of love and cheer,
Knowin' I've a welcome there
Truer an' warmer'n anywhere.

Home folks ain't jes' family kin,
They're the folks with whom you've been
Reared and raised for years an' years,
Minglin' all your smiles an' tears
Till they seem a part o' you
From yer childhood clear on through,
Standin' by you, lose or win,
Same as real blood, kith an' kin.

Makes no difference what you do,
Seems like homefolks still stay true;
Overlookin' wayward ways,

Jes' rememberin' happy days,
Er when praise is but yer due
Fer some thing you've tried to do,
Home folks hands are quick to clasp
Yours in proud an' hearty grasp.

Stranger folks are purty nice,
Distant things lure an' entice,
But I like home folks the bes'!
Bein' with 'em's like a res'.
When death comes an' I must go,
Wish that I could only know
That there'd be some home folks nigh,
Sorter watchin', lingerin' by.

—RUTH YOLAND SHAW

Home is the place where character is built,
where sacrifices to contribute to the happiness of others are made, and where love has
taken up its abode.

—ELIJAH KELLOGG

I turned an ancient poet's book
And found upon the page,
"Stone walls do not a prison make
Or iron bars a cage."
Yes, that is true, and something more,
You will find where'er you roam
That marble floors and gilded walls
Can never make a home.
But everywhere that love abides,
And friendship is a guest
Is surely home, and home sweet home,
For there the soul can rest.

—HENRY VAN DYKE

WHEN A MAN TURNS HOMEWARD

When a man turns homeward through the
    moonfall,
Swift in his path like a meteor bright,
Kindling his wonder and blinding his sight,
His feet will go on, his heartbeats will call
Deep in his breast like quick music, and all
The darkness that swirls like a flame of dead
    light
Cannot fetter his feet turned homeward at
    night.

Past thicket and trees like a towering wall
He will go on over hillside and stone,
Clinging like hope to the road that he knows;
Groping along like a shadow, alone,
He will reach for the latch where a candle,
    gold-eyed,
Watches with her for the door that will close,
Leaving the world like a kitten outside!

—DANIEL WHITEHEAD HICKY

Home to me is laughter . . .
Kisses on my cheek when they're least
    expected;
Glances filled with gladness;
The happiness in knowing
I'm a portion of
My family's fulfillment.
Home to me . . . is love!

—JUNE BROWN HARRIS

TWO TRAVELERS

She talked about her travels
Of ecstasies the rarest;
Of winter days in Denmark
And summer nights in Paris.

She talked about her children
Of leading small, plump hands
And making countless journeys
Into many wonderlands.

They both spoke quite sincerely
With no intent to boast.
I pondered long and wonderingly
Which one had traveled most.

—VARNEY

MOTHER

As long ago we carried to your knees
The tales and treasures of eventful days,
Knowing no deed too humble for your praise,
Nor any gift too trivial to please,

So still we bring with older smiles and tears,
What gifts we may to claim the old, dear
    right;
Your faith beyond the silence and the night;
Your love still close and watching through
    the years.

HOPE

"Tomorrow, friend, will be another day,"
A seer wise of old was wont to say
To him who came at eventide, in grief,
Because the day had borne no fruitful sheaf.

O Lord of Life, that each of us might learn
From vain todays and yesterdays to turn,
To face the future with a hope newborn
That what we hope for cometh with the
*   morn!*

—THOMAS CURTIS CLARK

The word which God has written on the brow of every man is *Hope*.

—VICTOR HUGO

THE PESSIMIST

The pessimist's a cheerless man;
  To him the world's a place
Of anxious thoughts and clouds and gloom;
  Smiles visit not his face.

Though brightest sunshine floods the earth,
  And flowers are all ablow,
He spreads depression where he can
  By dismal tales of woe.

The pessimist's a hopeless man,
  He's full of doubt and fear;
No radiant visions come to him
  Of glad days drawing near.

The pessimist's a joyless man,
  He finds no sweet delight
In making this a happier world,
  In fighting for the right.

He views the future with alarm,
  He sees no light ahead;
Most wretched of all men is he,
  Because his hope is dead.

Everything that is done in the world is done by hope.

—MARTIN LUTHER

THE TIDE WILL WIN

On the far reef the breakers
  Recoil in shattered foam,
While still the sea behind them
  Urges its forces home;
Its song of triumph surges
  O'er all the thunderous din,
The wave may break in failure,
  But the tide is sure to win!

The reef is strong and cruel;
  Upon its jagged wall
One wave, a score, a hundred,
  Broken and beaten fall;
Yet in defeat they conquer,
  The sea comes flooding in,
Wave upon wave it routed,
  But the tide is sure to win.

O mighty sea! thy message
  In clanging spray is cast;
Within God's plan of progress
  It matters not at last
How wide the shores of evil,
  How strong the reefs of sin,
The wave may be defeated,
  But the tide is sure to win!

—PRISCILLA LEONARD

THE ARROW

The life of men
  Is an arrow's flight,
Out of darkness
  Into light,
And out of light
  Into darkness again;
Perhaps to pleasure,
  Perhaps to pain.

There must be Something,
  Above, or below;
Something unseen
  A mighty Bow,
A Hand that tires not,
  A sleepless Eye
That sees the arrow
  Fly, and fly;
One who knows
  Why we live—and die.

—RICHARD HENRY STODDARD

Hope ever urges us on, and tells us tomorrow will be better.

—ALBIUS TIBULLUS

Hope awakens courage. He who can implant courage in the human soul is the best physician.

—VON KNEBEL

HOPE'S SONG

I hear it singing, singing sweetly,
  Softly in an undertone,—
Singing as if God had taught it,
  "It is better farther on!"

Night and day it sings the same song,
  Sings it while I sit alone,
Sings so that the heart may hear it,
  "It is better farther on!"

Sits upon the grave and sings it,
  Sings it when the heart would groan,
Sings it when the shadows darken,
  "It is better farther on!"

Farther on? Oh, how much farther?
  Count the milestones one by one—
No, not counting, only trusting,
  "It is better farther on!"

He who loses hope, may then part with anything.

—WILLIAM CONGREVE

Your heart's desires be with you!

—SHAKESPEARE

BE HOPEFUL

Be hopeful, friend, when clouds are dark and
  days are gloomy, dreary,
Be hopeful even when the heart is sick and
  sad and weary.
Be hopeful when it seems your plans are all
  opposed and thwarted;
Go not upon life's battlefield despondent and
  fainthearted.
And, friends, be hopeful of yourself. Do by-
  gone follies haunt you?
Forget them and begin afresh. And let no
  hindrance daunt you.
Though unimportant your career may seem
  as you begin it,
Press on, for victory's ahead. Be hopeful,
  friend, and win it.

—STRICKLAND GILLILAN

Be not anxious about to-morrow. Do to-day's duty, fight to-day's temptation, and do not weaken and distract yourself by looking forward to things which you cannot see, and could not understand if you saw them.

—CHARLES KINGSLEY

WHEN HOPE DIES

D'ja ever see a flock o' black crows
'Bout sun-down time o' day
A-sitting in an ole dead tree
And they seem to laugh sardonically
In an evil croaking way?

Seems to me they're ole dreams o' mine
Come home to roost at night
Perched on the limbs o' Dead Hope tree
And they mock and laugh and jeer at me
Ole black dreams that once were white.

—GLENN G. EDWARDS

BE HOPEFUL

Fain would I hold my lamp of life aloft
Like yonder tower built high above the reef;
Steadfast, though tempests rave or winds
  blow soft;
Clear, though the sky dissolve in tears of
  grief.

For darkness passes; storms shall not abide:
A little patience and the storm is past.
After the sorrow of the ebbing tide
The singing flood returns in joy at last.

The night is long and pain weighs heavily;
But God will hold His world above despair.

Look to the east, where up the lucid sky
The morning climbs! The day shall yet be
fair.

WORK WITHOUT HOPE

All Nature seems at work. Slugs leave their
lair—
The bees are stirring—birds are on the
wing—
And Winter, slumbering in the open air,
Wears on his smiling face a dream of Spring!
And I, the while, the sole unbusy thing,
Nor honey make, nor pair, nor build, nor
sing.

Yet well I ken the banks where amaranths
blow,
Have traced the fount whence streams of
nectar flow.
Bloom, O ye amaranths! bloom for whom ye
may,
For me ye bloom not! Glide, rich streams,
away!
With lips unbrighten'd, wreathless brow, I
stroll:
And would you learn the spells that drowse
my soul?
Work without Hope draws nectar in a sieve,
And Hope without an object cannot live.

—SAMUEL TAYLOR COLERIDGE

THE ONE WHO PLANS

Often darkness fills the pathway of the
pilgrim's onward track,
And we shrink from going forward—
trembling, feel like going back:
But the Lord, Who plans so wisely,
leads us on both day and night,
Till at last, in silent wonder,
we rejoice in Wisdom's light.

Though the tunnel may be tedious thro'
the narrow, darkened way,
Yet it amply serves its purpose—
soon it brings the light of day:
And the way so greatly dreaded,
as we backward take a glance,
Shows the skill of careful planning:
never the result of chance!

Trust the Engineer Eternal, surely all His
works are right,
Though we cannot always trace them,
faith will turn at last to sight:
Then no more the deepening shadows of the
dark and dismal way,
There for ever in clear sunlight,
we'll enjoy "the perfect day."

Hope is the dream of a waking man.

—DIOGENES

THE TREASURE OF HOPE

O fair Bird, singing in the woods
To the rising and the setting sun,
Does ever any throb of pain
Thrill through thee ere thy song be done:
Because the Summer fleets so fast;
Because the Autumn fades so soon;
Because the deadly Winter treads
So closely on the steps of June?

O sweet Maid, opening like a rose
In Love's mysterious, honeyed air,
Dost think sometimes the day will come
When thou shalt be no longer fair:
When love will leave thee, and pass on
To younger and to brighter eyes;
And thou shalt live unloved, alone,
A dull life, only dowered with sighs?

O brave Youth, panting for the fight,
To conquer wrong and win thee fame,
Dost see thyself grown old and spent,
And thine a still unhonored name:
When all thy hopes have come to naught,
And all thy fair schemes droop and pine,
And Wrong uplifts her hydra heads
To fall to stronger hearts than thine?

Nay: Song and Love and lofty Aims
May never be where Faith is not;
Strong souls within the Present life,
The Future veiled—the Past forgot:
Grasping what is, with hands of steel
They bend what shall be to their will;
And, blind alike to doubt and dread,
The End, for which they are, fulfil.

—LEWIS MORRIS

IMMORTALITY

The great Easter truth is not that we are to
live newly after death—that is not the
great thing—but that we are to be new here
and now by the power of the resurrection; not
so much that we are to live forever as that we
are to, and may, live nobly now because we
are to live forever.

—PHILLIPS BROOKS

There is a haven where storm-tossed souls
　　may go.
You call it death—we, immortality!

You call it death, this seeming endless sleep.
We call it birth, the soul at last set free.
'Tis hampered not by time or space—
　　you weep.
Why weep at death? 'Tis immortality!

Farewell, dear voyageur; 'twill not be long.
Your work is done—now may peace rest
　　with thee.
Your kindly thoughts and deeds,
　　they will live on.
This is not death—'tis immortality!

Farewell, dear voyageur. The river winds
　　and turns.
The cadence of your song wafts near me.
And now you know the thing that all men
　　learn:
There is no death—there's immortality.

Ah, why should we wear black for the guests of God?

—JOHN RUSKIN

GUESTS OF GOD

From the dust of the weary highway,
　　From the smart of sorrow's rod,
Into the royal presence,
　　They are bidden as guests of God.
The veil from their eyes is taken,
　　Sweet mysteries they are shown,
Their doubts and fears are over,
　　For they know as they are known.

For them there should be rejoicing
　　For them, the festal array,
As for the bride in her beauty
　　Whom love hath taken away;
Sweet hours of peaceful waiting,
　　Till the path that we have trod
Shall end at the Father's gateway,
　　And we are the guests of God.

Which is the more difficult, to be born, or to rise again? . . . Is it more difficult to come into being than to return to it?

—BLAISE PASCAL

When he understood it, he called for his friends, and told them of it. Then said he, 'I am going to my Father's; and though with great difficulty I have got hither, yet now I do not regret me of all the trouble I have been at to arrive where I am. My sword I give to him that shall succeed me in my pilgrimage, and my courage and skill to him that can get it. My marks and scars I carry with me, to be a witness for me that I have fought His battle who will now be my rewarder.' When the day that he must go hence was come, many accompanied him to the river-side, into which as he went, he said, 'Death, where is thy sting?' And as he went down deeper, he said, 'Grave, where is thy victory?' So he passed over, and all the trumpets sounded for him on the other side.

—JOHN BUNYAN

Heaven is the soul finding its own perfect personality in God.

—PHILLIPS BROOKS

A GREATER PLAN

There is a plan far greater than the plan
　　you know;
There is a landscape broader than the one
　　you see;

A GLIMPSE OF GLORY

I have caught a glimpse of glory
  Never seen by mortal eyes,
Just beyond the blue horizon
  Of evening's transient skies;
But the ear of hope has heard it
  And the eye of faith can see
Sound and sign of heaven's nearness
  Just beyond mortality.

I have caught a glimpse of glory,
  Of that bright eternal day,
When the mists of Time have lifted
  And we lay aside his clay;
  Then shall be the consummation
  Of our longing and desire,
For we'll sing the Song of Ages
  In the resurrection choir!

I have caught a glimpse of glory
  Just beyond the brink of Time,
And I travel toward the sunrise
  Of a better land and clime.
Soon I'll trade this earth for heaven
  And inside some golden door
I shall greet the ones I've cherished
  Safe with Jesus evermore.

THE ETERNAL LIFE

There is a land of pure delight,
  Where saints immortal reign;
Infinite day excludes the night,
  And pleasures banish pain.

There everlasting spring abides,
  And never-withering flowers;
Death like a narrow sea divides
  This heavenly land from ours.

Sweet fields beyond the swelling flood
  Stand dressed in living green;
So to the Jews old Canaan stood,
  While Jordan rolled between.

But timorous mortals start and shrink
  To cross this narrow sea,
And linger shivering on the brink,
  And fear to launch away.

Oh! could we make our doubts remove,
  These gloomy thoughts that rise,

And see that Canaan that we love
  With unbeclouded eyes—

Could we but climb where Moses stood,
  And view the landscape o'er,
Not Jordan's stream, nor death's cold flood,
  Could fright us from the shore.

There is a Land of Pure Delight.

—ISAAC WATTS

God who placed me here will do what He pleases with me hereafter, and He knows best what to do.

—BOLINGBROKE

FOR A BIRTHDAY

This would have been your birthday,
  had you stayed.
You would have been—how old?
  I cannot think.
I only know that still the golden link
Encircles us. Insatiate years have laid
Relentless hands upon me; have betrayed
The youth that rivaled yours. Now, on the
  brink
Of every birthday, impotent, I shrink
Before the years I cannot well evade.

But birthdays of the dead may come and go
Without recording; for these, Time stands
  still.
This is the benison the living know.
And somewhere—somewhere just beyond
  the chill,
You wait, where all the flowers, unfading,
  blow—
Forever twenty—on a little hill.

—RUTH CRARY

Immortality is not a gift,
Immortality is an achievement;
And only those who strive mightily
Shall possess it.

—EDGAR LEE MASTERS

LIFE

Alas for him who never sees
The stars shine through his cypress-trees!
Who, hopeless, lays his dead away,
Nor looks to see the breaking day
Across the mournful marbles play!
Who hath not learned, in hours of faith,
The truth to flesh and sense unknown,
That life is ever Lord of Death,
And Love can never lose its own!

—JOHN GREENLEAF WHITTIER

CATO'S SOLILOQUY

It must be so—Plato, thou reason'st well—
Else whence this pleasing hope, this fond
    desire,
This longing after immortality?
Or whence this secret dread, and inward
    horror
Of falling into nought? Why shrinks the
    Soul
Back on herself, and startles at destruction?
'Tis the Divinity, that stirs within us;
'Tis Heav'n itself, that points out a hereafter,
And intimates eternity to man.
Eternity! thou pleasing, dreadful thought!
Through what variety of untried being,
Through what new scenes and changes must
    we pass!
The wide, th' unbounded prospect lies
    before me;
But shadows, clouds, and darkness rest
    upon it.
Here will I hold. If there's a power above us,
(And that there is, all Nature cries aloud
Through all her works,) He must delight in
    virtue;
And that which He delights in must be
    happy.
But when or where? This world was made
    for Caesar.
I'm weary of conjectures—this must end 'em.
    Thus am I doubly arm'd—my death and
    life,
My bane and antidote are both before me.
This in a moment brings me to an end;
But this informs me I shall never die.
The Soul, secured in her existence, smiles

At the drawn dagger, and defies its point;
The stars shall fade away, the Sun himself
Grow dim with age, and Nature, sink in
    years;
But thou shalt flourish in immortal youth,
Unhurt amidst the war of elements,
The wreck of matter and the crash of worlds.

—JOSEPH ADDISON

LOVE'S STRENGTH

They sin who tell us Love can die:
With life all other passions fly,
All others are but vanity.
In Heaven ambition cannot dwell,
Nor avarice in the vaults of Hell;
Earthly these passions; as of Earth,
They perish where they have their birth.
    But Love is indestructible;
Its holy flame forever burneth;
From Heaven it came—to Heaven returneth.
Too oft on Earth a troubled guest,
At times deceived, at times opprest,
    It here is tried and purified,
And hath in Heaven its perfect rest.
It soweth here with toil and care,
But the harvest-time of Love is there.

—ROBERT SOUTHEY

REST REMAINETH

Easter day breaks!
    Christ rises! Mercy every way is infinite—
Earth breaks up; time drops away;
    In flows heaven with its new day
Of endless life!

—ROBERT BROWNING

OUR OWN FOREVER

Our own are our own forever, God taketh
    not back His gift:
They may pass beyond our vision, but our
    souls shall find them out,
When the waiting is all accomplished, and
    the deathly shadows lift,
And glory is given for grieving, and the
    surety of God for doubt.

We may find the waiting bitter and count
  the silence long;
God knoweth we are dust, and pitieth our
  pain;
And when faith hath grown to fullness and
  the silence changed to song,
We shall eat the fruit of patience and shall
  hunger not again.

So, sorrowing hearts, who wait in the
  darkness and all alone,
Missing a dear lost presence and the joy
  of a vanished day,
Be comforted with this message, that our
  own are forever our own,
And God, who gave the precious gift, He
  takes it never away.

—SUSAN COOLIDGE

HURRYING YEARS

For life seems so little when life is past,
And the memories of sorrow flee so fast.
And the woes which were bitter to you and
  to me,
Shall vanish as raindrops which fall in the
  sea;
And all that has hurt us shall be made good,
And the puzzles which hindered be
  understood,
And the long, hard march through the
  wilderness bare
Seem but a day's journey when once we are
  there.

—SUSAN COOLIDGE

And yet, dear heart! remembering thee,
  Am I not richer than of old?
Safe in thy immortality,
What change can reach the wealth I hold?
What chance can mar the pearl and gold
  Thy love hath left in trust for me?

And while in life's long afternoon,
  Where cool and long the shadows grow,
I walk to meet the night that soon
  Shall shape and shadow overflow,
I cannot feel that thou art far,

Since near at need the angels are;

And when the sunset gates unbar,
  Shall I not see thee waiting stand,
And, white against the evening star,
  The welcome of thy beckoning hand?

—JOHN GREENLEAF WHITTIER

A LEGACY

Friend of my many years!
When the great silence falls, at last, on me,
Let me not leave, to pain and sadden thee,
  A memory of tears,

But pleasant thoughts alone
Of one who was thy friendship's honored
  guest
And drank the wine of consolation pressed
  From sorrows of thy own.

I leave with thee a sense
Of hands upheld and trials rendered less—
The unselfish joy which is to helpfulness
  Its own great recompense;

The knowledge that from thine,
As from the garments of the Master, stole
Calmness and strength, the virtue which
  makes whole
  And heals without a sign;

Yea more, the assurance strong
That love, which fails of perfect utterance
  here,
Lives on to fill the heavenly atmosphere
  With its immortal song.

—JOHN GREENLEAF WHITTIER

THE WHOLE MAN IMMORTAL

Present and future are alike bound up in
  our belief of our Lord's resurrection and
ascension; and dreary indeed must this present be, and gloomy and clouded that future,
if our belief in our risen and ascended Lord be
uncertain, partial, precarious.

—BISHOP ELLICOTT

EASTER

Say not that death is king, that night is lord,
That loveliness is passing, beauty dies;
Nor tell me hope's a vain, deceptive dream
Fate lends to life, a pleasing, luring gleam
To light awhile the earth's despondent skies,
Till death brings swift and sure its dread
    reward.

Say not that youth deceives, but age is true,
That roses quickly pass, while cypress bides,
That happiness is foolish, grief is wise,
That stubborn dust shall choke our human
    cries.
Death tells new worlds, and life immortal
    hides
Beyond the veil, which shall all wrongs undo.
This was the tale God breathed to me at
    dawn
When flooding sunrise told the night was
    gone.

—Thomas Curtis Clark

AT A GRAVE

Valor, love, undoubting trust,
Patience, and fidelity
Lie beneath this carven stone.
If the end of these be dust,
And their doom oblivion,
Then is life a mockery.

—Thomas Bailey Aldrich

LIFE SHALL LIVE FOR EVERMORE

My own dim life should teach me this,
    That life shall live for evermore,
    Else earth is darkness at the core,
And dust and ashes all that is;

This round of green, this orb of flame,
    Fantastic beauty; such as lurks
    In some wild poet, when he works
Without a conscience or an aim.

What then were God to such as I?
    'Twere hardly worth my while to choose
    Of things all mortal; or to use
A little patience ere I die;

'Twere best at once to sink to peace,
    Like birds the charming serpent draws,
    To drop head-foremost in the jaws
Of vacant darkness and to cease.

—Alfred Tennyson

Blessed are they that are homesick for
they shall come at last to their father's
house.

—Jean Paul Richter

A COMRADE RIDES AHEAD

Time brings us change and leaves us fretting;
    We weep when ev'ry comrade goes—
Perhaps too much, perhaps forgetting
    That over yonder there are those
    To whom he comes and whom he knows.

I would not hold our loss too lightly;
    God knows, and we, how deep the pain;
But, friends, I see still shining brightly
    The brightest link in all our chain
    That links us to a new domain.

For this I swear, because believing,
    Time breaks no circle such as this.
However hurt, however grieving
    However much a friend we miss,
    Between the worlds is no abyss.

For friendship binds the worlds together—
    World over there, world over here.
From earth to heaven is the ether
    That brings the earth and heaven near
    And makes them both a bit more dear.

Not weaker now our chain, but stronger;
    In all our loss and all our ill
We shall now look a little longer
    At every star above the hill
    And think of him, and have him still.

Whatever vales we yet may wander
    What sorrows come, what tempests blow,
We have a friend, a friend out yonder
    To greet us when we have to go—
    Out yonder someone that we know.

To all eternity he binds us;
    He links this planet with the stars;

He rides ahead, the trail he finds us,
    And where he is and where we are
    Will never seem again so far.

—DOUGLAS MALLOCH

THE DOOR

And death itself, to her, was but
    The wider opening to the door
That had been opening, more and more,
    Through all her life, and ne'er was shut—

And never shall be shut. She left
    The door ajar for you and me;
And looking after her, we see
    The glory shining through the cleft.

—JOHN OXENHAM

The deeper man goes into life, the deeper is his conviction that this life is not all; it is an "unfinished symphony." A day may round out an insect's life, and a bird or a beast needs no tomorrow. Not so with him who knows that he is related to God and has felt the power of an endless life.

—HENRY WARD BEECHER

THE ETERNAL GOODNESS

I long for household voices gone
For vanished smiles I long,
But God hath led my dear ones on
And He can do no wrong.

I know not what the future holds
Of marvel or surprise
Assured alone that life and death
His mercy underlies.

And so beside the silent sea
I wait the muffled oar;
No harm from Him can come to me
On ocean or on shore.

I know not where His islands lift
Their fronded palms in air;
I only know I cannot drift
Beyond His love and care.

—JOHN GREENLEAF WHITTIER

PRE-VALEDICTORY

. . . by the Eternal, I am not expendable.
No, do not speculate on where I have gone.
The guides on this journey do not speak our
    language.
I have long contemplated reduction to my
    essential being.
Now regard me as having slipped into the
    finer interstices of the universe of Spirit.
Take heed to St. Paul, and do not ask
"With what manner of body . . . ?"
Why, I wouldn't be caught dead with a body.

Should you care to note my withdrawal
In the manner that best links spirit and
    matter,
Play the Emperor Concerto, second
    movement, and disperse
But cheerfully.

—DONALD C. BABCOCK

THE BEYOND

It seemeth such a little way to me,
Across to that strange country, the Beyond;
And yet, not strange, for it has grown to be
The home of those of whom I am so fond;
They make it seem familiar and most dear,
As journeying friends bring distant countries
    near.

And so for me there is no sting to death,
And so the grave has lost its victory;
It is but crossing with abated breath
And white, set face, a little strip of sea,
To find the loved ones waiting on the shore,
More beautiful, more precious than before.

—ELLA WHEELER WILCOX

I believe that when the soul disappears from this world, it disappears only to become manifest upon another scene in the wondrous drama of eternity.

—EDWIN MARKHAM

Why should it be thought a thing incredible with you, that God should raise the dead?

—ACTS 26:8

THE THREE TREASURES

COMPLAINT

*How seldom, Friend! a good great man
inherits
    Honor or wealth, with all his worth
    and pains!
It sounds like stories from the land of
spirits,
If any man obtain that which he merits,
    Or any merit that which he obtains.*

REPROOF

*For shame, dear Friend; renounce this
    canting strain!
What wouldst thou have a good great man
    obtain?
Place—titles—salary—a gilded chain—
Or throne of corses which his sword has
    slain?
Greatness and goodness are not means, but
    ends!
Hath he not always treasures, always friends,
The good great man? three treasures,—
    love and light,
And calm thoughts, regular as infant's
    breath;
And three firm friends, more sure than day
    and night—
Himself, his Maker, and the angel Death.*

—SAMUEL TAYLOR COLERIDGE

FRIENDS BEYOND

*I cannot think of them as dead,
    Who walk with me no more;
Along the path of life I tread—
    They have but gone before.*

*The Father's House is mansioned fair,
    Beyond my vision dim;
All souls are His, and here or there
    Are living unto Him.*

*And still their silent ministry
    Within my heart hath place,
As when on earth they walked with me,
    And met me face to face.*

*Their lives are made forever mine;
    What they to me have been*

*Hath left henceforth its seal and sign
    Engraven deep within.*

*Mine are they by an ownership
    Nor time nor death can free;
For God hath given to love to keep
    Its own eternally.*

—FREDRICK L. HOSMER

THE UNDYING SOUL

*Yet howsoever changed or tost,
Not even a wreath of mist is lost,
No atom can itself exhaust.*

*So shall the soul's superior force
Live on and run its endless course
In God's unlimited universe.*

—JOHN GREENLEAF WHITTIER

THE FUTURE LIFE

I feel within me the future life. I am like a forest that has once been razed; the new shoots are stronger and brisker. I shall most certainly rise toward the heavens. The sun's rays bathe my head. The earth gives to me its generous sap, but the heavens illuminate me with the reflection of—of worlds unknown.

Some say the soul results merely from bodily powers. Why, then, does my soul become brighter when my bodily powers begin to waste away? Winter is above me, but eternal spring is within my heart. I inhale even now the fragrance of lilacs, violets, and roses just as I did when I was twenty.

The nearer my approach to the end, the plainer is the sound of immortal symphonies of worlds which invite me. It is wonderful, yet simple. It is a fairy tale; it is history.

For half a century I have been translating my thoughts into prose and verse; history, philosophy, drama, romance, tradition, satire, ode, and song; all of these have I tried. But I feel that I haven't given utterance to the thousandth part of what lies within me. When I go to the grave I can say as others have said, "My day's work is done." But I cannot say, "My life is done." My day's work will recommence the next morning. The tomb is not a blind alley; it is a thoroughfare. It closes upon the twilight, but opens upon the dawn.

—VICTOR HUGO

HE IS NOT DEAD

Though he that, ever kind and true,
Kept stoutly step by step with you,
Your whole long lusty lifetime through,
Be gone a while before;
Yet, doubt not, soon the season shall restore,
Your friend to you.

He has but turned a corner; still
He pushes on with right good will,
Thru mire and marsh, by heugh and hill,
The self-same arduous way
That you and he through many a doubtful day
Attempted still.

He is not dead, this friend; not dead,
But on some road, by mortals tread,
Got some few trifling steps ahead,
And nearer to the end;
So that you, too, once past the bend,
Shall meet again, as face to face, this friend
You fancy dead.

Push gayly on, brave heart, the while
You travel forward mile by mile,
He loiters, with a backward smile,
Till you can overtake;
And strains his eyes to search his wake
Or, whistling as he sees you
through the brake,
Waits on a stile.

—ROBERT LOUIS STEVENSON

Though my soul may set in darkness,
it will rise in perfect light;
I have loved the stars too fondly
to be fearful of the night.

AUF WIEDERSEHEN

We walk along life's rugged road together
Such a little way.
We face the sunshine or the stormy weather
So brief a day.

Then paths diverge, from sorrow so appalling
We shrink with pain,
Yet, parted far and farther, still keep calling,
'Auf Wiedersehen.'

Despair not! See, through tear dimmed eyes,
before us
Such a little way.
Lies God's dear garden,
and His sun shines o'er us
A long, long day.
There all paths end,
long-parted loved ones, meeting,
Clasp hands again.
The past, the pain forgot
in rapturous greeting,—
'Auf Wiedersehen.'

—SUSIE E. ABBEY

THE LILY OF THE VALLEY

White bud, that in meek beauty so dost lean
Thy cloistered cheek as pale as moonlight
snow,
Thou seem'st beneath thy huge high leaf of
green,
An eremite beneath his mountain's brow.

White bud! thou 'rt emblem of a lovelier
thing,
The broken spirit that its anguish bears
To silent shades, and there sits offering
To Heaven the holy fragrance of its tears.

—GEORGE CROLY

THERE IS A GOD

For in the darkest of the black abode
There's not a devil but believes a God.
Old Lucifer has sometimes tried
To have himself deified;
But devils nor men the being of God denied,
Till men of late found out new ways to sin,
And turned the devil out to let the Atheist in.
But when the mighty element began,
And storms the weighty truth explain,
Almighty power upon the whirlwind rode,
And every blast proclaimed aloud
There is, there is, there is a God.

—DANIEL DEFOE

IN THE BEAUTIFUL MORNING

The storm and the darkness—
* the desolate night—*
But the ship saileth sure,
* and the harbor's in sight;*
*   And a melody swells*
*   From the chime o' the bells;—*
'Home in the beautiful morning.'

O, long was the seaway,
* with billows to breast;*
But we dreamed on those billows
* of havens of rest;*
*   O'er the ocean's sad knells*
*   Still the chime o' the bells—*
'Home in the beautiful morning.'

'Mid the wrecks that were tossed
* by the storm and the strife*
We had drifted so far
* from the love that is life;*
*   But the bells o'er the foam,*
*   Ever singing of home—*
'Home in the beautiful morning.'

O, storm, and black billows,
* not hopeless, we roam,*
For love guides the ship
* to the white shores of home;*
*   And the melody swells*
*   From the jubilant bells—*
'Home in the beautiful morning.'

—FRANK L. STANTON

In the summer of 1949 a good minister of Jesus Christ, Dr. J. R. P. Sclater, fell on sleep while visiting his beloved Scotland. For a quarter of a century he had been a singularly effective minister in the city of Toronto. Unusually gifted as a preacher, he was a churchman of vision and influence. When his death was announced, the newspapers carried many tributes to his character and work. One of the most beautiful came from a parishioner who was a patient in one of the hospitals. This man recalled the difference his friend and pastor had made in his life by his frequent visits to him. Just to see him strengthened his faith and recovered his courage, said the invalid. This is how he ended his tribute:

Some day—it may be soon—I shall meet my friend again. He will look just the same, smiling, radiant, as the saints at rest. "Come in," he will say. "I have been looking for you. We have work for you." And I, young and strong again, will take up the humble task allotted to me.

—GEORGE C. PIDGEON

FROM MIDSTREAM

I believe that we can live on earth according to the teachings of Jesus, and that the greatest happiness will come to the world when man obeys His commandment "Love ye one another."

I believe that every question between man and man is a religious question, and that every social wrong is a moral wrong.

I believe that we can live on earth according to the fulfillment of God's will, and that when the will of God is done on earth as it is done in heaven, every man will love his fellow men, and act towards them as he desires they should act towards him. I believe that the welfare of each is bound up in the welfare of all.

I believe that life is given us so we may grow in love, and I believe that God is in me as the sun is in the colour and fragrance of a flower—the Light in my darkness, the Voice in my silence.

I believe that only in broken gleams has the Sun of Truth yet shone upon men. I believe that love will finally establish the Kingdom of God on earth, and that the Cornerstones of that Kingdom will be Liberty, Truth, Brotherhood, and Service.

I believe that no good shall be lost, and that all man has willed or hoped or dreamed of good shall exist forever.

I believe in the immortality of the soul because I have within me immortal longings. I believe that the state we enter after death is wrought of our own motives, thoughts, and deeds. I believe that in the life to come I shall have the senses I have not had here, and that my home there will be beautiful with colour, music, and speech of flowers and faces I love.

Without this faith there would be little

meaning in my life. I should be "a mere pillar of darkness in the dark." Observers in the full enjoyment of their bodily senses pity me, but it is because they do not see the golden chamber in my life where I dwell delighted; for, dark as my path may seem to them, I carry a magic light in my heart. Faith, the spiritual strong searchlight, illumines the way, and although sinister doubts lurk in the shadow, I walk unafraid towards the Enchanted Wood where the foliage is always green, where joy abides, where nightingales nest and sing, and where life and death are one in the Presence of the Lord.

—HELEN KELLER

ONE OF THESE DAYS

One of these days it will all be over,
  Sorrow and parting, and loss and gain,
Meetings and partings of friends and lover,
  Joy that was ever so edged with pain.
One of these days will our hands be folded,
  One of these days will the work be done,
Finished the pattern our lives have molded,
  Ended our labor beneath the sun.

One of these days will the heartaches leave us,
  One of these days will the burden drop;
Never again shall a hope deceive us,
  Never again will our progress stop.
Freed from the blight of vain endeavor,
  Winged with the health of immortal life,
One of these days we shall quit forever
  All that is vexing in earthly strife.

One of these days we shall know the reason,
  Haply, of much that perplexes now;
One of these days in the Lord's good season
  Light of His peace shall adorn the brow,
Blest, though out of tribulation,
  Lifted to dwell in His sun-bright smile,
Happy to share in the great salvation,
  Well may we tarry a little while.

WHEN ALL IS DONE

Well, all is done and my last word is said,
And ye who love me murmur, 'He is dead';
Weep not for me, for fear that I should know,
And sorrow, too, that ye should sorrow so.

When all is done, say not that my day is o'er,
And that, through night,
  I seek a dimmer shore;
Say, rather, that my day has just begun;
I greet the dawn, and not the setting sun—
  When all is done.

—PAUL LAURENCE DUNBAR

ALIVE FOREVER

"I am alive forever!"
  This is the word He said:
In him there is no dying,
  In Him are no dead;
"I am alive forever!"—
  This is His word to me
Through season after season
  To live eternally.

"I am alive forever!"
  Oh tell it far and near;
No more can winter trouble,
  Or autumn bring its tear.
"I am alive forever!"
  Let seasons go or stay,
For Christ is mine forever,
  Forever and a day.

"Forever and forever!"
  Oh fling it to the breeze,
To live with Him forever,
  Creator of the trees,
To paint with Him the sunsets,
  To visit with the stars,
To flash across God's highways
  Beyond all earthly bars.

I know not how the future
  Shall change me or surprise,
But this will be my heaven,
  To look into His eyes,
To hear again His promise
  As He sweetly welcomes me—
"Thou art alive forever,
  Alive eternally!"

—RALPH SPAULDING CUSHMAN

I know we shall behold them raised,
  complete,
The dust swept from their beauty, glorified.

—ELIZABETH BARRETT BROWNING

THEY MET AND ARE SATISFIED

They met tonight—the one who closed his
*   eyes unto pain forever and the woe;*
And the one who found the mansions in the
*   skies in all their splendor long,*
*   long years ago.*

What will they say when first their eyes meet?
*   Or will a silence take the place of words?*
As only saints can know how strangely sweet
*   a rapture such as only Heaven affords.*

Will he who went before ask first for those
*   left far behind—*
*   those whom he loved so well?*
Or will the other, new to Heaven's repose,
*   question of all its meaning? Who can tell?*

One went so long ago, and one tonight took
*   the long journey, far across the tide.*
This only do I know—they met tonight, and
*   meeting—both, I know, are satisfied.*

—BRITISH WEEKLY

MY DREAM OF HEAVEN

What Heaven is, I know not; but I long have dreamed of its purple hills and its fields of light, blossoming with immortal beauty; of its brooks of laughter, and its rivers of song and its palace of eternal love. I long have dreamed that every bird which sings its life out here, may sing forever there in the tree of life; and every consecrated soul that suffers here may rest among its flowers, and live and love forever. I long have dreamed of opal towers and burnished domes; but what care I for gate of pearl or street of gold, if I can meet the loved ones who have blessed me here, and see the glorified faces of father and mother and the boy brother who died among the bursting buds of hope; and take in my arms again, my baby, who fell asleep ere his little tongue had learned to lisp, "Our Father who art in Heaven." What care I for crown of stars and harp of gold, if I can love and laugh and sing with them forever in the smile of my Saviour and my God!

—BOB TAYLOR

FRIENDS

Friend after friend departs;
*   Who hath not lost a friend?*
There is no union here of hearts,
*   That finds not here an end.*
Were this frail world our only rest,
Living or dying, none were blest.

Beyond the flight of time,
*   Beyond this vale of death,*
There surely is some blessed clime
*   Where life is not a breath,*
Nor life's affections transient fire,
Whose sparks fly upward to expire.

There is a world above
*   Where parting is unknown—*
A whole eternity of love
*   Formed for the good alone;*
And faith beholds the dying here,
Translated to that happier sphere.

Thus star by star declines,
*   Till all are passed away,*
As morning high and higher shines
*   To pure and perfect day;*
Nor sink those stars in empty night;
They hide themselves in heaven's own light.

—JAMES MONTGOMERY

STEPPING ASHORE

Oh! think to step ashore,
*   And find it Heaven;*
To clasp a hand outstretched,
*   And find it God's hand!*
To breathe new air,
*   And that celestial air;*
To feel refreshed,
*   And find it immortality;*
Ah, think to step from storm and stress
*   To one unbroken calm;*
To awake and find it Home.

—ROBERT E. SELLE

LIFE

Our lives are songs; God writes the words
And we set them to music at pleasure;
And the song grows glad, or sweet or sad,
As we choose to fashion the measure.

—Ella Wheeler Wilcox

Birth's gude, but breedin's better.

— SCOTCH PROVERB

For a man to *grow* a gentleman, it is of great consequence that his grandfather should have been an honest man; but if a man *be* a gentleman, it matters little what his grandfather, or grandmother either, was.

— GEORGE MacDONALD

A man asked to define the essential characteristics of a gentleman—using the term in its widest sense—would presumably reply, "The will to put himself in the place of others; the horror of forcing others into positions from which he would himself recoil; the power to do what seems to him to be right, without considering what others may say or think."

— JOHN GALSWORTHY

To be true—first to myself—and just and merciful. To be kind and faithful in the little things. To be brave with the bad; openly grateful for good; always moderate. To seek the best, content with what I find—placing principles above persons and right above riches. Of fear, none; of pain, enough to make my joys stand out; of pity, some; of work, a plenty; of faith in God and man, much; of love, all.

— LEIGH MITCHELL HODGES

Be sure of the foundation of your life. Know why you live as you do. Be ready to give a reason for it. Do not, in such a matter as life, build on opinion or custom, or what you guess is true. Make it a matter of certainty and science.

— THOMAS STARR KING

If we can say with Seneca, "This life is only a prelude to eternity," then we need not worry so much over the fittings and furnishings of this ante-room; and more than that, it will give dignity and purpose to the fleeting days to know they are linked with the eternal things as prelude and preparation.

— SAVAGE

Life is the childhood of our immortality.

— GOETHE

Life is beautiful when one sees beyond it.

— BONNAT

So live — decently, fearlessly, joyously — and don't forget that in the long run it is not the years in your life but the life in your years that counts.

— ADLAI E. STEVENSON

THAT'S LIVING!

To travel on a weary road
To stumble 'neath a heavy load
To rise again and trudge along
And smile and sing a cheery song;
    That's living!

To rise at dawning brave and strong
To help a weaker one along
To heal a wound or right a wrong
To fill a heart with gladder song;
    That's living!

To meet a stranger on the way
To shake his hand and pass the day
To speak a word of kindness too

And hide the sorrow deep in you
    That's living!

To stand for right with courage true
To show with pride the man in you
To fill your life with noble deeds,
A sacrifice to human needs;
    That's living!

To greet life's end with no disgrace
To meet your Maker face to face
To feel, along the path you've trod
That you have known both man and God
    That's living!

MY WINDOW

From kitchen window I can see
Eternal mountains smile on me.
They lift my cares at break of day,
They are a friend who seems to say,
"Oh, weary one, bowed down with grief,
Haste to the hills and find relief.
Your earthly cares away will flee
If you in solace, dwell with me."
So, when the cares of life enfold,
And sorrows seem to crush my soul,
I hasten to my window sill
And there my eyes with beauty fill.
Forget the toil, forget the strife;
How small the things that vex my life!
From kitchen window I still see
Eternal mountains smile on me!

          —LILLIE ROONEY

He only is advancing in life whose heart is getting softer, whose blood warmer, whose brain quicker, whose spirit is entering into living peace.

          —JOHN RUSKIN

HELP ME TO LIVE!

If I have wounded any soul today,
If I have caused one foot to go astray,
If I have walked in my own willful way—
    Dear Lord, forgive!

If I have uttered idle words or vain,
If I have turned aside from want or pain
Lest I myself should suffer
    through the strain—
      Dear Lord, forgive!

If I have been perverse or hard or cold,
If I have longed for shelter in Thy fold,
When Thou hast given me
    some part to hold—
      Dear Lord, forgive!

Forgive the wrong I have confessed to Thee,
Forgive the wrong, the secret wrongs,
   I do not see;
That which I know not, Master,
    teach Thou me—
      Help me to live!

          —CHARLES GABRIEL

Live in the *active* rather than the passive voice, intent upon what you can do rather than upon what may happen to you. Live in the *indicative* mood, not the subjunctive, concerned with facts as they are rather than as they might be. Live in the *present* tense, concentrating upon the duty at hand, without regrets for the past or worry about the future. Live in the *first person*, criticizing yourself rather than condemning others. Live in the *singular number*, caring more for the approval of your own conscience than for popularity with the many.

          —WILLIAM DeWITT HYDE

Do it that very moment!
Don't put it off—don't wait.
There's no use in doing a kindness
If you do it a day too late!

          —CHARLES KINGSLEY

Possessions, outward success, publicity, luxury—to me these have always been contemptible. I believe that a simple and unassuming manner of life is best for the body and the mind.

          —ALBERT EINSTEIN

IT'S SIMPLY GREAT

It's great to be alive, and be
  A part of all that's going on;
To live and work and feel and see
  Life lived each day from early dawn;
To rise and with the morning light
  Go forth until the hours grow late,
Then joyously return at night
  And rest from honest toil—it's great!

It's great to be a living part
  Of all the surging world alive,
And lend a hand in field and mart,
  A worker in this human hive;
To live and earn and dare to do,
  Nor ever shirk or deviate
From course or purpose we pursue!
  Until the goal is won—it's great!

It's great to realize that we
  Are of a latent power possessed
To be what we are willed to be,
  And equal unto any test;
That of ourselves we may achieve
  To worthy deeds and high estate,
If we but in our powers believe
  It can and will be done—it's great!

It's great and wonderful to know
  That all we have to do is do,
That if we will to grow we'll grow,
  And reach the mark we have to view;
To know that we're a vital part
  Of all that is, nor hesitate
With all of skill and mind and heart
  To work and win—it's simply great!

—SIDNEY WARREN MASE

A little work, a little play
To keep us going—and so, good-day!
A little warmth, a little light
Of love's bestowing—and so, good-night!
A little fun, to match the sorrow
Of each day's growing—
  and so, good morrow!
A little trust that when we die
We reap our sowing! And so—good-bye!

—GEORGE DU MAURIER

GIFTS THAT ENDURE

The Gift of Praise—Appropriate mention —right in front of the other fellow—of superior qualities or of jobs or deeds well done.

The Gift of Consideration—Putting yourself in the other fellow's shoes, thus proving your genuine understanding of his side of the case.

The Gift of Gratitude—Never forgetting to say "Thank you"—and never failing to mean it.

The Gift of Inspiration—Plant seeds of courage and action in the other fellow's heart. Help him to strive for greater accomplishment and lasting satisfaction.

LITTLE BOY BLUE

The little toy dog is covered with dust,
  But sturdy and staunch he stands;
The little toy soldier is red with rust,
  And his musket moulds in his hands.
Time was when the little toy dog was new,
  And the soldier was passing fair;
And that was the time when our Little
    Boy Blue
  Kissed them and put them there.

"Now don't you go till I come," he said,
  "And don't you make any noise!"
So, toddling off to his trundle bed,
  He dreamt of the pretty toys;
And, as he was dreaming, an angel song
  Awakened our Little Boy Blue—
Oh! the years are many, the years are long,
  But the little toy friends are true!

Ay, faithful to Little Boy Blue they stand,
  Each in the same old place,
Awaiting the touch of a little hand,
  The smile of a little face;
And they wonder, as waiting the long
    years through
  In the dust of that little chair,
What has become of our Little Boy Blue,
  Since he kissed them and put them there.

—EUGENE FIELD

MY LIFE

I have a life I can't escape,
A life that's mine to mold and shape,
Some things I lack of strength and skill,
I blunder much and fumble; still
I can in my own way design
What is to be this life of mine.

It is not mine to say how much
Of gold and silver I shall clutch,
What heights of glory I shall climb,
What splendid deeds achieve in time;
Lacking the genius of the great
The lesser tasks may be my fate.

But I can say what I shall be,
What in my life the world shall see;
Can mold my thoughts and actions here
To what is fine or what is drear.
Though small my skill, I can elect
To keep or lose my self-respect.

No man can kindlier be than I,
No man can more detest a lie,
I can be just as clean and true
As any gifted genius, who
Rises to earthly heights of fame
And wins at last the world's acclaim.

I can be friendly, blithe of heart,
Can build or tear my life apart,
Can happy-natured smile along
And shrug my shoulders at a wrong.
I only choose what is to be
This life which symbolizes me.

—EDGAR A. GUEST

G enius is eternal patience.

—MICHELANGELO

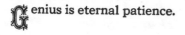 t is the prime secret of the Open Road that you are to pass nothing, reject nothing, despise nothing upon this earth. As you travel, many things both great and small will come to your attention; you are to regard all with open eyes and a heart of simplicity. Believe that everything belongs somewhere; each thing has its fitting and luminous place within this mosaic of human life. The Road is not open to those who withdraw the skirts of intolerance or lift the chin of pride. Rejecting the least of those who are called common or unclean, it is (curiously) you yourself that you reject.

If you despise that which is ugly you do not know that which is beautiful.

—DAVID GRAYSON

LIFE'S RECOMPENSE

There's a hidden thorn in ambush
Couched in every joy we feel;
There's oft a sob of sorrow
Quenched in laughter's merry peal.
There's a ruthless rod that's gilded
In the wand that pleasure sways;
There's a nightmare of awakening
From false dreams where conscience slays.

There's a note of wailing sadness
Blent in music's harmony,
While pain so close to rapture
Mingles in its ecstasy.
There's a wood-thrush singing gladly
In the prickly thorn-bush snare,
And soft angel choirs are chanting
Although raucous night winds blare.

There's a cross of heavy anguish
Oft concealed in shining crown—
It's the price we pay for glory,
Be it sainthood or renown.
But an unseen blessing's lurking
'Neath the torture that we bear;
There's a recompense in hiding,
Where we only found despair.

There's a compensation glorious
Culled where jarring discord's rife;
There's a Love Divine in chastening;
That is life—oh, that is life!

—JULIE CAROLINE O'HARA

I f you want to be miserable, think about yourself, about what you want, what you like, what respect people ought to pay you, and what people think of you.

—CHARLES KINGSLEY

Laughter, while it lasts, slackens and unbraces the mind, weakens the faculties, and causes a kind of remissness and dissolution in all the powers of the soul; and thus far it may be looked upon as a weakness in the composition of human nature. But if we consider the frequent reliefs we receive from it, and how often it breaks the gloom which is apt to depress the mind and damp our spirits, with transient, unexpected gleams of joy, one would take care not to grow too wise for so great a pleasure of life.

—Joseph Addison

LIFE

An infant—wailing in nameless fear;
  A shadow, perchance, in the quiet room,
Or the hum of an insect flying near,
  Or the screech owl's cry in the
    outer gloom.

A little child on the sun-checked floor;
  A broken toy, and a tear-stained face;
A young life clouded, a young heart sore,
  And the great clock, Time, ticks on apace.

A maiden weeping in bitter pain;
  Two white hands clasped on an
    aching brow;
A blighted faith, a fond hope slain,
  A shattered trust, and a broken vow.

A matron holding a baby's shoe;
  The hot tears gather and fall at will
On the knitted ribbon of white and blue,
  For the foot that wore it is cold and still.

An aged woman upon her bed,
  Worn and wearied, and poor and old,
Longing to rest with the happy dead;
  And thus the story of life is told.

Where is the season of careless glee;
  Where is the moment that holds no pain?
Life has its crosses from infancy
  Down to the grave—
    Are Its Hopes in Vain?

—Ella Wheeler Wilcox

HUMILITY

Oh, be at least able to say in that day,—
Lord, I am no hero. I have been careless, cowardly, sometimes all but mutinous. Punishment I have deserved, I deny it not. But a traitor I have never been; a deserter I have never been. I have tried to fight on Thy side in Thy battle against evil. I have tried to do the duty which lay nearest me; and to leave whatever Thou didst commit to my charge a little better than I found it. I have not been good, but I have at least tried to be good. Take the will for the deed, good Lord. Strike not my unworthy name off the roll-call of the noble and victorious army, which is the blessed company of all faithful people; and let me, too, be found written in the Book of Life; even though I stand the lowest and last upon its list. Amen.

—Charles Kingsley

LOST

What? Lost your temper, did you say?
  Well, dear, I would not mind it.
It is not such a dreadful loss—
  Pray do not try to find it.

It chased the dimples all away,
  And wrinkled up your forehead.
And changed a pretty, smiling face
  To one—well, simply horrid.

It put to flight the cheery words,
  The laughter and the singing
And clouds upon the shining sky
  It would persist in bringing.

And now it's gone. Then, do, my dear,
  Make it your best endeavor
To quickly find a better one,
  And lose it never, never.

INVITATION TO A FRESH START

There is something entrancing about opening a desk calendar at the beginning of the year. For a fleeting moment it is like holding a whole new year in your hands. All of the mistakes and shortcomings of the past fade into insignificance. Here are three hundred and sixty-five clean white spaces!

Each day is an invitation to a fresh start and a promise of untouched opportunity. Each one suggests an exciting adventure in living. Each one masks a carefully guarded secret, for no one knows the future.

Three hundred and sixty-five days!

CODE OF ROBERT LOUIS STEVENSON

To work "a little harder" and with
    determination and intelligence.
To remember enough of the past to profit by
    its mistakes.
To "worry never," but to think seriously of
    the future, and not only of today.
To "play the game" fair.
To be cheerful and keep smiling.
To perform my duties faithfully.
To develop courage and self-reliance.
To be kind to dogs and other dumb animals.
To cultivate economy and to waste nothing of
    value.
To look well after my health, and spend as
    much time as possible in the "great
    out-of-doors."
To keep thoroughly posted and "know more"
    about the business in which I am engaged.
To ignore courteously any display of jealousy
    or unfriendliness on the part of others.
To co-operate earnestly and sincerely with all
    my business associates.
These things let me resolve to do at all times
    and under all circumstances.

AS YOU GO THROUGH LIFE

Don't look for flaws as you go through life,
    And even when you find them,
It is wise and kind to be somewhat blind
    And look for the virtue behind them.

For the cloudiest night has a hint of light
    Somewhere in its shadows hiding;
It's better by far to hunt for a star
    Than the spots on the sun abiding.

The current of life runs ever away
    To the bosom of God's great ocean—

Don't set your force 'gainst the river's course,
    And think to alter its motion.

Don't waste a curse on the universe,
    Remember, it lived before you;
Don't butt at the storm with your puny
    form,
    But bend and let it go o'er you.

The world will never adjust itself
    To suit your whims to the letter;
Some things must go wrong your whole life
    long,
    And the sooner you know it the better.

It is folly to fight with the infinite,
    And go under at last in the wrestle;
The wiser man shapes into God's plan
    As water shapes into a vessel.

—ELLA WHEELER WILCOX

A LITTLE FELLOW FOLLOWS ME

A careful man I ought to be,
A little fellow follows me,
I do not dare to go astray
For fear he'll go the selfsame way.

Not once can I escape his eyes;
Whate'er he sees me do he tries.
Like me says he's going to be
That little chap who follows me.

He thinks that I am good and fine;
Believes in every word of mine.
The base in me he must not see
That little chap who follows me.

I must remember as I go,
Thro' summer sun and winter snow,
I'm building for the years to be
That little chap who follows me.

THE MEETING

After so long an absence
    At last we meet again:
Does the meeting give us pleasure,
    Or does it give us pain?

The tree of life has been shaken,
    And but few of us linger now,
Like the Prophet's two or three berries
    In the top of the uppermost bough.

We cordially greet each other
  In the old, familiar tone;
And we think, though we do not say it,
  How old and gray he is grown!

We speak of a Merry Christmas
  And many a Happy New Year;
But each in his heart is thinking
  Of those that are not here.

We speak of friends and their fortunes,
  And of what they did and said,
Till the dead alone seem living,
  And the living alone seem dead.

—HENRY WADSWORTH LONGFELLOW

RAINY DAY

Beside my window-casement clings
A butterfly with rain-drenched wings.

To me small matter if it rain—
Tomorrow brings the sun again;

But if my life were one brief day
And all my sky was sodden gray

And cold rain fell unceasingly—
What could amend the tragedy!

Beside my casement-window clings
A butterfly with rain-drenched wings.

—B. Y. WILLIAMS

Learn not only by a comet's rush, but by a rose's blush.

—ROBERT BROWNING

To live content with small means—to seek elegance rather than luxury, and refinement rather than fashion, to be worthy not respectable, and wealthy not rich—to study hard, think quietly, talk gently, act frankly, to listen to stars and birds, babes and sages, with open heart—to bear all cheerfully—do all bravely, await occasions—never hurry; in a word, to let the spiritual, unbidden and unconscious, grow up through the common. This is to be my symphony.

—W. E. CHANNING

WHATEVER THE WEATHER MAY BE

"Whatever the weather may be," says he—
  "Whatever the weather may be,
It's plaze, if ye will, an' I'll say me say,—
Supposin' to-day was the winterest day,
Wud the weather be changing because ye
    cried,
Or the snow be grass were ye crucified?
The best is to make yer own summer," says
    he,
"Whatever the weather may be," says he—
  "Whatever the weather may be!

"Whatever the weather may be," says he—
  "Whatever the weather may be,
It's the songs ye sing, an' the smiles ye wear,
That's a-makin' the sun shine everywhere;
An' the world of gloom is a world of glee,
Wid the bird in the bush, an' the bud in the
    tree,
An' the fruit on the stim o' the bough," says
    he,
"Whatever the weather may be," says he—
  "Whatever the weather may be!

"Whatever the weather may be," says he—
  "Whatever the weather may be,
Ye can bring the Spring, wid its green an'
    gold,
An' the grass in the grove where the snow
    lies cold;
An' ye'll warm yer back, wid a smiling face,
As ye sit at yer heart, like an owld fireplace,
An' toast the toes o' yer sowl," says he,
"Whatever the weather may be," says he—
  "Whatever the wheather may be!"

—JAMES WHITCOMB RILEY

There is more to life than increasing its speed.

—MAHATMA GANDHI

One who claims that he knows about it
  Tells me the earth is a vale of sin;
But I and the bees, and the birds, we doubt
    it,
  And think it a world worth living in.

—ELLA WHEELER WILCOX

WARN SOMEONE

If you have passed a dangerous place
Somewhere along life's way,
And know that others, too, will face
The same some future day,
You ought to place a red flag there,
Or firmly set a stake,
Thus warning them with honest care
For God and Heaven's sake.

Then sound a strong, clear, warning note
Revealing Satan's wiles,
Which may be done by word or vote,
Or by some self-denials;
But if you save a soul from sin,
A life from wreck and woe,
You'll help yourself a crown to win
Where Heaven's glories flow.

A DAY

What does it take to make a day?
A lot of love along the way:
It takes a morning and a noon,
A father's voice, a mother's croon;
It takes some task to challenge all
The powers that a man may call
His own: the powers of mind and limb;
A whispered word of love; a hymn
Of hope—a comrade's cheer—
A baby's laughter and a tear;
It takes a dream, a hope, a cry
Of need from some soul passing by;
A sense of brotherhood and love;
A purpose sent from God above;
It takes a sunset in the sky,
The stars of night, the winds that sigh;
It takes a breath of scented air,
A mother's kiss, a baby's prayer.
That is what it takes to make a day:
A lot of love along the way.

—WILLIAM L. STIDGER

The cost of a thing is the amount of what I will call life which is required to be exchanged for it, immediately or in the long run.

—HENRY DAVID THOREAU

Formula for living—Keep your chin up and your knees down.

FOR MY DAUGHTER

Now I do not want you any more
As I did before;

Now I do not cry, "You are my own—
My flesh and my bone!"

Catching at your hair, your hand, your
*   dress—*
Eager to possess.

Now I see you separate and free,
Different from me;

Different but hauntingly the same
Hinting that you came

From my body—from the passionate flood
Of its breath and blood;

Carrying life to some new beauty, bent
To some new intent;

Host to hunger fiercer in its need
Than my love can feed.

So I see you lift your hand and cry
Without tears, "Good-bye."

Watching till the road curves out of sight
Where the sky is bright.

—MARY BALLARD DURYEE

ON LIVING

The riders in a race do not stop short when they reach the goal. There is a little finishing canter before coming to a standstill. There is time to hear the kind voice of friends and to say to one's self: "The work is done." But just as one says that, the answer comes: "The race is over, but the work never is done while the power to work remains." The canter that brings you to a standstill need not be only coming to rest. It cannot be, while you still live. For to live is to function. That is all there is in living.

—OLIVER WENDELL HOLMES, JR.

COMPENSATION

I'd like to think when life is done
    That I had filled a needed post,
That here and there I'd paid my fare
    With more than idle talk and boast;
That I had taken gifts divine,
The breath of life and manhood fine,
And tried to use them now and then
In service for my fellow men.

I'd hate to think when life is through
    That I had lived my round of years
A useless kind, that leaves behind
    No record in this vale of tears;
That I had wasted all my days
By treading only selfish ways,
And that this world would be the same
If it had never known my name.

I'd like to think that here and there,
    When I am gone, there shall remain
A happier spot that might have not
    Existed had I toiled for gain;
That some one's cheery voice and smile
Shall prove that I had been worth while;
That I had paid with something fine
My debt to God for life divine.

—EDGAR A. GUEST

L ife is not life at all without delight.

—PATMORE

A MORNING PRAYER

Let me today do something that will take
    A little sadness from the world's vast
      store,
And may I be so favored as to make
    Of joy's too scanty sum a little more.

Let me not hurt, by any selfish deed
    Or thoughtless word, the heart of foe or
      friend.
Nor would I pass unseeing worthy need,
    Or sin by silence when I should defend.

However meager be my worldly wealth,
    Let me give something that shall aid my
      kind—
A word of courage, or a thought of health
    Dropped as I pass for troubled hearts to
      find.

Let me tonight look back across the span
    'Twixt dawn and dark, and to my
      conscience say—
Because of some good act to beast or man—
    "The world is better that I lived today."

—ELLA WHEELER WILCOX

ONE YEAR TO LIVE

If I had but one year to live;
One year to help; one year to give;
One year to love; one year to bless;
One year of better things to stress;
One year to sing; one year to smile;
To brighten earth a little while;
I think that I would spend each day,
In just the very self-same way
That I do now. For from afar
The call may come to cross the bar
At any time, and I must be
Prepared to meet eternity.
So if I have a year to live,
Or just a day in which to give
A pleasant smile, a helping hand,
A mind that tries to understand
A fellow-creature when in need,
'Tis one with me,—I take no heed;
But try to live each day He sends
To serve my gracious Master's ends.

—MARY DAVIS REED

T ruth . . . is the highest summit of art and
of life.

—HENRI FREDERIC AMIEL

I've seen the moonbeam's shining light;
I've watched the lamb clouds in the night,
As stars shone clear and bright.

I've heard the mighty ocean's roar,
Lashing the waves against the shore,
While stormy was the night.

I've seen the bitter, seen the sweet,
I've learned at last that it is meet,
To accept justly what is right.

LOVE

To love very much is to love inadequately;
we love—that is all. Love cannot be modified without being nullified. Love is a short word but it contains everything. Love means the body, the soul, the life, the entire being. We feel love as we feel the warmth of our blood, we breathe love as we breathe the air, we hold it in ourselves as we hold our thoughts. Nothing more exists for us. Love is not a word; it is a wordless state indicated by four letters. . . .

—GUY DE MAUPASSANT

And on her lover's arm she leant,
And round her waist she felt it fold,
And far across the hills they went
In that new world which is the old.

—ALFRED TENNYSON

A BIRTHDAY

My heart is like a singing bird
  Whose nest is in a watered shoot;
My heart is like an apple tree
  Whose boughs are bent with thickset
    fruit;
My heart is like a rainbow shell
  That paddles in a halcyon sea,
My heart is gladder than all these
  Because my love is come to me.

Raise me a dais of silk and down;
  Hang it with vair and purple dyes;
Carve it in doves, and pomegranates,
  And peacocks with a hundred eyes;
Work it in gold and silver grapes
  In leaves, and silver fleurs-de-lys;
Because the birthday of my life
  Is come, my love is come to me.

—CHRISTINA ROSSETTI

We too often love things and use people when we should be using things and loving people.

—REUEL HOWE

Be a spendthrift in love.
Don't economize in love.

Love is the one exception. It is the one treasure that grows bigger the more you take from it. Love is the one business in which it pays to be a spendthrift.

Give it away, throw it away, splash it over, empty your pockets, shake the basket, turn the glass upside down, and tomorrow you shall have more than ever.

—FRANK CRANE

GOD SCATTERS LOVE

God scatters love on every side
Freely among his children all,
And always hearts are lying open wide
Wherein some grains may fall.

—JAMES RUSSELL LOWELL

Love is the master key that opens the gates of happiness.

—OLIVER WENDELL HOLMES

WHAT IS LOVE?

Love is an attitude—Love is a prayer,
For a soul in sorrow, a heart in despair.
Love is good wishes for the gain of another,
Love suffers long with the fault of a brother.
Love giveth water to a cup that's run dry.
Love reaches low, as it can reach high.
Seeks not her own at expense of another.
Love reaches God when it reaches our
  brother.

NO TIME TO HATE

I had no time to hate, because
The grave would hinder me,
And life was not so ample I
Could finish enmity.

Nor had I time to love, but since
Some industry must be,
The little toil of love, I thought,
Was large enough for me.

—EMILY DICKINSON

To do him any wrong was to beget
A kindness from him for his heart was rich—
Of such fine mould that if you sowed therein
The seed of Hate, it blossomed Charity.

—ALFRED TENNYSON

CONVERSION

I have lived this life as the skeptic lives it;
    I have said the sweetness was less than the
        gall;
Praising, nor cursing, the Hand that gives it,
    I have drifted aimlessly through it all.
I have scoffed at the tale of a so-called
        heaven;
    I have laughed at the thought of a
        Supreme Friend;
I have said that it only to man was given
    To live, to endure; and to die was the end.

But I know that a good God reigneth,
    Generous-hearted and kind and true;
Since unto a worm like me he deigneth
    To send so royal a gift as you.
Bright as a star you gleam on my bosom,
    Sweet as a rose that the wild bee sips;
And I know, my own, my beautiful blossom,
    That none but a God could mould such
        lips.

And I believe, in the fullest measure
    That ever a strong man's heart could
        hold,
In all the tales of heavenly pleasure
    By poets sung or by prophets told;
For in the joy of your shy, sweet kisses,
    Your pulsing touch and your languid sigh
I am filled and thrilled with better blisses
    Than ever were claimed for souls on high.
And now I have faith in all the stories
    Told of the beauties of unseen lands;
Of royal splendors and marvellous glories
    Of the golden city not made with hands
Fo the silken beauty of falling tresses,
    Of lips all dewy and cheeks aglow,
With—what the mind in a half trance
        guesses
    Of the twin perfection of drifts of snow;

Of limbs like marble, of thigh and shoulder
    Carved like a statue in high relief—

These, as the eyes and the thoughts grow
        bolder,
    Leave no room for an unbelief.
So my lady, my queen most royal,
    My skepticism has passed away;
If you are true to me, true and loyal,
    I will believe till the Judgment-day.

—ELLA WHEELER WILCOX

The violet is much too shy,
    The rose too little so;
I think I'll ask the buttercup
    If I may be her beau.

When winds go by, I'll nod to her
    And she will nod to me,
And I will kiss her on the cheek
    As gently as may be.

And when the mower cuts us down,
    Together we will pass,
I smiling at the buttercup,
    She smiling at the grass.

—CHARLES G. BLANDEN

Should the wide world roll away,
Leaving black terror,
Limitless night,
Nor God, nor man, nor place to stand
Would be to me essential,
If thou and thy white arms were there
And the fall to doom a long way.

—STEPHEN CRANE

THE LAMP

If I can bear your love like a lamp before me,
When I go down the long steep Road of
        Darkness,
I shall not fear the everlasting shadows,
    Nor cry in terror.

If I can find out God, then I shall find Him,
If none can find Him, then I shall sleep
        soundly,
Knowing how well on earth your love
    sufficed me,
        A lamp in darkness.

—SARA TEASDALE

EVENING SONG

Look off, dear Love, across the sallow sands,
And mark yon meeting of the sun and
sea,
How long they kiss in sight of all the lands.
Ah! longer, longer, we.

Now in the sea's red vintage melts the sun,
As Egypt's pearl dissolved in rosy wine,
And Cleopatra night drinks all. 'This done,
Love, lay thine hand in mine.

Come forth, sweet stars, and comfort
heaven's heart;
Glimmer, ye waves, round else-unlighted
sands.
O Night! divorce our sun and sky apart,
Never our lips, our hands.

—SIDNEY LANIER

I t is cynicism and fear that freeze life; it is
faith that thaws it out, releases it, sets it free.

—HARRY EMERSON FOSDICK

WHEN THE WIND IS LOW

When the wind is low, and the sea is soft,
And the far heart-lightning plays
On the rim of the west where dark clouds
nest
On a darker bank of haze;
When I lean o'er the rail with you that I
love
And gaze to my heart's content;
I know that the heavens are there above—
But you are my firmament.

When the phosphor-stars are thrown from
the bow
And the watch climbs up the shroud;
When the dim mast dips as the vessel slips
Through the foam that seethes aloud;
I know that the years of our life are few,
And fain as a bird to flee,
That time is as brief as a drop of dew—
But you are Eternity.

—CALE YOUNG RICE

A loving heart is the truest wisdom.

—CHARLES DICKENS

YOU COME TOO LATE

You come too late—my need for you has
gone;
For I have triumphed over time and pain,
And learned of sorrow how to stand alone
And smile and face the world again.
My soul the wine, my heart the broken bread.
You feasted lightly and as lightly went,
And left me here with something in me dead.
My life is empty now and cleansed of grief;
I rise again—the pride of life is strong,
And in the place of love and old belief,
Courage goes marching with a merry song.
Come in, my friend, but do not hope to find
A trace of anything you left behind.

—GEORGE PINK ROBERTSON

FORGIVENESS

"I NOW forgive. If any have offended
Through ignorance or malice, be it known
The debt is canceled and the matter ended,
There's nothing to atone.

"I NOW forgive, my thought goes out in
blessing,
And love erases every trace of wrong—
Father, what lifts the weight that has been
pressing
So sorely, and so long?"

"CHILD, 'twas the weight of your own
condemnation,
The self-inflicted load that burdened you,
By your own act of reconciliation,
You are forgiven, too.

"FOR while you held your brother as a
debtor,
Your bitter thinking shackled your own soul,
The self-same act that broke for him the
fetter
Has made you free and whole."

—BONNIE DAY

SONG TO CELIA

Drink to me only with thine eyes,
    And I will pledge with mine;
Or leave a kiss but in the cup,
    And I'll not look for wine.
The thirst that from the soul doth rise
    Doth ask a drink divine:
But might I of Jove's nectar sup,
    I would not change from thine.

I sent thee late a rosy wreath,
    Not so much honoring thee
As giving it a hope, that there
    It could not withered be.
But thou thereon didst only breathe,
    And sent'st it back to me:
Since when it grows, and smells, I swear,
    Not of itself, but thee.

—BEN JONSON

YOU WILL FORGET ME

You will forget me. The years are so tender,
    They bind up the wounds which we think
    are so deep;
This dream of our youth will fade out as the
    splendor
    Fades from the skies when the sun sinks
    to sleep;
The cloud of forgetfulness, over and over
    Will banish the last rosy colors away,
And the fingers of time will weave garlands
    to cover
    The scar which you think is a life-mark
    to-day.

You will forget me. The one boon you covet
    Now above all things will soon seem no
    prize;
And the heart, which you hold not in keeping
    to prove it
    True or untrue, will lose worth in your
    eyes.
The one drop to-day, that you deem only
    wanting
    To fill your life-cup to the brim, soon
    will seem
But a valueless mite; and the ghost that is
    haunting
    The aisles of your heart will pass out with
    the dream.

You will forget me; will thank me for saying
    The words which you think are so pointed
    with pain.
Time loves a new lay; and the dirge he is
    playing
    Will change for you soon to a livelier
    strain.
I shall pass from your life—I shall pass out
    forever,
    And these hours we have spent will be
    sunk in the past.
Youth buries its dead; grief kills seldom or
    never,
    And forgetfulness covers all sorrows at
    last.

—ELLA WHEELER WILCOX

If I can put one touch of a rosy sunset into
the life of any man or woman, I shall feel
that I have worked with God.

—HENRY DAVID THOREAU

SONG

You bound strong sandals on my feet,
    You gave me bread and wine,
And sent me under sun and stars,
    For all the world was mine.

Oh take the sandals off my feet,
    You know not what you do;
For all my world is in your arms,
    My sun and stars are you.

—SARA TEASDALE

The only way to speak the truth is to speak
lovingly.

—HENRY DAVID THOREAU

A HEALTH

I fill this cup to one made up of loveliness
    alone,
A woman, of her gentle sex the seeming
    paragon;
To whom the better elements and kindly
    stars have given

A form so fair, that, like the air, 'tis less of
   earth than heaven.

Her every tone is music's own, like those of
   morning birds,
And something more than melody dwells
   ever in her words;
The coinage of her heart are they, and from
   her lips each flows
As one may see the burthened bee forth
   issue from the rose.

Affections are as thoughts to her, the
   measure of her hours;
Her feelings have the fragrancy, the
   freshness of young flowers;
And lovely passions, changing oft, so fill her,
   she appears
The image of themselves by turns,—the
   idol of past years!

Of her bright face one glance will trace a
   picture on the brain,
And of her voice in echoing hearts a sound
   must long remain,
But memory such as mine of her so very
   much endears,
When death is nigh my latest sigh will not
   be life's but hers.

I fill this cup to one made up of loveliness
   alone,
A woman, of her gentle sex the seeming
   paragon—
Her health! and would on earth there stood
   some more of such a frame,
That life might be all poetry, and weariness
   a name.

—EDWARD COOTE PINKNEY

THE ULTIMATE

How far together? Till the road
   Ends at some churchyard wall; until the
   bell
Tolls for the entrance to the lone abode;
   Until the only whisper is 'Farewell'?

How far together? Till the light
   No longer wakens in the loving eyes;
Until the shadow of the final night
   Has swept the last star-glimmer from the
   skies?

How far together? Past the end
   Of this short road, beyond the starry
   gleam;
Till day and night and time and space shall
   blend
   Into the vast Forever of our Dream.

—ELDREDGE DENISON

IDEALS

Some men deem
Gold their god, and some esteem
Honor is the chief content
That to man in life is lent;
And some others do contend,
Quite none like to a friend;
Others hold there is no wealth
Compared to a perfect health;
Some man's mind in quiet stands
When he is lord of many lands:
But I did sigh, and said all this
Was but a shade of perfect bliss;
And in my thoughts I did approve
Naught so sweet as is true love.

—ROBERT GREENE

LOVE'S STRENGTH

The face of all the world is changed, I think,
Since first I heard the footsteps of thy soul
Move still, oh, still, beside me, as they stole
Betwixt me and the dreadful outer brink
Of obvious death, where I, who thought to
   sink,
Was caught up into love, and taught the
   whole
Of life in a new rhythm. The cup of dole
God gave for baptism I am fain to drink,
And praise its sweetness, Sweet, with thee
   anear.
The names of country, heaven, are changed
   away
For where thou art or shalt be, there or here;
And this . . . this lute and song . . . loved
   yesterday,
(The singing angels know) are only dear
Because thy name moves right in what they
   say.

—ELIZABETH BARRETT BROWNING

LOVE IS A SICKNESS

Love is a sickness full of woes,
  All remedies refusing;
A plant that with most cutting grows,
  Most barren with best using.
    Why so?
More we enjoy it, more it dies;
If not enjoy'd, it sighing cries—
    Heigh ho!

Love is a torment of the mind,
  A tempest everlasting;
And Jove hath made it of a kind
  Not well, nor full nor fasting.
    Why so?
More we enjoy it, more it dies;
If not enjoy'd, it sighing cries—
    Heigh ho!

—SAMUEL DANIEL

ove spends his all, and still hath store.

—PHILLIP JAMES BAILEY

THE MASTER-PLAYER

An old, worn harp that had been played
Till all its strings were loose and frayed,
Joy, Hate, and Fear, each one essayed,
To play. But each in turn had found
No sweet responsiveness of sound.

Then Love the Master-Player came
With heaving breast and eyes aflame;
The Harp he took all undismayed,
Smote on its strings, still strange to song,
And brought forth music sweet and strong.

—PAUL LAURENCE DUNBRAR

AT THE GARDEN GATE

They lingered at the garden gate,
  The moon was full above;
He took her darling hand in his,
  The trembling little dove,
And pressed it to his fervent lips,
  And softly told his love.

About her waist he placed his arm,
  He called her all his own;
His heart, he said, it ever beat
  For her, and her alone;
And he was happier than a king
  Upon a golden throne.

"Come weal, come woe," in ardent tones
  This youth continued he,
"As is the needle to the pole,
  So I will constant be;
No power on earth shall tear thee, love,
  Away, I swear, from me!"

From out the chamber window popped
  A grizzly night-capped head;
A hoarse voice yelled: "You, Susan Jane,
  Come in and go to bed!"
And that was all—it was enough;
  The young man wildly fled.

he supreme happiness of life is the conviction of being loved for yourself, or, more correctly, being loved in spite of yourself.

—VICTOR HUGO

TIME IS

Too Slow for those who Wait,
Too Swift for those who Fear,
Too Long for those who Grieve,
Too Short for those who Rejoice;
  But for those who Love, Time is eternity.

—HENRY VAN DYKE

ove is like having a fever . . . When a man is in love, he endures more than at other times; he submits to everything.

—FRIEDRICH NIETZCHE

ove is the enchanted dawn of every heart.

—LAMARTINE

LOVE'S STRENGTH

In Love, if Love be Love, if Love be ours,
Faith and unfaith can ne'er be equal powers;
Unfaith in aught is want of faith in all.

It is the little rift within the lute
That by and by will make the music mute,
And, ever widening, slowly silence all.

The little rift within the lover's lute,
Or little pitted speck in garner'd fruit,
That, rotting inward, slowly moulders all.

It is not worth the keeping; let it go!
But shall it? Answer, darling; answer, No;
And trust me not at all or all in all.

—ALFRED TENNYSON

Let me not to the marriage of true minds
Admit impediments: love is not love
Which alters when it alteration finds.

—SHAKESPEARE

YOU

It isn't the money you are making,
   It isn't the clothes you wear;
It isn't the skill of your good right hand
   That makes folks really care.
But it's the smile on your face
   And the light of your eyes,
And the burdens that you bear;
   It's how do you live, and neighbor,
It's how do you work and play,
   And it's how do you say "Good
      Morning"
To the people along the way;
   And it's how do you face your troubles
Whenever the skies are gray.

—BYRNE

WHY I LOVE YOU

It is not because your heart is mine—mine
   only,
   Mine alone,
It is not because you choose me weak and
   lonely

For your own;
Not because the earth is fairer, and the skies,
   Spread above you,
Are more radiant for the shining of your
   eyes—
   That I love you!

Nay, not even because your hand holds
   heart and life
   At your will,
Soothing, hushing all its discord, making
   strife
   Calm and still;
Teaching Trust to fold her wings, nor
   ever roam
   From her nest;
Teaching Love that her securest, safest home
   Must be res .

But because this human Love, though true
   and sweet—
   Yours and mine—
Has been sent by Love more tender, more
   complete,
   More divine,
That it leads our hearts to rest at last in
   Heaven,
   Far above you;
Do I take you as a gift that God has given—
   And I love you!

—ADELAIDE ANNE PROCTER

I love you for what you are, but I love you yet more for what you are going to be.

I love you not so much for your realities as for your ideals. I pray for your desires that they may be great, rather than for your satisfactions, which may be so hazardously little.

A satisfied flower is one whose petals are about to fall. The most beautiful rose is one hardly more than a bud wherein the pangs and ecstasies of desire are working for larger and finer growth.

Not always shall you be what you are now.

You are going forward toward something great. I am on the way with you and therefore I love you.

—CARL SANDBURG

MANKIND

No man is an Iland intire of it selfe;
Every man is a peece of the Continent,
A part of the maine; if a Clod bee washed
    away by the sea,
Europe is the leese, as well as if a
    Promontorie were,
As well as if a Mannor of thy friends or of
    thine owne were,
Any man's death diminishes me, because I
    am involved in Mankinde;
And therefore never send to know for whom
    the bell tolls;
It tolls for thee.

—JOHN DONNE

Man's rank is his power to uplift.

—GEORGE MACDONALD

Teach me to feel another's woe,
To hide the fault I see;
That mercy I to others show,
That mercy show to me.

—ALEXANDER POPE

WHAT IS OUR CONCERN?

Dietrich Bonhoeffer was a great theologian and Christian martyr. He was imprisoned and put to death under the Hitler regime.

"I believe," he said, "that God can and will bring good out of all things, even the most evil. For this he needs men who will let all things work for the best in respect to them. I believe that in every trial God will give us as much power to resist as we need. But in order that we will rely on him alone and not on ourselves, he does not give it ahead of time. Such faith must overcome all anxiety about the future. I believe that even our mistakes and errors are not in vain, and it is no harder for God to deal with them than with what we regard as our good deeds. I believe that God is no timeless fate, but that he waits for and answers upright prayer and responsible deeds."

—DIETRICH BONHOEFFER

Man! thou pendulum betwixt a smile and tear.

—LORD BYRON

No man can hold another man in the gutter without remaining there himself.

—BOOKER T. WASHINGTON

I am a man; nothing that concerns mankind is alien to me.

—PUBLIUS TERENCE

We believe we can win the friendship of people only by working beside them, humans-to-humans, toward goals they understand and seek themselves. Our instrument for this shall be medicine.

—THOMAS A. DOOLEY

BROTHERS AND SISTERS

There is so much of loneliness
On this unchartered earth
It seems each one's a prisoner
Within a cell from birth.

There is such need for union,
Such need for clasping hands,
Yet we deny the brotherhood
The human heart demands.

Whatever you have received more than others in health, in talents, in ability, in success, in a pleasant childhood, in harmonious conditions of home life, all this you must not take to yourself as a matter of course. You must pay a price for it. You must render an unusually great sacrifice of your life for other life.

—ALBERT SCHWEITZER

There's nothing so kingly as kindness,
And nothing so royal as truth.

—ALICE CARY

To be rich in admiration and free from envy; to rejoice greatly in the good of others; to love with such generosity of heart that your love is still a dear possession in absence or unkindness—these are the gifts of fortune which money cannot buy and without which money can buy nothing. He who has such a treasury of riches, being happy and valiant himself, in his own nature, will enjoy the universe as if it were his own estate; and help the man to whom he lends a hand to enjoy it with him.

—ROBERT LOUIS STEVENSON

 thin skin is a poor asset.

We are all travellers in the wilderness of this world, and the best that we find in our travels is an honest friend.

—ROBERT LOUIS STEVENSON

INFLUENCE

Give a smile to someone passing;
Thereby make his morning glad.
It may greet you in the evening
When your own heart may be sad.

Do a deed of simple kindness,
Though its end you may not see.
It may reach, like widening ripples,
Down a long eternity.

—JOSEPH NORRIS

THE QUARREL

I quarreled with my brother.
I don't know what about.
One thing led to another.
Somehow we fell out.

The start of it was slight;
The end of it was strong.
He said he was right.
I knew he was wrong.

We hated one another.
The afternoon turned black
Then suddenly my brother
Thumped me on the back

And said, "Oh, come along,
We can't go on all night.
I was in the wrong."
So he was in the right.

—ELEANOR FARJEON

THY NEIGHBOR

Who is thy neighbor? He whom thou
Hast power to aid or bless,
Whose aching heart or burning brow
Thy soothing hand may press.

Thy neighbor? 'Tis the fainting poor
Whose eye with want is dim.
Oh, enter thou his humble door
With aid and peace for him.

Thy neighbor? He who drinks the cup
When sorrow drowns the brim;
With words of high sustaining hope
Go thou and comfort him.

Thy neighbor? 'Tis the weary slave,
Fettered in mind and limb;
He hath no hope this side the grave.
Go thou and ransom him.

Thy neighbor? Pass no mourner by.
Perhaps thou canst redeem
A breaking heart from misery.
Go share thy lot with him.

There is nothing so great that I fear to do it for my friend; nothing so small that I will disdain to do it for him.

—PHILIP SIDNEY

The tragedy is not that things are broken. The tragedy is that they are not mended again.

—ALAN PATON

THANKS

For sunlit hours and visions clear,
For all remembered faces dear,
For comrades of a single day
Who sent us stronger on our way,
For friends who shared the year's long road
And bore with us the common load,
For hours that levied heavy tolls
But brought us nearer to our goals,
For insights won through toil and tears,
We thank the Keeper of the Years.

—CLYDE McGEE

Believe nothing against another but on good authority; nor report what may hurt another, unless it be a greater hurt to conceal it.

—WILLIAM PENN

FIRST IMPRESSIONS

It is not right to judge a man
By hasty glance or passing whim,
Or think that first impressions can
Tell all there is to know of him.

Who knows what weight of weariness
The man we rashly judge may bear,
The burden of his loneliness.
His blighted hopes, his secret care.

A pompous guise or air of pride
May only be an outward screen,
A compensation meant to hide
A baffled will, a grief unseen.

However odd a person seems,
However strange his ways may be,
Within each human spirit gleams
A spark of true divinity.

So what can first impressions tell?
Unthinking judgments will not do,
Who really knows a person well
May also come to like him too!

—ALFRED GRANT WALTON

YOU PRAYED FOR ME

You did not know my need,
Or that my heart was sore indeed,
Or that I had a fear I could not quell.
You sensed that with me all was not quite
well,

And so—you prayed for me.

My path had seemed so black,
And yet I know there was no turning back,
Then in my loneliness I felt God near,
And down the long dark road a light showed
clear.

Because—you prayed for me.

And as your prayer, like incense sweet did
soar,
God did in love, on me, a blessing pour,

The day—you prayed for me.

To be popular yourself you must first learn to like other people. There is just no other way.

—ETTINGER

THE HATE AND THE LOVE OF THE WORLD

I have seen men binding their brothers in
chains, and crafty traders reaching for the
bread that women and children lifted to
their mouths;
I have seen suffering go unaided.
I have heard the iron din of war, and have
seen the waxen face of early death;
And I have cried in my heart, "The world is
hate!"

I have heard birds calling their mates in the
still forests, and insects chirping to their
loves in the tangled grass of meadows;
I have seen mothers caressing their babes,
and aged men supporting with devotion
the slow steps of stooping women;
I have seen cheerful hearthstones surrounded
by laughing children and strong men and
happy women;
I have heard the tender words of lovers in
the pure passion of youth;
And I have cried in my heart, "The world is
love!"

—MAX EHRMANN

A MAN'S WORTH

Down with your pride of birth
And your golden gods of trade!
A man is worth to his mother, Earth,
All that a man has made!

    —JOHN G. NEIHARDT

A MAN'S A MAN FOR A' THAT

Is there, for honest poverty,
 That hings his head, an' a' that?
The coward slave, we pass him by,
 We dare be poor for a' that!
  For a' that, an' a' that,
   Our toils obscure, an' a' that;
  The rank is but the guinea's stamp;[1]
  The man's the gowd[2] *for a' that.*

What tho' on hamely fare we dine,
 Wear hodden gray,[3] *an' a' that?*
Gie fools their silks, and knaves their wine,
 A man's a man for a' that!
  For a' that, an' a' that,
   Their tinsel show, an' a' that;
  The honest man, tho' e'er sae poor,
  Is king o' men for a' that.

Ye see yon birkie,[4] *ca'd a lord,*
 Wha struts, an' stares, an' a' that?
Tho' hundreds worship at his word,
 He's but a coof[5] *for a' that!*
  For a' that, an' a' that,
   His riband, star, an' a' that;
  The man o' independent mind,
   He looks and laughs at a' that.

A prince can mak a belted knight,
 A marquis, duke, an' a that;
But an honest man's aboon his might,[6]
 Guid faith he mauna fa'[7] *that!*
  For a' that, an' a' that,
   Their dignities, an' a' that;

The pith o' sense, an' pride o' worth,
 Are higher rank than a' that.

Then let us pray that come it may,
 As come it will for a' that,
That sense and worth, o'er a' the earth,
 May bear the gree,[8] *an' a' that;*
 For a' that, an' a' that,
  It's coming yet, for a' that,
 That man to man, the warld o'er,
  Shall brothers be for a' that!

    —ROBERT BURNS

LINES WRITTEN IN EARLY SPRING

I heard a thousand blended notes,
While in a grove I sate reclined,
In that sweet mood when pleasant thoughts
Bring sad thoughts to the mind.

To her fair works did Nature link
The human soul that through me ran;
And much it grieved my heart to think
What man had made of man.

Through primrose tufts, in that green bower,
The periwinkle trailed its wreaths;
And 'tis my faith that every flower
Enjoys the air it breathes.

The birds around me hopped and played,
Their thoughts I cannot measure—
But the least motion which they made,
It seemed a thrill of pleasure.

The budding twigs spread out their fan,
To catch the breezy air;
And I must think, do all I can,
That there was pleasure there.

In this belief from heaven be sent,
If such be Nature's holy plan,
Have I not reason to lament
What man has made of man?

    —WILLIAM WORDSWORTH

---

[1]*guinea's stamp,* the imprint of the King's head on a coin as a statement of its value.

[2]*gowd,* gold.

[3]*hodden gray,* coarse gray woolen cloth, undyed.

[4]*birkie,* young fellow.

[5]*coof,* fool.

[6]*aboon his might,* above the might of a prince.

[7]*mauna fa',* must not claim or get.

[8]*bear the gree,* have the prize.

All men are equal, but it is what they are equal to—that makes the difference.

—PIERCE HARRIS

SELF-KNOWLEDGE

It is dangerous to make man see too clearly his equality with the brutes without showing him his greatness. It is also dangerous to make him see his greatness too clearly, apart from his vileness. It is still more dangerous to leave him in ignorance of both. But it is very advantageous to show him both. Man must not think that he is on a level with the brutes or with the angels, nor must he be ignorant of both sides of his nature; but he must know both.

—BLAISE PASCAL

THE HOUSE BY THE SIDE OF THE ROAD

"He was a friend to man, and lived in a
house by the side of the road"—Homer.

There are hermit souls that live withdrawn
In the peace of their self-content;
There are souls, like stars, that dwell apart,
In a fellowless firmament;
There are pioneer souls that blaze their paths
Where highways never ran;
But let me live by the side of the road
And be a friend to man.

Let me live in a house by the side of the road,
Where the race of men go by—
The men who are good and the men who are
bad,
As good and as bad as I.
I would not sit in the scorner's seat,
Or hurl the cynic's ban;
Let me live in a house by the side of the road
And be a friend to man.

I see from my house by the side of the road,
By the side of the highway of life,
The men who press with the ardor of hope,
The men who are faint with the strife.
But I turn not away from their smiles nor
their tears—
Both parts of an infinite plan;
Let me live in my house by the side of the
road
And be a friend to man.

I know there are brook-gladdened meadows
ahead,
And mountains of wearisome height,
That the road passes on through the long
afternoon
And stretches away to the night.
But still I rejoice when the travelers rejoice,
And weep with the strangers that moan,
Nor live in my house by the side of the road
Like a man who dwells alone.

Let me live in my house by the side of the
road
Where the race of men go by—
They are good, they are bad, they are weak,
they are strong,
Wise, foolish—so am I.
Then why should I sit in the scorner's seat
Or hurl the cynic's ban?—
Let me live in my house by the side of the
road
And be a friend to man.

—SAM WALTER FOSS

THE MEASURE OF A MAN

Who thrives on competition
And criticism too,
Yet gives the opposition
Unstintingly its due,
Who takes it when it's coming
And gives it when he must,
Yet smiles and keeps on humming—
Is a fellow you can trust.

—DAVID RAYMOND INNES

MEMORY

A memory without blot or contamination must be an exquisite treasure, an inexhaustible source of pure refreshment.

—Charlotte Bronte

Memories are such fragile things;
So soft, fading into dreams—
Dimly obscured by the bitter smoke
That rises up from fires of other years.
Tinged faintly with laughter, and blackened
With loss, and washed with tears.

Places I have been and people
I have known pass before me.
One by one . . . So strange. So wistful.
Old hopes, barely able to walk. Old desires,
Somewhat unrecognizable in their gaudy
    dress.
Old ideals, like bright, shining stars.

I remember old streets, steaming with heat,
Or glistening in the rain, or wearing white.
Old, accustomed haunts—I like to think
They're lonely now, missing the old crowds.
The old hill, baring its head to the wind,
Wearing a little wistfully its mantle of
    clouds.

All of these and more—old books,
Old loves, old friends, all are dreams . . .
Dreams I have loved,
And dreams I have remembered.

             —GEORGE DRAUT

THE LIGHT OF OTHER DAYS

Oft in the stilly night,
   Ere slumber's chain has bound me,
Fond Memory brings the light
   Of other days around me:

The smiles, the tears
   Of boyhood's years,
The words of love then spoken;
   The eyes that shone,
   Now dimm'd and gone,
The cheerful hearts now broken!
Thus in the stilly night,
   Ere slumber's chain has bound me,
Sad Memory brings the light
   Of other days around me.

When I remember all
   The friends so link'd together
I've seen around me fall
   Like leaves in wintry weather,
   I feel like one
   Who treads alone
Some banquet-hall deserted,
   Whose lights are fled
   Whose garlands dead,
And all but he departed!
Thus in the stilly night,
   Ere slumber's chain has bound me,
Sad Memory brings the light
   Of other days around me.

             —THOMAS MOORE

So sad, so strange, the days that are no more.

             —ALFRED TENNYSON

TEARS, IDLE TEARS

Tears, idle tears, I know not what they mean,
Tears from the depth of some divine despair
Rise in the heart, and gather to the eyes,
In looking on the happy autumn-fields,
And thinking of the days that are no more.

Fresh as the first beam glittering on a sail,
That brings our friends up from the
    under-world,
Sad as the last which reddens over one
That sinks with all we love below the verge;
So sad, so fresh, the days that are no more.

Ah, sad and strange as in dark summer dawns
The earliest pipe of half-awakened birds
To dying ears, when unto dying eyes
The casement slowly grows a glimmering
    square;
So sad, so strange, the days that are no more.

Dear as remembered kisses after death,
And sweet as those by hopeless fancy feigned
On lips that are for others; deep as love,
Deep as first love, and wild with all regret;
O Death in Life, the days that are no more!

—ALFRED TENNYSON

THE SECRET PACK

My memory hath a secret pack
  Wherein I store the loveliest things;
And in my heart, not on my back,
  My dear and guarded treasure swings.
With every passing year it grows,
  And as it grows life fairer gleams;
And lesser weigh my daily woes,
  And brighter, rarer shine my dreams.

My memory hath a secret pack;
  It steads me, cheers me all the while.
Within it enters nothing black,
  But each kind word, each loving smile.
It matters not if darkness fall,
  I never let my heart be dumb
For love knows not until it call
  What faithful echoes back will come.

My memory hath a secret pack
  When I am sad I open it
And soon of solace I've no lack,
  And all my soul with joy is lit;
And over land, and over sea,
  My thought flies swifter than a dove,
For are not those who smiled on me
  Still keeping bright the lamp of love?

—SAMUEL MINTURN PECK

ONE WHO WATCHES

We are all near to death. But in my friends
I am forewarned too closely of that nearness.
Death haunts their days that are; in him
  descends
The darkness that shall change their living
  dearness
To something different, made within my
  mind
By memories and recordings and convenings
Of voices heard through veils and faces blind
To the kind light of my autumnal gleamings.

Not so much for myself I feel that fear
As for all those in whom my loves must die;
Thus, like some hooded death, I stand apart;
And in their happiest moments I can hear
Silence unending, when those lives must lie
Hoarded like happy summers in my heart.

—SIEGFRIED SASSOON

RELICS OF JOY

Let Fate do her worst, there are relics of joy,
Bright dreams of the past, which she cannot
  destroy;
Which come in the night-time of sorrow and
  care,
And bring back the features that joy used to
  wear,
Long, long be my heart with such memories
  fill'd!
Like the vase, in which roses have once been
  distill'd—
You may break, you may shatter the vase, if
  you will,
But the scent of the roses will hang round
  it still.

—THOMAS MOORE

FAITHFULNESS

Thy voice is near me in my dreams;
  In accents sweet and low,
Telling of happiness and love
  In days long, long ago.

Word after word I think I hear,
  Yet strange it seems to me
That, though I listen to thy voice,
  Thy face I never see.

From night to night my weary heart
  Lives on the treasured past,
And ev'ry day I fondly say,
  He'll come to me at last.

Yet still I weep, and watch, and pray,
  As time rolls slowly on;
And yet I have no hope but thee,
  Thou first, thou dearest one.

—M. LINDSAY

WHEN PA SAID GRACE

When pa said grace and bowed his head,
We knew he meant each word he said,
'Pears like to me we all could feel
Much more enjoyment in our meal.
For he was earnest and his face
Showed thankfulness, when pa said grace.

When pa said grace his words were few,
But how they'd touch you through and
    through,
He'd simply ask God's blessin' rare,
Upon his family gathered there,
And, "Bless this food, Lord to its place,
We thank thee God" when pa said grace.

When pa said grace, it reached the spot,
God's throne above and what it taught,
Has always been so much to me,
Since pa has passed away you see,
And as I nearly close life's race,
I oft recall when pa said grace.

—CARL B. IKE

EMPTY INTERLUDE

Remembrance is a bitter food;
Since I am left to dine alone
Time is an empty interlude
That I have vainly tried to fill
With little songs that once were known
To haunt your lips now strangely still . . .
Remembrance is a bitter food.

—HALLIE DAVIS MAAS

When to the sessions of sweet silent thought
I summon up remembrance of things past,
I sigh the lack of many a thing I sought,
And with old woes new wail my dear time's
    waste:
Then can I drown an eye, unused to flow,
For precious friends hid in death's dateless
    night,
And weep afresh love's long since cancell'd
    woe,
And moan the expense of many a vanish'd
    sigh:
Then can I grieve at grievances foregone,
And heavily from woe to woe tell o'er
The sad account of fore-bemoaned moan,

Which I new pay as if not paid before.
But if the while I think on thee, dear
    friend,
All losses are restored and sorrows end.

—SHAKESPEARE

What, though, are the stretching miles,
What the darkness of the night
When each of the golden whiles
Glimmers in the friendly light
Of the memories we hold
Of the days when field and tree
And the meadow-lands outrolled
Were the world for you and me?

Friend o' mine, I blindly reach
Till again I touch your hand—
Thoughts we cannot put in speech
Come to me. You understand!
Friend o' mine, I fill the cup
To the past of you and me—
Pledge it, ere we drink it up,
To the days that used to be!

—WILBUR NESBIT

My mind lets go a thousand things,
Like dates of wars and deaths of kings,
And yet recalls the very hour—
'Twas noon by yonder village tower,
And on the last blue moon in May—
The wind came briskly up this way,
Crisping the brook beside the road;
Then, pausing here, set down its load
Of pine-scents, and shook listlessly
Two petals from that wild-rose tree.

—THOMAS BAILEY ALDRICH

Memory is a capricious and arbitrary creature.

You never can tell what pebble she will pick up from the shore of life to keep among her treasures, or what inconspicuous flower of the field she will preserve as the symbol of thoughts that do often "lie too deep for tears."

And yet I do not doubt that the most important things are always the best remembered.

—HENRY VAN DYKE

⁕MUSIC⁕

Music is the universal language of mankind.

—HENRY WADSWORTH LONGFELLOW

Music has been called the speech of angels; I will go further, and call it the speech of God Himself.

—CHARLES KINGSLEY

Music is a revelation; a revelation loftier than all wisdom and all philosophy.

—LUDWIG VON BEETHOVEN

LIFE FOR SONG

Come Muse, O Muse, so often scorned by me,
  The hope of sorrow and the balm of care,
Give to me speech and song, that I may be
Unchid by grief; grant me such graces rare
  As other ministering souls may never see
Who boast thy laurel, and thy myrtle wear.
I know no joy wherein thou hast not part,
  My speeding wind, my anchor, and my
    goal.
Come, fair Parnassus, lift thou up my heart;
  Come, Helicon, renew my thirsty soul.
A cypress crown, O Muse, is thine to give,
  And pain eternal: take this weary frame,
Touch me with fire, and this my death shall
    live
  On all men's lips and in undying fame.

—GIORDANO BRUNO

Music is Nature's love and tears transformed into Harmonies that reach the spirit of man.

—DORA-FLICK FLOOD

Besides theology, music is the only art capable of affording peace and joy of the heart like that induced by the study of the science of divinity. The proof of this is that the Devil, the originator of sorrowful anxieties and restless troubles, flees before the sound of music almost as much as he does before the Word of God. This is why the prophets preferred music before all the other arts, proclaiming the Word in psalms and hymns.

My heart, which is full to overflowing, has often been solaced and refreshed by music when sick and weary.

—MARTIN LUTHER

Music is love in search of a word.

—SIDNEY LANIER

MANY LOVE MUSIC

Many love music but for music's sake,
Many because her touches can awake
Thoughts that repose within the breast
    half-dead,
And rise to follow where she loves to lead.
What various feelings come from days
    gone by!
What tears from far-off sources dim the eye!
Few, when light fingers with sweet voices
    play,
And melodies swell, pause, and melt away,
Mind how at every touch, at every tone,
A spark of life hath glistened and hath gone.

—WALTER SAVAGE LANDOR

Where words fail, music speaks.

—HANS CHRISTIAN ANDERSEN

WHEN THERE IS MUSIC

Whenever there is music, it is you
  Who come between me and the sound of
    strings;
The cloudy portals part to let you through,
  Troubled and strange with long
    rememberings.

Your nearness gathers ghostwise down the
room,
And through the pleading violins they
play,
There drifts the dim and delicate perfume
That once was you, come dreamily astray.
Behind what thin and shadowy doors you
wait
That such frail things as these should set
you free!
When all my need, like armies at a gate,
Would storm in vain to bring you back
to me;
When in this hush of strings you draw more
near
Than any sound of music that I hear.

—DAVID MORTON

God has a few of us whom He whispers in
the ear:
The rest may reason and welcome; 'tis we
musicians know.

—ROBERT BROWNING

A piper in the streets today
Set up, and tuned, and started to play,
And away, away, away on the tide
Of his music we started.

—SEUMAS O'SULLIVAN

Our lives are songs;
God writes the words,
And we set them to music at leisure;
And the song is sad, or the song is glad
As we choose to fashion the measure.

We must write the song,
Whatever the words,
Whatever its rhyme, or meter;
And if it is sad, we must make it glad,
And if sweet, we must make it sweeter.

—GIBBON

usic to the mind is as air to the body.

—PLATO

hose who are not touched by music, I
hold to be like sticks and stones.

—MARTIN LUTHER

THE BEGINNING

When Jubal struck the chorded shell,
His listening brethren stood around,
And, wondering, on their faces fell
To worship the celestial sound:
Less than a god they thought there could
not dwell
Within the hollow of that shell
That spoke so sweetly and so well.

hen I hear music I fear no danger, I am
invulnerable, I see no foe. I am related
to the earliest times, and to the latest.

—HENRY D. THOREAU

nd music too—dear music! that can touch
Beyond all else the soul that loves it
much.

—MOORE

hen words fail to express the exalted
sentiments and finer emotions of the
human heart, music becomes the sublimated
language of the soul, the divine instrumental-
ity for its higher utterance.

—WENDTE

here is music in the beauty, and the silent
note that Cupid strikes, far sweeter than
the sound of an instrument; for there is
music wherever there is harmony, order or
proportion; and thus far we may maintain
the music of the spheres.

—THOMAS BROWNE

And the night shall be filled with music,
And the cares, that infest the day,
Shall fold their tents, like the Arabs,
And as silently steal away.

—HENRY WADSWORTH LONGFELLOW

There is something marvelous in music. I might almost say it is, in itself, a marvel. Its position is somewhere between the region of thought and that of phenomena; a glimmering medium between mind and matter, related to both and yet differing from either. Spiritual, and yet requiring rhythm; material, and yet independent of space.

—HEINRICH HEINE

SKY-BORN MUSIC

Let me go where'er I will
I hear a sky-born music still:
It sounds from all things old,
It sounds from all things young,
From all that's fair. . . .
Peals out a cheerful song.
It is not only in the rose,
It is not only in the bird,
Not only where the rainbow glows,
Nor in the song of woman heard,
But in the darkest, meanest things
There always, always something sings.
'Tis not in the high stars alone,
Nor in the cups of budding flowers,
Nor in the redbreast's mellow tone,
Nor in the bow that smiles in showers,
But in the mud and scum of things
There always, always something sings.

RALPH WALDO EMERSON

Music is to me an ethereal rain, an ever-soft distillation, fragrant and liquid and wholesome to the soul, as dew to flowers; an incomprehensible delight, a joy, a voice of mystery, that seems to stand on the boundary between the sphere of the senses and the soul, and plead with pure, unrefined human nature to ascend into regions of seraphic uncontained life.

O wondrous power! Art thou not the nearest breath of God's own beauty, born to us amid the infinite, whispering gallery of His reconciliation! Type of all love and reconciliation, solvent of hard, contrary elements— blender of soul with soul, and all with the Infinite Harmony.

—JOHN S. DWIGHT

The lads that come from Kerry
Are not like the lads at home;
They show you where the fairie
Dance circles on the loam,
And tell old tales and sing old songs
That lift your heart like foam.

—THEODOSIA GARRISON

THE PASSIONS

When Music, heavenly maid! was young,
While yet in early Greece she sung,
The Passions oft, to hear her shell,
Thronged around her magic cell.
Exulting, trembling, raging, fainting,
Possest beyond the Muse's painting;
By turns they felt the glowing mind
Disturbed, delighted, raised, refined:
Till once, 'tis said, when all were fired,
Filled with fury, rapt, inspired,
From the supporting myrtles round
They snatched her instruments of sound,
And as they oft had heard apart
Sweet lessons of her forceful art,
Each—for Madness ruled the hour—
Would prove his own expressive power.

First Fear his hand, its skill to try,
    Amid the chords bewildered laid;
And back recoiled, he knew not why,
    E'en at the sound himself had made.

Next Anger rushed; his eyes on fire,
    In lightnings owned his secret stings:
In one rude clash he struck the lyre,
    And swept with hurried hand the strings.

With woful measures wan Despair—
    Low solemn sounds—his grief beguiled,
A sullen, strange, and mingled air;
    'Twas sad by fits, by starts 'twas wild.
    But thou, O Hope! with eyes so fair,
        What was thy delighted measure?
        Still it whispered promised pleasure,
    And bade the lovely scenes at distance hail!
        Still would her touch the strain prolong,
    And from the rocks, the woods, the vale,

She called on Echo still through all the
    song;
And where her sweetest theme she chose,
And Hope enchanted smiled, and waved her
    golden hair.
A soft responsive voice was heard at every
    close,

And longer had she sung—but with a frown,
    Revenge impatient rose;
He threw his blood-stained sword in thunder
    down,
    And with a withering look
    The war-denouncing trumpet took,
    And blew a blast so loud and dread,
Were ne'er prophetic sounds so full of woe!
    And ever and anon he beat
    The doubling drum with furious heat;
And though sometimes, each dreary pause
    between,
    Dejected Pity, at his side,
    Her soul-subduing voice applied,
Yet still he kept his wild unaltered mien,
While each strained ball of sight seemed
    bursting from his head.

Thy numbers, Jealousy, to naught were fixed,
    Sad proof of thy distressful state!
Of differing themes the veering song was
    mixed,
And now it courted Love, now raving called
    on Hate.

With eyes upraised, as one inspired,
    Pale Melancholy sat retired;
    And from her wild sequestered seat,
    In notes by distance made more sweet,
Poured through the mellow horn her pensive
    soul:
    And dashing soft from rocks around,
    Bubbling runnels joined the sound.
Through glades and glooms the mingled
    measure stole,
Or o'er some haunted streams with fond
    delay,
    Round an holy calm diffusing,
    Love of peace and lonely musing,
    In hollow murmurs died away.

But oh, how altered was its sprightlier tone
    When Cheerfulness, a nymph of healthiest
    hue,
    Her bow across her shoulders flung,

    Her buskins gemmed with morning dew,
Blew an inspiring air that dale and thicket
    rung!
    The hunter's call, to Faun and Dryad
    known.
The oak-crowned Sisters, and their
    chaste-eyed Queen,
    Satyrs and sylvan boys were seen,
    Peeping from forth their alleys green;
    Brown Exercise rejoiced to hear,
And Sport leapt up, and seized his beechen
    spear.

    Last came Joy's ecstatic trial;
    He with viny crown advancing,
First to the lively pipe his hand addrest;
    But soon he saw the brisk awakening viol,
Whose sweet entrancing voice he loved the
    best.
    They would have thought who heard the
    strain,
They saw in Tempe's vale her native maids,

    Amidst the festal sounding shades,
    To some unwearied minstrel dancing;
While, as his flying fingers kissed the strings,
Love framed with Mirth a gay fantastic
    round;
Loose were her tresses seen, her zone
    unbound;
    And he, amidst his frolic play,
As if he would the charming air repay,
Shook thousand odors from his dewy wings.

There is no truer truth obtainable by man
than comes of music.

—ROBERT BROWNING

THE MAN THAT HATH NO MUSIC IN HIMSELF

The man that hath no music in himself,
Nor is not moved with concord of sweet
    sounds,
Is fit for treasons, stratagems, and spoils;
The motions of his spirit are dull as night,
And his affections dark as Erebus.
Let no such man be trusted.

                      —SHAKESPEARE

O Music! sphere-descended maid,
Friend of pleasure, Wisdom's aid!
Why, goddess, why, to us denied,
Lay'st thou thy ancient lyre aside?
As in that loved Athenian bower,
You learned an all-commanding power,
Thy mimic soul, O nymph endeared!
Can well recall what then it heard.
Where is that native simple heart,
Devote to Virtue, Fancy, Art?
Arise, as in that elder time,
Warm, energetic, chaste, sublime!
Thy wonders, in that godlike age,
Fill thy recording Sister's page.
'Tis said—and I believe the tale—
Thy humblest reed could more prevail,
Had more of strength, diviner rage,
Than all which charms this laggard age!
E'en all at once together found
Cecilia's mingled world of sound.
Oh bid our vain endeavors cease,
Revive the just designs of Greece;
Return in all thy simple state!
Confirm the tales her sons relate!

—WILLIAM COLLINS

HOW SONGS ARE BEGOT AND BRED

How are songs begot and bred?
  How do golden measures flow?
From the heart or from the head?
  Happy Poet! let me know.

Tell me first how folded flowers
Bud and bloom in vernal bowers;
How the south-wind shapes its tune—
The harper he of June!

None may answer, none may know;
Winds and flowers come and go,
And the self-same canons bind
Nature and the Poet's mind.

So with thoughts my brain is peopled
  And they sing there all day long;
But they will not fold their pinions
  In the little cage of song.

—RICHARD HENRY STODDARD

There's music in the sighing of a reed;
There's music in the gushing of a rill;

There's music in all things, if men had ears;
The earth is but the music of the spheres.

—LORD BYRON

HARMONY

It is my temper . . . to affect all harmony: and sure there is music even in the beauty and the silent note which Cupid strikes, far sweeter than the sound of an instrument: for there is music wherever there is harmony, order, or proportion; and thus far we may maintain the *music of the spheres;* for these well-ordered motions, and regular paces, though they give no sound to the ear, yet to the understanding they strike a note most full of harmony. . . . It is a . . . shadowed lesson of the whole world, and creatures of God; such a melody to the ear, as the whole world, well understood, would afford the understanding. . . .

—THOMAS BROWNE

Music is the art of the prophets, the only art that can calm the agitations of the soul; it is one of the most magnificent and delightful presents God has given us.

—MARTIN LUTHER

Listen, O listen, my soul, to the voice of God speaking through the melody of music. Be still in the cool of the day and hear Him in the soft breezes ask "Where art thou?" Bend your ear close to the flowers, let them whisper His love and beauty. Open your ears and hear Him through the song of the bird. Look up at the stars and recall His infinity and constancy. Tune your heart to the bubbling brook that brings peace and gladness from His throne. Remember in the storms the Power that can speak, "Peace be still." Open thy window, soul of mine, to the beauty and glory of God. And the most wonderful peace that ever slumbered in the heart of God shall fill your life, even through its darkest hours.

❧ NATURE ❧

Let others crowd the giddy Court
Of mirth and revelry,
The simple joys that Nature yields
Are dearer far to me.

—Robert Tannahill

I like trees because they seem more resigned to the way they have to live than other things do.

—WILLA CATHER

My garden, with its silence and the pulses of fragrance that come and go on the airy undulations, affects me like sweet music. Care stops at the gates, and gazes at me wistfully through the bars. Among my flowers and trees, Nature takes me into her own hands, and I breathe freely as the first man.

—ALEXANDER SMITH

Beauty is God's handwriting. Welcome it in every fair face, every fair sky, every fair flower.

—CHARLES KINGSLEY

Spring unlocks the flowers to paint the laughing soil.

—REGINALD HEBER

ON IDEALS

A walk. The atmosphere incredibly pure—a warm, caressing gentleness in the sunshine—joy in one's whole being. . . . Every way I was happy—as idler, as painter, as poet. Forgotten impressions of childhood and youth came back to me—all those indescribable effects wrought by colour, shadow, sunlight, green hedges, and songs of birds, upon the soul just opening to poetry. I became again young, wondering, and simple, as candour and ignorance are simple. I abandoned myself to life and to nature, and they cradled me with an infinite gentleness. To open one's heart in purity to this ever pure nature, to allow this immortal life of things to penetrate into one's soul, is at the same time to listen to the voice of God.

—HENRI FREDERIC AMIEL

Nature gives to every time and season some beauties of its own; and from morning to night, as from the cradle to the grave, is but a succession of changes so gentle and easy that we can scarcely mark their progress.

—CHARLES DICKENS

EARTH'S COMMON THINGS

Seek not afar for beauty. Lo! it glows
In dew-wet grasses all about thy feet;
In birds, in sunshine, childish faces sweet,
In stars and mountain summits topped with
snows.

Go not abroad for happiness. For see,
It is a flower that blooms at thy door.
Bring love and justice home, and then
no more
Thou'lt wonder in what dwelling joy may be.

Dream not of noble service elsewhere
wrought;
The simple duty that awaits thy hand
Is God's voice uttering a divine command,
Life's common deeds build all that saints
have thought.

In wonder-workings, or some bush aflame,
Men look for God and fancy him
concealed;
But in earth's common things he stands
revealed
While grass and flowers and stars spell out
his name.

—MINOT JUDSON SAVAGE

It is not raining rain for me,
It's raining daffodils;
In every dimpled drop I see
Wild flowers on the hills.

The clouds of gray engulf the day
And overwhelm the town;
It is not raining rain to me,
It's raining roses down.

It is not raining rain to me,
But fields of clover bloom,
Where any buccaneering bee
Can find a bed and room.

A health unto the happy,
A fig for him who frets!
It is not raining rain to me,
It's raining violets.

—ROBERT LOVEMAN

ROADSIDE FLOWERS

We are the roadside flowers,
Straying from garden grounds;
Lovers of idle hours,
Breakers of ordered bounds.

If only the earth will feed us,
If only the wind be kind,
We blossom for those who need us,
The stragglers left behind.

And lo, the Lord of the Garden,
He makes His sun to rise,
And His rain to fall like pardon
On our dusty paradise.

On us He has laid the duty—
The task of the wandering breed—
To better the world with beauty,
Wherever the way may lead.

Who shall inquire of the season,
Or question the wind where it blows?
We blossom and ask no reason,
The Lord of the Garden knows.

—BLISS CARMAN

AUTUMNAL GLORY

There is an autumnal as well as a vernal glory. What is more beautiful than a tree in autumn dress, than a forest aflame with colour, as the frost paints his tints of red fire and yellow gold into the landscape? There is pathos in the tree whose leaves wither in mid-summer before the time, but when nature does her work, the fading leaf is not an emblem of defeat but the season's victorious banner flung out to say that the woods are ready for winter.

—JAMES I. VANCE

MY GARDEN

A garden is a lovesome thing, God wot!
Rose plot,
Fringed pool,
Fern grot—
The veriest school
Of peace; and yet the fool
Contends that God is not—
Not God! in gardens! when the eve is cool?
Nay, but I have a sign:
'Tis very sure God walks in mine.

—THOMAS EDWARD BROWN

Now in the place where he was crucified there was a garden; and in the garden a new sepulchre, wherein was man never yet laid.

—JOHN 19:41

LIFE'S MEANING

These things make life worth while to me:
A sunset sky, a maple tree,
A mountain standing grim and gray
Against the sky line far away;
A baby's laugh, a summer breeze,
A roadway winding 'neath the trees;
A friend to trust, a book to read,
And work which meets some human need.
And through it all, a sense of God
Lifting my soul above the sod,
The hope and peace which He can give—
These make it worth my while to live.

HYACINTHS TO FEED THY SOUL

If of thy mortal goods thou art bereft,
And from thy slender store two loaves alone
*   to thee are left,*
Sell one, and with the dole
Buy hyacinths to feed thy soul.

—GULISTAN OF MOSLIH EDDIN SAADI

If spring came but once in a century, instead of once a year, or burst forth with the sound of an earthquake, and not in silence, what wonder and expectation there would be in all hearts to behold the miraculous change. But now the silent succession suggests nothing but necessity. To most men only the cessation of the miracle would be miraculous, and the perpetual exercise of God's power seems less wonderful than its withdrawal would be.

—HENRY WADSWORTH LONGFELLOW

Science has found that nothing disappears without a trace. Nature does not know extinction. All it knows is transformation.

—WERNHER VON BRAUN

AN AUTUMN SONG

There is something in the Autumn that
*   is native to my blood,*
Touch of manner, hint of mood;
And my heart is like a rhyme,
With the yellow and the purple and the
*   crimson keeping time.*

The scarlet of the maples can shake me
*   like a cry*
Of bugles going by.
And my lonely spirit thrills
To see the frosty asters like smoke
*   upon the hills.*

There is something in October sets the
*   gipsy blood astir;*
We must follow her,
When from every hill aflame,
She calls and calls each vagabond by name.

—BLISS CARMAN

—our life, exempt from public haunt,
Finds tongues in trees, books in the
*   running brooks,*
Sermons in stones, and good in everything.

—SHAKESPEARE

SPRING

Spring, with that nameless pathos in the air
Which dwells with all things fair,
Spring, with her golden suns and silver rain,
*   is with us once again.*

Out in the lonely woods the jasmine burns
Its fragrant lamps, and turns
Into a royal court with green festoons
The banks of dark lagoons.

In the deep heart of every forest tree
The blood is all aglee,
And there's a look about the leafless bowers
As if they dreamed of flowers.

Yet still on every side we trace the hand
Of Winter in the land,
Save where the maple reddens on the lawn,
Flushed by the season's dawn;

Or where, like those strange semblances
*   we find*
That age to childhood blind,
The elm puts on, as if in Nature's scorn,
The brown of Autumn corn.

—HENRY TIMROD

SYMBOL

My faith is all a doubtful thing,
*   Wove on a doubtful loom,—*
Until there comes, each showery spring,
*   A cherry tree in bloom;*

And Christ who died upon a tree
*   That death had stricken bare,*
Comes beautifully back to me,
*   In blossoms, everywhere.*

—DAVID MORTON

I need not shout my faith. Thrice eloquent
*   Are quiet trees and the green listening sod;*

Hushed are the stars; whose power is never
   spent;
The hills are mute: yet how they speak
   of God!

—CHARLES HANSON TOWNE

He who wanders widest lifts
No more of Beauty's jealous veils
Than he who from his doorway sees
The miracle of flowers and trees.

I am sorry for the man who never goes fish-
ing,—who does not know what it is to bait
a hook and cast a line, and wait for that
strange electric thrill to leap from the stream
up the line and rod, up the arm and spine,
into his nerve centers, when something down
there out of sight begins to play with the bait,
I am sorry for the man who never sits on the
bank under the shade of trees and listens to
the shining river sing its song, and to the
birds sing theirs in the treetops, while he forgets all his cares and waits for the fish to bite.

—VANCE

THE GARDEN

My heart was once a garden
   By dim, enchanted trees,
With hint of untouched violets
   And shy anemones.

I showed my love the garden
   Where April dreams I'd hide,
But heedlessly he lost the key
   And now—we're both inside!

—NOEL LANE

To him who in the love of nature holds
communion with her visible forms, she
speaks a various language.

—WILLIAM CULLEN BRYANT

Nature is the living, visible garment of God.

—GOETHE

TREES

Many a tree is found in the wood,
And every tree for its use is good:
Some for the strength of the gnarled root,
Some for the sweetness of flower or fruit,
Some for shelter against the storm,
And some to keep the hearthstone warm;
Some for the roof and some for the beam,
And some for a boat to breast the stream.
In the wealth of the wood since the world
   began,
The trees have offered their gifts to man.

But the glory of trees is more than their gifts:
'Tis a beautiful wonder of life that lifts
From a wrinkled seed in an earthbound clod
A column, an arch in the temple of God,
A pillar of power, a dome of delight,
A shrine of song and a joy of sight!
Their roots are the nurses of rivers in birth,
Their leaves are alive with the breath of the
   earth;
They shelter the dwellings of man, and they
   bend
O'er his grave with the look of a loving
   friend.

I have camped in the whispering forest of
   pines
I have slept in the shadow of olives and
   vines,
In the knees of an oak, at the foot of a palm,
I have found good rest and slumber's balm.
And now, when the morning gilds the boughs
Of the vaulted elm at the door of my house,
I open the window and make a salute:
"God bless thy branches and feed thy root!
Thou hast lived before, live after me,
Thou ancient, friendly, faithful tree!"

—HENRY VAN DYKE

REFUGE

When grief had made her music still
   She watered plants upon her sill.
When pain came by and took its turn
   She put wood earth around her fern.
When haunting fears were at her heart,
   She pinched a little slip to start.
I never knew until she went

How much her green things must have
*   meant—*
Until I saw them through a blur
And tended them with grief for her.

—BARBARA H. JONES

SUMMER

Today, as I was reading in the garden, a waft of summer perfume—some hidden link of association in what I read—I know now what it may have been—took me back to schoolboy holidays; I recovered with strange intensity that lightsome mood of long release from tasks, of going away to the seaside, which is one of childhood's blessings. I was in the train; no rushing express, such as bears you great distances; the sober train which goes to no place of importance, which lets you see the white steam of the engine float and fall upon a meadow ere you pass. Thanks to a good and wise father, we youngsters saw nothing of seaside places where crowds assemble; I am speaking, too, of a time more than forty years ago, when it was still possible to find on the coasts of northern England, east or west, spots known only to those who loved the shore for its beauty and its solitude. At every station the train stopped; little stations, decked with beds of flowers, smelling warm in the sunshine where country folk got in with baskets, and talked in an unfamiliar dialect an English which to us sounded almost like a foreign tongue. Then the first glimpse of the sea; the excitement of noting whether the tide was high or low—stretches of sand and weedy pools, or halcyon wavelets, frothing at their furthest reach, under the sea-banks starred with convolutions. Of a sudden, *our* station!

Ah, that taste of the brine on a child's lips! Nowadays, I can take holiday when I will, and go whithersoever it pleases me; but that salt kiss of the sea air I shall never know again. My senses are dulled; I cannot get so near to Nature; I have a sorry dread of her clouds, her winds, and must walk with tedious circumspection where once I ran and leapt exultingly. Were it possible, but for one half-hour, to plunge and bask in the sunny surf, to roll on the silvery sand hills, to leap from rock to rock on shining sea-ferns, laughing if I slipped into the shallows among starfish and anemones!

—GEORGE GISSING

One touch of nature makes the whole world kin.

—SHAKESPEARE

THE BRAVE OLD OAK

A song to the oak, the brave old oak,
Who hath ruled in the greenwood long;
Here's health and renown to his broad
*   green crown,*
And his fifty arms so strong.
There's fear in his frown when the sun
*   goes down.*
And the fire in the west fades out;
And he showeth his might on a wild
*   midnight,*
When the storms through his branches shout.

Then here's to the oak, the brave old oak,
Who stands in his pride alone;
And still flourish he, a hale green tree,
When a hundred years are gone!

In the days of old, when the spring with cold
Had brightened his branches gray,
Through the grass at his feet crept maidens
*   sweet,*
To gather the dew of May.
And on that day to the rebeck gay
They frolicked with lovesome swains;
They are gone, they are dead, in the
*   churchyard laid,*
But the tree it still remains.

He saw the rare times when the Christmas
*   chimes*
Were a merry sound to hear,
When the squire's wide hall and the cottage
*   small*
Were filled with good English cheer.
Now gold hath sway we all obey,
And a ruthless king is he;
But he never shall send our ancient friend
To be tossed on the stormy sea.

—HENRY FOTHERGILL CHORLEY

Nature has some perfections to show that she is the image of God, and some defects to show that she is only His image.

—BLAISE PASCAL

I went to the woods because I wished to live deliberately, to front only the essential facts of life, and see if I could not learn what it had to teach, and not, when I came to die, discover that I had not lived.

—HENRY DAVID THOREAU

THOUGHTS IN A GARDEN

What wondrous life is this I lead!
Ripe apples drop about my head;
The luscious clusters of the vine
Upon my mouth do crush their wine;
The nectarine and curious peach
Into my hands themselves do reach;
Stumbling on melons, as I pass,
Ensnared with flowers, I fall on grass.

Meanwhile the mind from pleasure less
Withdraws into its happiness;
The mind, that ocean where each kind
Does straight its own resemblance find;
Yet it creates, transcending these,
Far other worlds, and others seas;
Annihilating all that's made
To a green thought in a green shade.

How well the skilful gardener drew
Of flowers, and herbs, this dial new,
Where, from above, the milder sun
Does through a fragrant zodiac run,
And as it works, the industrious bee
Computes its time as well as we!
How could such sweet and wholesome hours
Be reckoned but with herbs and flowers?

—ANDREW MARVELL

DOWN TO EARTH

Some persons may think, that **Flowers** are things of no use; that they are nonsensical things. The same may be, and, perhaps with more reason, said of pictures. An Italian, while he gives his fortune for a picture, will laugh to scorn a Hollander, who leaves a tulip root as a fortune to his son. For my part, as a thing to keep and not to sell; as a thing, the possession of which is to give me pleasure, I hesitate not a moment to prefer the plant of a fine carnation to a gold watch set with diamonds.

—WILLIAM COBBETT

Lord, now that spring is in the world, and
every tulip is a cup filled with Thy great
love, lift Thou me up. Raise Thou my
heart as flowers arise to greet the glory of
Thy day, with soul as clean as lilies are,
and white as they.
Let me not fear the darkness now, since Life
and Light break through Thy tomb;
Teach me that doubts no more oppress, no
more consume.
Show me that You art April, Lord, and Thou
the flowers and the grass;
Then, when awake the soft spring winds, I'll
hear Thee pass.

—CHARLES HANSON TOWNE

The poignant hush and the blue haze of Indian summer when the cornstalks stand like sentinels guarding the yellow pumpkins upon the ground . . . The graceful lines of a startled deer as it stands poised to run when I invade its private sanctuary . . . Millions of stars dotting the canopy of heaven on a night when frost nips the air . . . Wisps of smoke curling from chimneys and the contented happy sounds of living coming from the home I pass as I walk down the street in the twilight . . . Autumn leaves casting a cloak of many colors over the hillsides . . . A tawny squirrel peering at me from the crotch of a tree, his bushy tail waving like a warning flag to tell me he has staked his claim to this tree where he has hidden his store of food for winter.

All this . . . and so much more. "Oh, God, give us eyes to see, and ears to hear. One lifetime is not long enough in which to drink in all this loveliness."

—GRACE WILSON

A haze on the far horizon,
The infinite, tender sky,
The ripe, rich tint of the cornfields,
And the wild geese sailing high;
And all over upland and lowland
The charm of the goldenrod—
Some of us call it Autumn,
And others call it God.

—WILLIAM HERBERT CARRUTH

The morns are meeker than they were,

The nuts are getting brown;

The berry's cheek is plumper,

The rose is out of town.

The maple wears a gayer scarf,

The field a scarlet gown.

Lest I should be old-fashioned,

I'll put a trinket on.

—EMILY DICKINSON

You love the Roses—so do I. I wish
The sky would rain down Roses, as they rain
From off the shaken bush. Why will it not?
Then all the valley would be pink and white
And soft to tread on. They would fall as light
As feathers, smelling sweet; and it would be
Like sleeping and yet waking, all at once!

—GEORGE ELIOT

Our Lord has written the promise of the Resurrection, not in books alone, but in every leaf in springtime.

—MARTIN LUTHER

SUNRISE AND SUNSET

I'll tell you how the sun rose,—
A ribbon at a time.
The steeples swam in amethyst,
The news like squirrels ran.

The hills untied their bonnets,
The bobolinks begun.

Then I said softly to myself,
"That must have been the sun!"

But how he set, I know not.
There seemed a purple stile
Which little yellow boys and girls
Were climbing all the while

Till when they reached the other side,
A dominie in gray
Put gently up the evening bars,
And led the flock away.

—EMILY DICKINSON

Nature is the art of God.

—THOMAS BROWNE

Die when I may, I want it said by those who knew me best, that I always plucked a thistle and planted a flower where I thought a flower would grow.

—ABRAHAM LINCOLN

INDIAN SUMMER

It is the Indian summer. The rising sun blazes through the misty air like a conflagration. A yellowish, smoky haze fills the atmosphere, and a filmy mist lies like a silver lining on the sky. The wind is soft and low. It wafts to us the odor of forest leaves, that hang wilted on the dripping branches, or drop into the stream. Their gorgeous tints are gone, as if the autumnal rains had washed them out. Orange, yellow and scarlet, all are changed to one melancholy russet hue. The birds, too, have taken wing, and have left their roofless dwellings. Not the whistle of a robin, not the twitter of an eavesdropping swallow, not the carol of one sweet, familiar voice. All gone. Only the dismal cawing of a crow, as he sits and curses that the harvest is over; or the chit-chat of an idle squirrel, the noisy denizen of a hollow tree, the mendicant friar of a large parish, the absolute monarch of a dozen acorns.

—HENRY WADSWORTH LONGFELLOW

✦OPPORTUNITY✦

To improve the golden moment of opportunity and catch the good that is within our reach, is the great art of life.

—SAMUEL JOHNSON

Great opportunities come to all, but many do not know they have met them. The only preparation to take advantage of them, is simple fidelity to what each day brings.

—A. E. DUNNING

Master of human destinies am I.
Fame, love, and fortune on my footsteps
   wait,
Cities and fields I walk; I penetrate
Deserts and seas remote, and, passing by
Hovel, and mart, and palace, soon or late
I knock unbidden, once at every gate!
If sleeping, wake—if feasting, rise before
I turn away. It is the hour of fate,
And they who follow me reach every state
Mortals desire, and conquer every foe
Save death; but those who doubt or hesitate,
Condemned to failure, penury and woe,
Seek me in vain and uselessly implore—
I answer not, and I return no more.

              —JOHN JAMES INGALLS

THE ROSE

Of all flowers
Methinks a rose is best,
It is the very emblem of a maid;
For when the west wind courts her gently,
How modestly she blows, and paints the sun
With her chaste blushes! When the north
   comes near her
Rude and impatient, then, like chastity,
She locks her beauties in her bud again,
And leaves him to base briars.

             —BEAUMONT AND FLETCHER

In life's small things be resolute and great
To keep thy muscles trained; knowest thou
   when Fate
Thy measure takes, or when she'll say to
   thee,
"I find thee worthy, do this thing for me?"

             —JAMES RUSSELL LOWELL

A man must make his opportunity as oft as find it.

             —FRANCIS BACON

IF YOU BUT KNEW

You are not higher than your lowest thought,
Or lower than the peak of your desire.
And all existence has no wonder wrought
To which ambition may not yet aspire.
O Man! There is no planet, sun or star
Could hold you, if you but knew what
   you are.

There are more opportunities than there are young men to take advantage of them. You say the country has grown larger, that life is more complex and that as a result the personal incentive has vanished in proportion. Everything in that is perfectly correct except the conclusion. The country is bigger and life is more complex, but who will gainsay that if the country has grown bigger and the opportunities have with it, and that if life is more complex, it at least results in a greater variety of opportunities.

             —JAMES J. HILL

God's best gift to us is not things, but opportunities.

             —ALICE W. ROLLINS

JANE JONES

Jane Jones keeps talkin' to me all the time,
   An' says you must make it a rule
To study your lessons 'nd work hard 'nd
   learn,

An' never be absent from school.
Remember the story of Elihu Burritt,
  An' how he clum up to the top,
Got all the knowledge 'at he ever had
  Down in a blacksmithing shop?
Jane Jones she honestly said it was so!
  Mebbe he did—I dunno!
O' course what's a-keepin' me 'way from
    the top,
Is not never havin' no blacksmithing shop.

Jane Jones said Abe Lincoln had no books
    at all,
  An' used to split rails when a boy;
An' General Grant was a tanner by trade
  An' lived way out in Ill'nois.
So when the great war in the South first
    broke out
  He stood on the side o' the right,
An' when Lincoln called him to take charge
    o' things,
  He won nearly every blamed fight.
Jane Jones she honestly said it was so!
  Mebbe he did—I dunno!
Still I ain't to blame, not by a big sight,
For I ain't never had any battles to fight.

She said 'at Columbus was out at the knees
  When he first thought up his big scheme,
An' told all the Spaniards 'nd Italians, too,
  An' all of 'em said 'twas a dream.
But Queen Isabella jest listened to him,
  'Nd pawned all her jewels o' worth,
'Nd bought him the Santa Maria 'nd said,
  "Go hunt up the rest o' the earth!"
Jane Jones she honestly said it was so!
  Mebbe he did—I dunno!
O' course that may be, but then you must
    allow
They ain't no land to discover jest now!

—Ben King

START WHERE YOU STAND

Start where you stand and never mind the
    past;
  The past won't help you in beginning new;
If you have left it all behind at last
  Why, that's enough, you're done with it,
    you're through;
This is another chapter in the book;

This is another race that you have
    planned;
Don't give the vanished days a backward
    look;
  Start where you stand.

The world won't care about your old defeats
  If you can start anew and win success;
The future is your time, and time is fleet
  And there is much of work and strain
    and stress;
Forget the buried woes and dead despairs;
  Here is a brand-new trial right at hand;
The future is for him who does and dares;
  Start where you stand.

Old failures will not halt, old triumphs aid;
  Today's the thing, tomorrow soon will be;
Get in the fight and face it unafraid,
  And leave the past to ancient history;
What has been, has been; yesterday is dead
  And by it you are neither blessed nor
    banned;
Take courage, man, be brave and drive
    ahead;
  Start where you stand.

—Berton Braley

Once to every man and nation comes the
    moment to decide;
In the strife of Truth with Falsehood,
    for the good or evil side;
Some great cause, God's new Messiah,
    offering each the bloom or blight,
Parts the goats upon the left hand and
    the sheep upon the right,
And the choice goes by forever 'twixt that
    darkness and that light.

—James Russell Lowell

Small opportunities are often the beginning
of great enterprises.

—Demosthenes

TOMORROW'S OPPORTUNITY

If we might have a second chance
  To live the days once more,
And rectify mistakes we've made
  To even up the score.

If we might have a second chance
To use the knowledge gained,
Perhaps we might become at last
As fine as God ordained.
But though we can't retrace our steps
However, stands the score,
Tomorrow brings another chance
For us to try once more.

—FARR

THE GOD OF ONE MORE CHANCE

A man named Peter stumbled bad,
Lost all the love he ever had.
Fouled his own soul's divinest spring,
Cursed, swore, and all that sort of thing.
He got another chance, and then
He reached the goal of God-like men!

A boy goes wrong, the same as he
Who fed swine in the far country;
He seems beyond the utmost reach
Of hearts that pray, of lips that preach;
Give him another chance, and see
How beautiful his life may be.

Paul cast the young man, Mark, aside,
But Barnabas his metal tried,
Called out his courage, roused his vim,
And made a splendid man of him.
Then Paul, near death, longed for one glance
At Mark, who had another chance.

King David, one dark day, fell down,
Lost every jewel from his crown;
He had another chance and found
His kingly self redeemed, recrowned.
Now lonely souls and countless throngs
Are lifted by his deathless songs!

Far-fallen souls, arise! Advance!
Ours is the God of one more chance!

WORLD FOREVER NEW

Consider that the perpetual admonition of Nature to us is, The world is new, untried. Do not believe in the past. I give you the universe new and unhandled every hour. You think in your idle hours that there is literature, history, science behind you so accumulated as to exhaust thought and prescribe your own future and the future. In your sane hour you shall see that not a line has yet been written; that for all the poetry that is in the world your first sensation on entering a wood or standing on the shore of a lake has not been chanted yet. It remains for you, so does all thought, all object, all life remain unwritten still.

—RALPH WALDO EMERSON

PROCRASTINATION

He was going to be all that a mortal could
be—
Tomorrow;
No one should be kinder nor braver than
he—
Tomorrow;
A friend who was troubled and weary he
knew
Who'd be glad of a lift and who needed
it, too;
On him he would call and see what he could
do—
Tomorrow.

Each morning he stacked up the letters he'd
write—
Tomorrow;
And he thought of the folks he would fill
with delight—
Tomorrow;
It was too bad, indeed, he was busy today,
And hadn't a minute to stop on his way;
"More time I'll have to give others," he'd
say—
"Tomorrow."

The greatest of workers this man would have
been—
Tomorrow;
The world would have known him had he
ever seen—
Tomorrow;
But the fact is he died, and he faded from
view,
And all that he left here when living was
through
Was a mountain of things he intended to
do—
Tomorrow.

Within me is the sum of all things past;
Within me are the years that yet remain;
And heaven has not a space too high or vast
That I may not within myself contain;
Nor is there an accomplishment divine
That is not slumbering in this soul of mine.

In Margaret Irwin's story, after the execution of Montrose, his betrothed ran away and entered a nunnery. All sorts of unsavoury reports got abroad about her reasons for such a step, but she meant what she did, and in time became the abbess. Years after her sister asked her bluntly,—"Why did you take vows?" and she answered: "Because the story of God Who gave up His Godhead and His human life for the world of humans has always moved me, not with sorrow or pity, but with exaltation. Could anything be more glorious than to have so much to give and to give it all?"

—THEODORE F. ADAMS

LOST OPPORTUNITY

He came to you, for in His gentle voice
He'd much that He would say.
Your ears were turned to earth's discordant
sounds,
And so—He went away.

He came; and in His hand He had a task
That he would have you do,
But you were occupied with other things,
And so you missed that too.

He would have touched you; and His touch
could thrill,
And give you quickening power;
But earthly things enveloped, and you could
Not feel Him in that hour.

HEIRS OF TOMORROW

Children of yesterday,
Heirs of tomorrow,
What are you weaving?
Labor and sorrow?
Look to your looms again.
Faster and faster

Fly the great shuttles
Prepared by the Master;
Life's in the loom,
Room for it—
Room!

Children of yesterday,
Heirs of tomorrow,
Lighten the labor
And sweeten the sorrow.
Now, while the shuttles fly
Faster and faster,
Up and be at it,
At work with the Master;
He stands at your loom,
Room for Him—
Room!

Children of yesterday,
Heirs of tomorrow,
Look at your fabric
Of labor and sorrow.
Seamy and dark
With despair and disaster,
Turn it, and—lo,
The design of the Master!
The Lord's at the loom;
Room for Him—
Room!

—MARY ARTEMISIA LATHBURY

You wake up in the morning, and lo! your purse is magically filled with twenty-four hours of the magic tissue of the universe of your life. No one can take it from you. No one receives either more or less than you receive. Waste your infinitely precious commodity as much as you will, and the supply will never be withheld from you. Moreover, you cannot draw on the future. Impossible to get into debt. You can only waste the passing moment. You cannot waste tomorrow; it is kept for you.

—ARNOLD BENNETT

CHALLENGE

Yes, read the pages of the old-world story,
Of kings of noble deed and noble thought
Of heroes whose resplendent crown of glory

Bound their wide brows, unsought.

But be not sad because their work is ended,
And they have rest which life so long
denied:
They still live in the world which they
befriended,
For which they lived and died.

Great deeds can never die: all through the
ages
Their fruits increasing ever grow and
spread,
And many a deed unnamed in written pages
Lived once—and is not dead.

And, God be praised, man's work is not
completed,
There still is work on earth for men to do;
Not yet, not yet are all the false defeated,
Not yet crowned all the true.

Still the world needs brave deeds and true
hearts many,
Not yet are all the noble battles won!
We too, we too may yet do deeds great as
any
That ever yet were done.

—Wilbur Nesbit

NOTHING EVER HAPPENS HERE

"Well, nuthin' ever happens out here." The year is 1809, the setting is the small village of Hardin, Kentucky. Two men dressed in homespun—one with a gun slung over his right shoulder standing deep in the snow—the other mounted on a horse. The man on foot turns to the man on horseback and asks, "Any news down in the village?" And the other replies, "Well, they tell me that Tom Singleton has gone down to Washington to see Madison sworn in. They're saying, too, that a man called Bonaparte has captured almost all of Spain . . . What's the news out here?" The man standing in the snow commented, "Well, I heard that down at Tom Lincoln's hut there is a new baby boy." And as the man started to ride away he was mumbling, "Nuthin' ever happens out here."

THIS IS YOUR HOUR

This is your hour—creep upon it!
Summon your power, leap upon it!
Grasp it, clasp it, hold it tight!
Strike it, spike it, with full might!
If you take too long to ponder,
Opportunity may wander.
Yesterday's a bag of sorrow;
No man ever finds Tomorrow.
Hesitation is a mire—
Climb out, climb up, climb on higher!
Fumble, stumble, risk a tumble,
Make a start, however humble!
Do your best and do it now!
Pluck and grit will find out how.
Persevere, although you tire—
While a spark is left, there's fire.
Distrust doubt; doubt is a liar.
Even if all mankind jeer you,
You can force the world to cheer you.

—Herbert Kaufman

Let us ask ourselves as we arise each morning, "What is my work today?" We do not know where the influence of today will end. Our lives may outgrow all our present thoughts and outdazzle all our dreams. God puts each fresh morning, each new chance of life, into our hands as a gift, to see what we will do with it.

—Anna R. Brown Lindsay

Opportunities do not come with their values stamped upon them. Everyone must be challenged. A day dawns, quite like other days; in it a single hour comes, quite like other hours; but in that day and in that hour the chance of a lifetime faces us. To face every opportunity of life thoughtfully and ask its meaning bravely and earnestly, is the only way to meet the supreme opportunities when they come, whether open-faced or disguised.

—Maltbie D. Babcock

PATRIOTISM

And so my fellow Americans: Ask not what your country can do for you—ask what you can do for your country.

—JOHN FITZGERALD KENNEDY

has been termed by some religious writers, who overthrew the established church in his own State, and then, with prophetic statesmanship, made it impossible for any church to establish itself under our national Constitution or in any way to abridge the rights of conscience.

—OSCAR S. STRAUS

The ideal state is that in which an injury done to the least of its citizens is an injury done to all.

—SOLON

America is a tune; it must be sung together.

—GERALD STANLEY LEE

If we were to single out the men who from the beginning of our Colonial state until the present time have most eminently contributed to fostering and securing religious freedom, who have made this country of ours the haven of refuge from ecclesiastical tyranny and persecution, who have set an example more puissant than army or navy for freeing the conscience of men from civil interference, and have leavened the mass of intolerance wherever the name of America is known, I would mention first the Baptist, Roger Williams, who maintained the principle that the civil powers have no right to meddle in matters of conscience, and who founded a State with that principle as its keystone. I would mention second the Catholic, Lord Baltimore, the proprietor of Maryland, to whom belongs the credit of having established liberty in matters of worship which was second only to Rhode Island. I would name third the Quaker, William Penn, whose golden motto was, "We must yield the liberties we demand." Fourth on the list is Thomas Jefferson, that "arch-infidel," as he

UNMANIFEST DESTINY

To what new gates, my country, far
And unforseen of foe or friend,
Beneath what unexpected star,
Compelled to what unchosen end.

Across the sea that knows no beach
The Admiral of Nations guides
Thy blind obedient keels to reach
The harbor where thy future rides!

The guns that spoke at Lexington
Knew not that God was planning then
The trumpet word of Jefferson
To bugle forth the rights of men.

To them that wept and cursed Bull Run,
What was it but despair and shame?
Who saw behind the cloud the sun?
Who knew that God was in the flame?

Had not defeat upon defeat,
Disaster on disaster come,
The slave's emancipated feet
Had never marched behind the drum.

There is a Hand that bends our deeds
To mightier issues than we planned,
Each son that triumphs, each that bleeds,
My country, serves Its dark command.

I do not know beneath what sky
Nor on what seas shall be thy fate;
I only know it shall be high,
I only know it shall be great.

—RICHARD HOVEY

The war inevitably brought its own tremendous social problems and opened new avenues of social service in China. We were suddenly called upon among innumerable other things, to care for the millions of refugees, hundreds of thousands of families of recruits, and vast numbers of children who had lost their parents. The burden was heavy and our means meager, but they were augmented by the generous assistance received from America and other friendly nations. This gesture of sympathy and good will was deeply appreciated by all our Chinese people.

—MADAME CHIANG KAI-SHEK

That nation is proudest and noblest and most exalted which has the greatest number of really great men.

—SINCLAIR LEWIS

THE FLAG

O banner blazoned in the sky,
  Fling out your royal red;
Each deeper hue to crimson dye
  Won by our sainted dead.

Ye bands of snowy whiteness clean
  That bar the waning day,
Stand as the prophecy of things unseen
  Toward which we hew our way.

Fair field of blue, a symbol true
  Of Right, of Faith, of God,
O'erarch us as we seek anew
  The path our fathers trod.

Ye clustered stars that gleam above,
  Our darkness turn to light;
Reveal to men Heaven's law of love—
  Then ends the world's long night.

—HENRY C. POTTER

A PATRIOTIC CREED

To serve my country day by day
At any humble post I may;
To honor and respect her flag,
To live the traits of which I brag;

To be American in deed
As well as in my printed creed.

To stand for truth and honest toil,
To till my little patch of soil,
And keep in mind the debt I owe
To them who died that I might know
My country, prosperous and free,
And passed this heritage to me.

I always must in trouble's hour
Be guided by the men in power;
For God and country I must live,
My best for God and country give;
No act of mine that men may scan
Must shame the name American.

To do my best and play my part,
American in mind and heart;
To serve the flag and bravely stand
To guard the glory of my land;
To be American in deed:
God grant me strength to keep this creed!

—EDGAR A. GUEST

Let our object be our country, our whole country, and nothing but our country. And, by the blessing of God, may that country itself become a vast and splendid monument, not of oppression and terror, but of wisdom, of peace and of liberty, upon which the world may gaze with admiration forever.

—DANIEL WEBSTER

We make daily great improvements in natural, there is one I wish to see in moral philosophy; the discovery of a plan, that would induce and oblige nations to settle their disputes without first cutting one another's throats.

When will human reason be sufficiently improved to see the advantage of this? When will men be convinced, that even successful wars become misfortunes, who unjustly commenced them, and who triumphed blindly in their success, not seeing all its consequences.

—BENJAMIN FRANKLIN

THE FOUR FREEDOMS

In the future days, which we seek to make secure, we look forward to a world founded upon four essential human freedoms.

The first is freedom of speech and expression—everywhere in the world.

The second is freedom of every person to worship God in his own way—everywhere in the world.

The third is freedom from want—which, translated into world terms, means economic understandings which will secure to every nation a healthy peacetime life for its inhabitants—everywhere in the world.

The fourth is freedom from fear—which, translated into world terms, means a world-wide reduction of armaments to such a point and in such a thorough fashion that no nation will be in a position to commit an act of physical aggression against any neighbor—anywhere in the world.

That is no vision of a distant millennium. It is a definite basis for a kind of world attainable in our own time and generation. That kind of world is the very antithesis of the so-called new order of tyranny which the dictators seek to create with the crash of a bomb.

—FRANKLIN D. ROOSEVELT

MY AIN MOUNTAIN LAND

*Oh! wae's me on gowd, wi' its glamour and
   fame,*
*It tint me my love, and it wiled me frae
   hame,*
Syne dwindled awa' like a neivefu' o' sand,
*And left me to mourn for my ain mountain
   land.*

*I lang for the glens, and the brown heather
   fells,*
*The green birken shades, where the wild
   lintie dwells,*
*The dash o' the deep, on the gray rocky
   strand*
*That girds the blue hills of my ain mountain
   land.*

*I dream o' the dells where the clear burnies
   flow,*

*The bonnie green knowes where the green
   gowans grow;*
*But I wake frae my sleep like a being that's
   bann'd,*
*And shed a saut tear for my ain mountain
   land.*

I ken there's a lass that looks out on the sea,
*Wi' tears in the e'en that are watchin' for
   me;*
*Lang, lang she may wait for the clasp o' my
   hand,*
*Or the fa' o' my foot in my ain mountain
   land.*

—THOMAS ELLIOTT

MEMORIAL DAY

These heroes are dead. They died for liberty—they died for us. They are at rest. They sleep in the land they made free, under the flag they rendered stainless, under the solemn pines, the sad hemlocks, the tearful willows, the embracing vines. They sleep beneath the shadow of the clouds, careless alike of sunshine or storm, each in the windowless palace of rest. Earth may run red with other wars—they are at peace. In the midst of battles, in the roar of conflicts, they found the serenity of death.

—ROBERT G. INGERSOLL

THE LAST MESSAGE
FROM THE ALAMO

Commandancy of the Alamo, Bexar, February 24, 1836.—To the people of Texas and all Americans in the world. Fellow citizens and compatriots: I am besieged by a thousand or more of the Mexicans under Santa Anna. I have sustained a continual bombardment and cannonade for twenty-four hours and have not lost a man. The enemy has demanded a surrender at discretion; otherwise the garrison are to be put to the sword if the fort is taken. I have answered the demand with a cannon shot, and our flag still waves proudly from the walls. *I shall never surrender nor retreat.* Then, I call on you in the name of liberty, of patriotism, and everything dear to the American character, to come to our aid with all dispatch. The enemy is receiving reinforcements daily and will no doubt increase to three or four thousand in four or five days. If this call is neglected, I am determined to sustain myself as long as possible and die like a soldier who never forgets what is due to his own honor and that of our country. **VICTORY OR DEATH.**

—WILLIAM BARRET TRAVIS
Lieutenant Colonel Commandant

P.S. The Lord is on our side. When the enemy appeared in sight we had not three bushels of corn. We have since found in deserted houses eighty or ninety bushels and got into the walls twenty or thirty head of beeves.

THE AMERICAN FLAG

*Flag of my country! in thy folds
   Are wrapped the treasures of the heart,
Where'er that waving sheet is fanned
By breezes of the sea or land,
   It bids the life-flood start.*

*It is not that among those stars
   The fiery crest of Mars shines out;
It is not that on battle plain,
'Mid heaps of harnessed warriors slain
   It flaps triumphant o'er the rout.*

*Short-lived the joy that conquest yields;
   Flushed victory is bathed in tears;
The burden of that bloody fame
Which shouting myriads proclaim
   Sounds sad to widowed ears.*

*Thou hast a deeper, stronger hold,
   Flag of my country! on my heart,
Than when o'er mustered hosts unfurled,
Thou art a signal to the world
   At which the nations start.*

*Thou art a symbol of the power
   Whose sheltering wings our homes
      surround;
Guarded by thee was childhood's morn,
And where thy cheering folds are borne
   Order and peace are found.*

*Flag of our mighty Union, hail!
   Blessings abound where thou dost float
Best robe for living Freedom's form,
Fit pall to spread upon her tomb,
   Should Heaven to death devote.*

*Wave over us in glory still,
   And be our guardian as now
Each wind of heaven salute thy streaks!
And withered be the arm that seeks
   To bring that banner low!*

—WILLIAM PARSONS LUNT

AMERICAN LIBERTY

Caesar had his Brutus; Charles the First his Cromwell; and George the Third ("Treason!" cried the Speaker)—may profit by their example. If *this* be treason, make the most of it!

(In the Virginia Convention, 1765)

There is a just God who presides over the destinies of nations; and who will raise up friends to fight our battles for us. The battle, sir, is not to the strong alone; it is to the vigilant, the active, the brave. Besides, sir, we have no election. If we were base enough to desire it, it is now too late to retire from the contest. There is no retreat, but in submission and slavery! Our chains are forged! Their clanking may be heard on the plains of Boston! The war is inevitable—and let it come! I repeat it, sir, let it come!

It is in vain, sir, to extenuate the matter. Gentlemen may cry peace, peace—but there is no peace. The war is actually begun! The next gale that sweeps from the north will bring to our ears the clash of resounding arms! Our brethren are already in the field! Why stand we here idle? What is it that gentlemen wish? What would they have? Is life so dear, or peace so sweet, as to be purchased at the price of chains and slavery? Forbid it, Almighty God! I know not what course others may take; but as for me, give me liberty, or give me death!

—PATRICK HENRY

America is a willingness of the heart.

—F. SCOTT FITZGERALD

THE NEW COLOSSUS

Not like the brazen giant of Greek fame,
With conquering limbs astride from
  land to land,
Here at our sea-washed, sunset gates shall
  stand
A mighty woman with a torch, whose flame
Is the imprisoned lightning, and her name
Mother of Exiles. From her beacon-hand
Glows world-wide welcome;
  her mild eyes command
The air-bridged harbor that twin cities frame.
"Keep, ancient lands, your storied pomp!"
  cries she
With silent lips. "Give me your tired,
  your poor,
Your huddled masses yearning to breathe
  free,
The wretched refuse of your teeming shore.
Send these, the homeless, tempest-tost to me,
I lift my lamp beside the golden door!"

This tablet, with her Sonnet to the Bartholdi Statue of
Liberty engraved upon it, is placed upon these walls in
loving memory of
EMMA LAZARUS
Born in New York City, July 22, 1849
Died November 18, 1887

TRIBUTE TO THE FLAG

I have seen the glories of art and architecture and of river and mountain. I have seen the sun set on the Jungfrau and the moon rise over Mont Blanc. But the fairest vision on which these eyes ever rested was the flag of my country in a foreign port. Beautiful as a flower to those who love it, terrible as a meteor to those who hate it, it is the symbol of the power and the glory and the honor of millions of Americans.

—GEORGE F. HOAR

PRIVILEGE AND OBLIGATION

To millions of people all over the world America is a magic name. Here are schools, roads, parks, libraries, and playgrounds; peaceful living and the right to choose our jobs and plan our lives. Such an ample way of life we may too readily assume to be our natural right. But every benefit, every right, was bought for us—at a price. When we think of the cost paid by our forefathers, we begin to realize that living in a great land is a responsibility as well as a privilege. As we share the experiences of Americans past and present, we may discover new reasons for wanting to keep our country the home of the brave and the free and the good.

THE AMERICAN CREED

I believe in the United States of America as a government of the people, for the people, by the people; whose just powers are derived from the consent of the governed; a democracy in a republic; a sovereign Nation of many sovereign states; a perfect union, one and inseparable; established upon those principles of freedom, equality, justice, and humanity for which American patriots sacrificed their lives and fortunes.

I therefore believe it is my duty to my country to love it; to support its Constitution; to obey its laws; to respect its flag; and to defend it against all enemies.

—WILLIAM TYLER PAGE

AN AMERICAN

I was born an American; I will live an American; I shall die an American; and I intend to perform the duties incumbent upon me in that character to the end of my career. I mean to do this with absolute disregard of personal consequences. What are the personal consequences? What is the individual man, with all the good or evil that may betide him, in comparison with the good or evil which may befall a great country, and in the midst of great transactions which concern that country's fate? Let the consequences be what they will, I am careless. No man can suffer too much, and no man can fall too soon, if he suffer, or if he fall, in the defense of the liberties and constitution of his country.

—DANIEL WEBSTER

POETRY

If I had my life to live over again, I would have made a rule to read some poetry and listen to some music at least once a week; for perhaps the parts of my brain now atrophied would thus have been kept active through use.

The loss of these tastes is a loss of happiness, and may possibly be injurious to the intellect, and more probably to the moral character, by enfeebling the emotional part of our nature.

—CHARLES DARWIN

We can read poetry, and recite poetry, but to *live* poetry—is the symphony of life.

—S. FRANCES FOOTE

THE VOICELESS

We count the broken lyres that rest
  Where the sweet wailing singers slumber,
But o'er their silent sister's breast
  The wild flowers who will stoop to
    number?
A few can touch the magic string,
  And noisy Fame is proud to win them:—
Alas for those that never sing,
  But die with all their music in them!

O hearts that break and give no sign
  Save whitening lip and fading tresses,
Till Death pours out his longed-for wine
  Slow-dropped from Misery's crushing
    presses,—
If singing breath or echoing chord
  To every hidden pang were given,
What endless melodies were poured,
  As sad as earth, as sweet as heaven!

—OLIVER WENDELL HOLMES

Poetry makes immortal all that is best and most beautiful in the world.

—PERCY BYSSHE SHELLEY

COMRADES

I walked with poets in my youth,
  Because the world they drew
Was beautiful and glorious
  Beyond the world I knew.

The poets are my comrades still,
  But dearer than in youth,
For now I know that they alone
  Picture the world of truth.

—WILLIAM ROSCOE THAYER

I who am dead a thousand years,
  And wrote this sweet archaic song,
Send you my words for messengers
  The way I shall not pass along.

I care not if you bridge the seas,
  Or ride secure the cruel sky,
Or build consummate palaces
  Of metal or of masonry.

But you have wine and music still,
  And statues and a bright-eyed love,
And foolish thoughts of good and ill,
  And prayers to them that sit above?

How shall we conquer? Like a wind
  That falls at eve our fancies blow,
And old Moeonides the blind
  Said it three thousand years ago.

O friend, unseen, unborn, unknown,
  Student of our sweet English tongue,
Read out my words at night, alone:
  I was a poet, I was young.

Since I can never see your face,
  And never shake you by the hand,
I send my soul through time and space
  To greet you. You will understand.

—JAMES ELROY FLECKER

Poetry should please by a fine excess and not by singularity. It should strike the reader as a wording of his own highest thoughts, and appear almost as a remembrance.

—JOHN KEATS

Genius is mainly an affair of energy, and poetry is mainly an affair of genius; therefore a nation characterized by energy may well be eminent in poetry.

—MATTHEW ARNOLD

The functions of the poetical faculty are twofold; by one it creates new materials of knowledge, and power, and pleasure; by the other it engenders in the mind a desire to reproduce and arrange them according to a certain rhythm and order which may be called the beautiful and good. The cultivation of poetry is never more to be desired than at periods when, from an excess of the selfish and calculating principle, the accumulation of the materials of external life exceed the quantity of the power of assimilating them to the internal laws of human nature. The body has then become too unwieldy for that which animates it.

Poetry is indeed something divine. It is at once the center and circumference of knowledge; it is that which comprehends all science, and that to which all science must be referred. It is at the same time the root and blossom of all other systems of thought; it is that from which all spring, and that which adorns all; and that which, if blighted, denies the fruit and the seed, and witholds from the barren world the nourishment and the succession of the scions of the tree of life.

—PERCY BYSSHE SHELLEY

WHAT THE CHIMNEY SANG

Over the chimney the night wind sang
And chanted a melody no one knew;
And the Woman stopped as her babe she
    tossed
And thought of the one she had long
    since lost,
And said, as her tear drops back she forced,
"I hate the wind in the chimney."

Over the chimney the night wind sang
And chanted a melody no one knew;
And the Children said as they closer drew,
" 'Tis some witch that is cleaving the
    black night through,—

'Tis the fairy trumpet that just then blew,
And we fear the wind in the chimney."

Over the chimney the night wind sang
And chanted a melody no one knew;
And the Man, as he sat on his hearth below,
Said to himself, "It will surely snow,
And fuel is dear and wages low,
And I'll stop the leak in the chimney."

Over the chimney the night wind sang
And chanted a melody no one knew;
But the Poet listened and smiled, for he
Was Man, and Woman, and Child, all three
And said, "It is God's own harmony,
This wind we hear in the chimney."

—BRET HARTE

WORLD AND POET

"Sing to us, Poet, for our hearts are broken;
Sing us a song of happy, happy love,
Sing of the joy that words leave all
    unspoken,—
The lilt and laughter of life, oh sing thereof!
Oh, sing of life, for we are sick and dying;
Oh, sing of joy, for all our joy is dead;
Oh, sing of laughter, for we know but
    sighing;
Oh, sing of kissing, for we kill instead!"
How should he sing of happy love, I pray,
Who drank love's cup of anguish long ago?
How should he sing of life and joy and day,
Who whispers Death to end his night
    of woe?
    And yet the Poet took his lyre and sang,
    Till all the dales with happy echoes rang.

—RICHARD HOVEY

WHAT IS POETRY?

Poetry is the universal language which the heart holds with nature and itself. He who has a contempt for poetry cannot have much respect for himself or for anything else . . . for all that is worth remembering in life is the poetry of it. Fear is poetry, hope is poetry, love is poetry, hatred is poetry, contempt, jealousy, remorse, admiration, wonder, pity, despair, or madness are all poetry.

—WILLIAM HAZLITT

From HESPERIDES

I sing of brooks, of blossoms,
  birds and bowers,
Of April, May, of June and July flowers;
I sing of Maypoles, hock-carts, wassails,
  wakes,
Of bridegrooms, brides, and of their bridal
  cakes;
I write of youth, of love, and have access
By these to sing of cleanly wantonness;
I sing of dews, of rains, and piece by piece
Of balm, of oil, of spice and ambergris;
I sing of times trans-shifting, and I write
How roses first came red and lilies white;
I write of groves, of twilight, and I sing
The Court of Mab, and of the Fairy King;
I write of hell; I sing (and ever shall)
Of heaven, and I hope to have it after all.

—ROBERT HERRICK

Poetry is vocal painting, as painting is silent poetry.

—SIMONIDES OF CEOS

THE POET

The poet is chiefly distinguished from other men by a greater promptness to think and feel without immediate eternal excitement, and a greater power in expressing such thoughts and feelings as are produced in him in that manner.

But these passions and thoughts and feelings are the general passions and thoughts and feelings of men. And with what are they connected? Undoubtedly with our moral sentiments and animal sensations, and with the causes which excite these; with the operations of the elements, and the appearances of the visible universe; with storm and sunshine, with the revolutions of the seasons, with cold and heat, with loss of friends and kindred, with injuries and resentments, gratitude and hope, with fear and sorrow. These, and the like, are the sensations and objects which the Poet describes, as they are the sensations of other men and the objects which interest them.

—WILLIAM WORDSWORTH

THE POET'S REWARD

Thanks untraced to lips unknown
Shall greet me like the odors blown
From unseen meadows newly mown,
Or lilies floating in some pond,
Wood-fringed, the wayside gaze beyond;
The traveller owns the grateful sense
Of sweetness near, he knows not whence,
And, pausing, takes with forehead bare
The benediction of the air.

—JOHN GREENLEAF WHITTIER

The riches of scholarship, the benignities of literature, defy fortune and outlive calamity.

—JAMES RUSSELL LOWELL

The great charm of Scottish poetry consists in its simplicity and genuine, unaffected sympathy with the common joys and sorrows of daily life. It is a home-taught, household melody. It calls to mind the pastoral bleat on the hillsides, the kirk-bells of a summer Sabbath, the song of the lark in the sunrise.

—JOHN GREENLEAF WHITTIER

THE SONNET

What is a sonnet? It's the pearly shell
That murmurs of the far-off murmuring sea;
A precious jewel carved most curiously;
It is a little picture painted well.
What is a sonnet? It's the tear that fell
From a great poet's hidden ecstasy;
A two-edged sword, a star, a song—ah me!
Sometimes a heavy-tolling funeral bell.
This was the flame that shook with Dante's
  breath;
The solemn organ whereon Milton played,
And the clear glass where Shakespeare's
  shadow falls;
A sea this is—beware who ventureth!
For like a fjord the narrow floor is laid
Mid-ocean deep to the sheer mountain walls.

—RICHARD WATSON GILDER

SOLACE

Never does a man know the force that is in him till some mighty affection or grief has humanized the soul.

—FREDERICK W. ROBERTSON

Sorrow is a fruit: God does not make it grow on limbs too weak to bear it.

—VICTOR HUGO

As you live this new life, we pray that you will be strengthened from God's boundless resources, so that you will find yourselves able to pass through any experience and endure it with courage. You will even be able to thank God in the midst of pain and distress because you are privileged to share the lot of those who are living in the Light. For we must never forget that He rescued us from the power of darkness, and re-established us in the Kingdom of His beloved Son, that is, in the Kingdom of Light. For it is by His Son alone that we have been redeemed and have had our sins forgiven.

—PHILIPPIANS 1:11 ff. (*Philips Translation*)

ALONG THE ROAD

I walked a mile with Pleasure;
She chattered all the way,
But left me none the wiser
For all she had to say.

I walked a mile with Sorrow
And ne'er a word said she;
But oh, the things I learned from her
When Sorrow walked with me!

—ROBERT BROWNING HAMILTON

OUR DEBT TO SORROW

No words can express how much the world owes to sorrow. Most of the Psalms were born in a wilderness. Most of the Epistles were written in a prison. The greatest thoughts of the greatest thinkers have all passed through fire. The greatest poets have "learned in suffering what they taught in song." In bonds Bunyan lived the allegory that he afterwards indited, and we may thank Bedford Jail for the "Pilgrim's Progress." Take comfort afflicted Christian! When God is about to make pre-eminent use of a man, He puts him in the fire.

—GEORGE MACDONALD

Joys are our wings; sorrows our spurs.

—JEAN PAUL RICHTER

ALCHEMY

I lift my heart as spring lifts up
A yellow daisy to the rain;
My heart will be a lovely cup
Altho' it holds but pain.

For I shall learn from flower and leaf
That color every drop they hold,
To change the lifeless wine of grief
To living gold.

—SARA TEASDALE

I THINK THAT GOD IS PROUD

I think that God is proud of those who bear
A sorrow bravely—proud indeed of them
Who walk straight through the dark
to find Him there,
And kneel in faith to touch His garment's
hem.
Oh, proud of them who lifts their heads
to shake
Away the tears from eyes that have
grown dim,
Who tighten quivering lips and turn to take
The only road they know that leads
to Him.

How proud He must be of them—
He who knows
All sorrows, and how hard grief is to bear!
I think He sees them coming, and He goes

With outstretched arms and hands
   to meet them there.
And with a look, a touch on hand or head,
Each finds his hurt heart strangely comforted.

       —GRACE NOLL CROWELL

OUR BURDEN BEARER

The little sharp vexations
   And the briars that cut the feet,
Why not take all to the Helper
   Who has never failed us yet?
Tell Him about the heartache,
   And tell Him the longings too,
Tell Him the baffled purpose
   When we scarce know what to do.
Then, leaving all our weakness
   With the One divinely strong,
Forget that we bore the burden
   And carry away the song.

       —PHILLIPS BROOKS

HOLD ON!

When you come to the place where the
   shadows are,
And light ahead is withdrawn:
Put your hand in God's and keep it there
Till he carries you over and on.

You may have to tarry a while in the dark,
Till God is ready to lead,
But while you are waiting just pray and pray
To Him in your great need.

Then hold on to God's hand with a
   solid grip,
Let nothing deter your stand:
Keep waiting and waiting and holding on
Till the shadows pass from the land.

WHEN SHE MUST GO

When she must go, so much will go with her!
   Stories of country summers, far and bright,
Wisdom of berries, flowers and chestnut bur,
   And songs to comfort babies in the night;

Old legends and their meanings,
   half-lost tunes,

Wise craftsmanship in all the
   household ways,
And roses taught to flower in summer noons,
   And children taught the shaping of
   good days;

A heart still steadfast, stable, that can know
   A son's first loss, a daughter's first
   heartbreak,
And say to them, "This, too,
   shall pass and go;
   This is not all!" while anguished for
   their sake;

Courage to cling to when the day is lost,
   Love to come back to when all love
   grows cold,
Quiet from tumult; hearth fire from the frost.
   Oh, must she ever go, and we be old?

       —MARGARET WIDDEMER

VANISHED

She died—this is the way she died;
   And when her breath was done,
Took up her simple wardrobe
   And started for the sun.

Her little figure at the gate
   The angels must have spied,
Since I could never find her
   Upon the mortal side.

       —EMILY DICKINSON

LIFE'S LESSONS

I learn, as the years roll onward
   And leave the past behind,
That much I had counted sorrow
   But proves that God is kind;
That many a flower I had longed for
   Had hidden a thorn of pain,
And many a rugged bypath
   Led to fields of ripened grain.

The clouds that cover the sunshine
   They can not banish the sun;
And the earth shines out the brighter
   When the weary rain is done.
We must stand in the deepest shadow
   To see the clearest light;

And often thro' wrong's own darkness
  Comes the very strength of light.

The sweetest rest is at even,
  After a wearisome day,
When the heavy burden of labor
  Has born from our hearts away;
And those who have never known sorrow
  Can not know the infinite peace
That falls on the troubled spirit
  When it sees at last 'release.

We must live thro' the dreary winter
  If we would value the spring;
And the woods must be cold and silent
  Before the robins sing.
The flowers must be buried in darkness
  Before they can bud and bloom,
And the sweetest, warmest sunshine
  Comes after the storm and gloom.

Lead, kindly Light, amid the encircling
    gloom;
  Lead thou me on!
. . . . I do not ask to see
The distant scene; one step enough for me.

          —JOHN HENRY NEWMAN

Ere sin could blight or sorrow fade,
Death came with timely care.

       —SAMUEL TAYLOR COLERIDGE

A GOLDEN SORROW

I swear 'tis better to be lowly born,
And range with humble livers in content,
Than to be perked up in a glistering grief,
And wear a golden sorrow.

            —SHAKESPEARE

THIS, TOO, WILL PASS

This, too, will pass. O heart,
  say it over and over,
Out of your deepest sorrow,
  out of your grief.
No hurt can last forever—

perhaps tomorrow
Will bring relief.

This, too, will pass. It will spend itself—
  its fury
Will die as the wind dies down with the
  setting sun;
Assuaged and calm, you will rest again,
  forgetting
A thing that is done.

Repeat it again and again, O heart,
  for your comfort;
This, too, will pass, as surely as passed before
The old forgotten pain, and the other
  sorrows
That once you bore.

As certain as stars at night, or dawn
  after darkness,
Inherent as the lift of the blowing grass,
Whatever your despair or your frustration—
This, too, will pass.

       —GRACE NOLL CROWELL

Life, believe is not a dream
  So dark as sages say,
Oft a little rain,
  Foretells a pleasant day.

       —CHARLOTTE BRONTE

IN THE HOUR OF MY DISTRESS

In the hour of my distress,
When temptations me oppress,
And when I my sins confess,
  Sweet Spirit comfort me!

When the house doth sigh and weep,
And the world is drowned in sleep,
Yet mine eyes the watch do keep;
  Sweet Spirit comfort me!

When (God knows) I'm tost about,
Either with despair or doubt;
Yet before the glass be out,
  Sweet Spirit comfort me!

When the Judgment is revealed,
And that opened which was sealed,
When to Thee I have appealed;
  Sweet Spirit comfort me!

       —ROBERT HERRICK

THICK IS THE DARKNESS

Thick is the darkness—
Sunward, O, sunward!
Rough is the highway—
Onward, still onward!

Dawn harbors surely
East of the shadows.
Facing us somewhere
Spread the sweet meadows.

Upward and forward!
Time will restore us:
Light is above us,
Rest is before us.

—WILLIAM ERNEST HENLEY

Never bear more than one kind of trouble at a time. Some people bear three—all they have had, all they have now, and all they expect to have.

—EDWARD EVERETT HALE

I believe if we could only see beforehand what it is that our Heavenly Father means us to be, the soul beauty and perfection and glory, the glorious and lovely spiritual body that this soul is to dwell in through all eternity, if we could have a glimpse of this, we should not grudge all the trouble and pains he is taking with us now to bring us up to that ideal which is his thought of us.

—ANNIE KEARY

THE BETTER WAY

God never would send you the darkness
If He thought you could bear the light;
But you would not cling to His guiding hand,
If the way were always bright;
And you would not care to walk by faith
Could you always walk by sight.

'Tis true He has many an anguish
For your sorrowing heart to bear,
And many a cruel thorn crown
For your tired head to wear;
He knows how few would reach Heaven
at all

If pain did not guide them there.

So He sends you the blinding darkness,
And the furnace of sevenfold heat;
'Tis the only way, believe me,
To keep you close to His feet,
For 'tis always so easy to wander
When our lives are glad and sweet.

Then nestle your hand in your Father's,
And sing if you can, as you go,
Your song may cheer someone behind you
Whose courage is sinking low;
And, well, well if your lips do quiver
God will love you better so.

THE JOY OF INCOMPLETENESS

If all our life were one broad glare
Of sunlight clear, unclouded:
If all our path were smooth and fair,
By no soft gloom enshrouded;
If all life's flowers were fully blown
Without the sweet unfolding,
And happiness were rudely thrown
On hands too weak for holding—
Should we not miss the twilight hours,
The gentle haze and sadness?
Should we not long for storms and showers
To break the constant gladness?

If none were sick and none were sad,
What service could we render?
I think if we were always glad
We scarcely could be tender.
Did our beloved never need
Our patient ministration,
Earth would grow cold and miss indeed
Its sweetest consolation:
If sorrow never claimed our heart
And every wish were granted
Patience would die, and hope depart—
Life would be disenchanted.

—ALBERT CROWELL

Shadow owes its birth to light.

—JOHN GAY

IN THE HOUR OF DARKNESS

Am I and my misery alone together in the universe? Is my misery without any meaning, and I without hope? If there be no God, then all that is left for me is despair and death. But if there be, then I can hope that there is a meaning in my misery; that it comes to me not without cause, even though that cause be my own fault. I can plead with God like poor Job of old, even though in wild words like Job; and ask—What is the meaning of this sorrow? What have I done? What should I do? "I will say unto God, Do not condemn me; shew me wherefore thou contendest with me. Surely I would speak unto the Almighty, and desire to reason with God."

"I would speak unto the Almighty, and desire to reason with God." Oh my friends, a man, I believe, can gain courage and wisdom to say that, only by the inspiration of the Spirit of God.

But when once he has said that from his heart, he begins to be justified by faith. For he has had faith in God; he has trusted God enough to speak to God who made him; and so he has put himself, so far at least, into his just and right place, as a spiritual and rational being, made in the image of God.

But more, he has justified God. He has confessed that God is not a mere force or law of nature; nor a mere tyrant and tormenter: but a reasonable being, who will hear reason, and a just being, who will do justice by the creatures whom He has made.

And so the very act of prayer justifies God, and honours God, and gives glory to God; for it confesses that God is what He is, a good God, to whom the humblest and the most fallen of His creatures dare speak out the depths of their abasement, and acknowledge that His glory is this—That in spite of all His majesty, He is one who heareth prayer; a being as magnificent in His justice as He is magnificent in His Majesty and His might.

—CHARLES KINGSLEY

Thou knowest, not alone as God all-knowing;
As Man our mortal weakness Thou hast
    proved;

On earth, with purest sympathies
    o'er-flowing,
O Saviour, Thou hast wept, and Thou
    hast loved;
And love and sorrow still to Thee may come,
And find in Thee a hiding-place, a rest,
    a home.

FOR ALL OF TROUBLED HEART

The snow is falling softly on the earth,
Grown hushed beneath its covering of white;
O Father, let another peace descend
On all of troubled heart this winter night.

Look down upon them in their anxious dark,
On those who sleep not for their fear
    and care,
On those with tremulous prayers on
    their lips,
The prayers that stand between them
    and despair.

Let fall Thy comfort as this soundless snow;
Make troubled hearts aware in Thine own
    way
Of Love beside them in this quiet hour,
Of Strength with which to meet the
    coming day.

—A. WARREN

LOSS AND GAIN

The greater our love may be, the greater the surface that we expose to majestic sorrow, wherefore none the less does the sage never cease his endeavors to enlarge this beautiful surface.

—MAURICE MAETERLINCK

I KNOW

I know thy sorrow, child; I know it well,
Thou needst not try with broken voice to tell.
Just let Me lay thy head here on My breast,
And find here sweetest comfort, perfect rest;
Thou needst not bear the burden, child,
    thyself,

I yearn to take it all upon Myself;
Then trust it all to Me today—tomorrow,
Yes, e'en forever; for I know thy sorrow.

Long years ago I planned it all for thee;
Prepared it that thou mightst find need
    of Me.
Without it, child, thou wouldst not come to
Find this place of comfort in this love of
    Mine.
Hadst thou no cross like this for Me to bear,
Thou wouldst not feel the need of My
    strong care;
But in thy weakness thou didst come to Me,
And through this plan I have won thee.

I know thy sorrow and I love thee more,
Because for such as thee I came and bore
The wrong, the shame, the pain of Calvary,
That I might comfort give to such as thee.
So, resting here, My child, thy hand in Mine,
Thy sorrow to My care today resign;
Dread not that some new care will come
    tomorrow,—
What does it matter? I know all thy sorrow.

And I will gladly take it all for thee,
If only thou wilt trust it all to Me,
Thou needest not stir, but in My love lie still,
And learn the sweetness of thy Father's
    will—
That will has only planned for the best;
So, knowing this, lie still and sweetly rest.
Trust Me. The future shall not bring to thee
But that will bring thee closer still to Me.

ENDURANCE

How much the heart may bear and yet not
    break!
    How much the flesh may suffer and not
        die!
I question much if any pain or ache
    Of soul or body brings our end more nigh:
Death chooses his own time;
        till that is sworn,
    All evil may be borne.

Behold, we live through all things—
        famine, thirst,
    Bereavement, pain, all grief and misery,
All woe and sorrow; life inflicts its worst

On soul and body—but we cannot die,
Though we be sick, and tired, and faint
    and worn—
    Lo, all things can be borne!

—Elizabeth Akers Allen

THE SORROW TUGS

It seems as you look back over things,
        that all that you treasure dear
Is somehow blent in a wondrous way
        with a heart pang and a tear.
Though many a day is a joyous one when
        viewed by itself apart,
    The golden threads in the warp of life
        are the sorrows that tug at your heart.

—Edgar A. Guest

SOME TIME

Some time, when all life's lessons have
        been learned,
    And sun and stars for evermore have set,
The things which our weak judgment
        here has spurned,
    The things o'er which we grieved with
        lashes wet,
Will flash before us out of life's dark night,
    As stars shine most in deeper tints of blue;
And we shall see how all God's plans were
        right,
    And how what seemed reproof
        was love most true.

And we shall see that while we frown
        and sigh,
    God's plans go on as best for you and me:
How, when we called, He heeded not our cry,
    Because His wisdom to the end could see.
And e'en as prudent parents disallow
    Too much of sweet to craving babyhood,
So God, perhaps, is keeping from us now
    Life's sweetest things because it
        seemeth good.

And if, sometimes, comingled with life's
        wine,
    We find the wormwood, and rebel
        and shrink,
Be sure a wiser hand than yours or mine

Pours out this portion
    for our lips to drink.
And if some friend we love is lying low,
    Where human kisses cannot reach his face,
Oh, do not blame the loving Father so,
    But bear your sorrow with obedient grace.

And you shall shortly know that
      lengthened breath
    Is not the sweetest gift God sends
      his friends;
And that, sometimes, the sable pall of death
    Conceals the fairest boon
      His love can send.
If we could push ajar the gates of life,
    And stand within, and all God's
      working see,
We might interpret all this doubt and strife,
    And for each mystery find a key.

But not today. Then be content, poor heart;
    God's plans, like lilies pure and white,
      unfold.
We must not tear the close-shut leaves
      apart—
    Time will reveal the calyxes of gold.
And if, through patient toil,
      we reach the land
    Where tired feet, with sandals loose,
      may rest,—
When we shall clearly know and
      understand,—
    I think that we will say that
      God knew best.

—MAY RILEY SMITH

IN MEMORY

What mean you by this weeping
    To break my very heart?
We both are in Christ's keeping,
    And therefore cannot part.
You there, I here, though parted
    We still at heart are one;
I only just in sunshine,
    The shadow scarcely gone.
What though the clouds surround you,
    You can the brightness see,
'Tis only a little way
    That leads from you to me.

I was so very weary,
    Surely you would not mourn,
That I a little sooner
    Should lay my burden down.
Then weep not, weep not, Darling,
    God wipes away all tears;
'Tis only a little way
    Though you may call it years.

YESTERDAY'S GRIEF

The rain that fell a-yesterday is ruby
      on the roses
    Silver on the poplar leaf
      and gold on willow stem;
The grief that chanced a-yesterday
      is silence that incloses
    Holy loves when time and change shall
      never trouble them.
The rain that fell a-yesterday
      makes all the hillsides glisten,
    Coral on the laurel and beryl on the grass;
The grief that chanced a-yesterday
      has taught the soul to listen
    For whispers of eternity in all the winds
      that pass.

O faint-of-heart, storm-beaten, this rain
      will gleam tomorrow,
    Flame within the columbine and jewels
      on the thorn,
Heaven in the forget-me-not;
      though sorrow now be sorrow,
    Yet sorrow shall be beauty in the magic
      of the morn.

—KATHERINE LEE BATES

Forget thyself; console the sadness near thee:
    Thine own shall then depart,
And songs of joy, like heavenly birds,
      shall cheer thee
    And dwell within thy heart.

SPACE

For each age is a dream that is dying,
Or one that is coming to birth.

—ARTHUR WILLIAM O'SHAUGNESSY

Men grow when inspired by a high purpose when contemplating vast horizons. The sacrifice of oneself is not very difficult for one burning with the passion for a great adventure.

—ALEXIS CARREL

From IN THE DAWN

We are standing in the great dawn of a day
*   they did not know,*
On a height they only dreamed of,
*   toiling darkly far below;*
But our gaze is toward a summit,
*   loftier, airier, mist-encurled,*
Soaring skyward through the twilight
*   from the bases of the world.*
Up and up, achieving, failing,
*   weak in flesh but strong of soul.*
We may never live to reach it—
*   ah, but we have seen the goal!*

—ODELL SHEPARD

When I behold your heavens, the work of
*   your fingers, the moon and the stars which*
*   you set in place—*
What is man that you should be mindful of
*   him, or the son of man that you should*
*   care for him?*
You have made him little less than the angels,
*   and crowned him with glory and honor.*
You have given him rule over the works of
*   your hands, putting all things under his*
*   feet . . .*

—PSALMS 8:3-6

To know the mighty works of God; to comprehend His wisdom and majesty and power; to appreciate in degree, the wonderful working of His laws, surely all this must be a pleasing and acceptable mode of worship to the Most High, to whom ignorance can not be more grateful than knowledge.

—NICOLAUS COPERNICUS

Greater than any army with banners is an idea whose time has come.

—VICTOR HUGO

United States Astronaut Neil Armstrong placed his foot firmly on the fine-grained surface of the moon. The time was 10:56 p.m. (E.D.T.), July 20, 1969. Pausing briefly, the first man on the moon spoke the first words on lunar soil:

"That's one small step for a man, one giant leap for mankind."

Above the indistinguishable roar of the many feet I feel the presence of the sun, of the immense forces of the universe, and beyond these the sense of the eternal now, of the immortal. Full aware that all has failed, yet, side by side with the sadness of that knowledge, there lives on in me an unquenchable belief, thought burning like the sun, that there is yet something to be found, something real, something to give each separate personality sunshine and flowers in its own existence now. Something to shape this million-handed labor to an end and outcome, leaving accumulated sunshine and flowers to those who shall succeed. It must be dragged forth by might of thought from the immense forces of the universe.

—RICHARD JEFFERIES

OUT OF THE VAST

There's a part of the sun in the apple,
*   There's a part of the moon in a rose;*
There's a part of the flaming Pleiades
*   In every leaf that grows.*
Out of the vast comes nearness;
*   For the God whose love we sing*
Lends a little of His heaven
*   To every living thing.*

—AUGUSTUS WRIGHT BAMBERGER

From THE EXPLORER

"There's no sense in going farther—
*   it's the edge of civilization,"*
So they said, and I believed it—
*   broke my land and sowed my crop—*
Built my barns and strung my fences in the
*   little border station*
*   Tucked away below the foothills*
*   where the trails run out and stop.*

Till a voice, as bad as Conscience,
*   rang interminable changes*
On one everlasting Whisper—
*   day and night repeated—so:*
"Something hidden. Go and find it,
*   Go and look behind the Ranges—*
*   Something lost behind the Ranges.*
*   Lost and waiting for you. Go!"*

—RUDYARD KIPLING

Oh could I tell ye surely would believe it!
*   Oh could I only say what I have seen!*
How should I tell or how can ye receive it,
*   How, till he bringeth you where I have*
*   been?*

—FREDERICK W. H. MYERS

Ye stars! which are the poetry of heaven,
If in your bright leaves we would read the
*   fate*
Of men and empires—'t is to be forgiven
That in our aspirations to be great
Our destinies o'erleap their mortal state,
And claim a kindred with you; for ye are
A beauty and a mystery, and create
In us such love and reverence from afar,
That fortune, fame, power, life,
*   have named themselves a star.*

—LORD BYRON

Every generation enjoys the use of a vast hoard bequeathed to it by antiquity, and transmits that hoard, augmented by fresh acquisitions to future ages.

—THOMAS MACAULAY

COLUMBUS

Behind him lay the gray Azores,
Behind the Gates of Hercules;
Before him not the ghost of shores;
Before him only shoreless seas.
The good mate said: "Now must we pray,
For lo! the very stars are gone.
Brave Adm'r'l, speak; what shall I say?"
"Why, say: 'Sail on! and on!' "

"My men grow mutinous day by day;
My men grow ghastly wan and weak."
The stout mate thought of home; a spray
Of salt wave washed his swarthy cheek.
"What shall I say, brave Adm'r'l, say,
If we sight naught but seas at dawn?"
"Why, you shall say at break of day:
'Sail on! sail on! sail on! and on!' "

They sailed and sailed, as winds might blow,
Until at last the blanched mate said:
"Why, now not even God would know
Should I and all my men fall dead.
These very winds forget their way,
For God from these dread seas is gone.
Now speak, brave Adm'r'l; speak and say—"
He said: "Sail on! sail on! and on!"

They sailed. They sailed. Then spake the
*   mate:*
"This mad sea shows his teeth tonight.
He curls his lip, he lies in wait,
With lifted teeth, as if to bite!
Brave Adm'r'l, say but one good word:
What shall we do when hope is gone?"
The words leapt like a leaping sword:
"Sail on! sail on! sail on! and on!"

Then, pale and worn, he kept his deck,
And peered through darkness. Ah, that night
Of all dark nights! And then a speck—
A light! A light! A light! A light!
It grew, a starlit flag unfurled!
It grew to be Time's burst of dawn.
He gained a world; he gave that world
Its grandest lesson: "On! sail on!"

—JOAQUIN MILLER

God gave man an upright countenance to survey the heavens, and to look upward to the stars.

—OVID

Many times a day I realize how much my own outer and inner life is built upon the labors of my fellowmen, both living and dead, and how earnestly I must exert myself in order to give in return as much as I have received.

—ALBERT EINSTEIN

A SERMON OF THE SKY

The heavens declare the glory of God. PS. 19:1

When the Hebrew came and walked out among the starry constellations, he saw it was God that has brought the glory down and let it be, and let the noon light shine on him with its glorious torch. He could not let the solar luster be unhuman. He could not let the glory fall in his eyes and ask no amazing, passionate question. But, instead, when he saw the glory, he saw through it the heavenly face as through an open window, and saw him—him! And the heavens, to the Hebrew mind, declared the glory of God. That is why the Hebrew vocabulary and the Hebrew understanding and the Hebrew poesy and the Hebrew profundity answer to the human heart. And this race of people, this nation, as it was the nation of thousands of years ago, was never content to let things rest as things. Behind the mathematics they sought the mathematician; behind the door they sought the maker of the door, and behind the stairway they sought the carpenter who built the stair, and behind the constellations they looked for the fingers of fire that flung the stars out into space. Then they called, "The heavens declare the glory of God."

—WILLIAM A. QUAYLE

ORION

Before the glory that was ancient Rome
Whose mighty legions made the world
   resound
With clash of arms—who brought their
   trophies home

And to the chariot wheels their captives
   bound;
Before "the beauty that was Greece"
   had birth
In breathing marble and fair Sappho's lay,
Or Babylon or Egypt ruled the earth
You marched in splendor down the
   starry way.

Kings, potentates, and empires lie in dust.
Our modern world is racked with strife
   and fears,
But you, oh great Orion, we can trust,
You have not failed us in ten million years.
We grovel with our eyes upon the sod,
You sing the praise and glory of our God.

—EMILIE D. STONEHILL

THE STARS

If a man would be alone, let him look at the stars. The rays that come from those heavenly worlds will separate between him and what he touches.

One might think the atmosphere was made transparent with this design, to give man, in the heavenly bodies, the perpetual presence of the sublime. Seen the streets of cities, how great they are!

If the stars should appear one night in a thousand years, how would men believe, and adore, and preserve for many generations, the remembrance of the city of God which had been shown? But every night come out these envoys of beauty, and light the universe with their admonishing smile.

—RALPH WALDO EMERSON

THE LURE OF THE UNKNOWN

Is it yesterday, or tomorrow, which makes today what it is? Which has the more power, the push of the past or the pull of the future? Both of these forces are operating steadily, but the future seems to have the upper hand. "Your young men shall see visions and your old men shall dream dreams."

They will be pulled along by that which their imaginations picture as possible. They go feeling their way after something, if haply they may find it. They find great sections of it—they catch up with their dreams, and then dream of something yet higher. It is the way of wholesome advance. The future is more powerful than the past, as a source of motive.

—CHARLES R. BROWN

YOUR FRIEND, GOD

In this vast universe
There is but one supreme truth—
That God is our friend!
By that truth meaning is given
To the remote stars, the numberless
   centuries,
The long and heroic struggle of mankind . . .
O my Soul, dare to trust this truth!
Dare to rest in God's kindly arms,
Dare to look confidently into His face,
Then launch thyself into life unafraid!
Knowing thou art within thy Father's house,
That thou art surrounded by His love,
Thou wilt become master of fear
Lord of life, conqueror even of death!

A NEW EARTH

God grant us wisdom in these coming days,
And eyes unsealed, that we clear visions see
Of that new world that He would have
   us build,
To Life's ennoblement and His high ministry.

God give us sense,—God-sense of Life's
   new needs,
And souls aflame with new-born chivalries—
To cope with those black growths that
   foul the ways,—
To cleanse our poisoned founts with
   God-born energies.

To pledge our souls to nobler, loftier life,
To win the world to His fair sanctities,
To bind the nations in a Pact of Peace,
And free the Soul of Life for finer loyalties.

Not since Christ died upon His lonely cross
Has Time such prospect held of Life's
   new birth;
Not since the world of chaos first was born
Has man so clearly visaged hope of a new
   earth.

Not of our own might can we hope to rise
Above the ruts and soilures of the past,
But, with His help who did the first
   earth build,
With hearts courageous we may fairer
   build this last.

—JOHN OXENHAM

OTHER WORLDS

Moon Colonies: An observatory on the moon would be a wonderful way to investigate the heavens, because the difficulties of the [Earth's] atmosphere would disappear. The atmosphere is the reason stars twinkle. This effect would be avoided, and one would be much better able to explore the heavens from the moon. Sometime, there might be such an observatory on the moon. I would not exclude the possibility at all.

Mars: I think that, simply because the moon doesn't have any life on it doesn't mean that there may not be life on Mars. If there's life on Mars, it is very probably a different life than on the Earth.

—HAROLD UREY

We are intelligent beings; and intelligent beings can not have been formed by a blind brute, insensible being. There is certainly some difference between a clod and the ideas of Newton. Newton's intelligence came from some greater Intelligence.

—AROUET DE VOLTAIRE

God's gift was that man should conceive
   of truth
And yearn to gain it, catching at mistake,
As midway help till he reach fact indeed.

—ROBERT BROWNING

ROAD MAKERS

We shall not travel by the road we make,
Ere day by day the sound of many feet
Is heard upon the stones that now we break,
We shall but come to where the cross-roads
    meet.

For us the heat by day, the cold by night,
The inch-slow progress and the heavy load,
And death at last to close the long, grim fight
With man and beast and stone: for them—
    the road.

For them the shade of trees that now we
    plant,
The safe, smooth, journey and the ultimate
    goal—
Yea, birthright in the land of covenant:
For us day-labour, travail of the soul.

And yet the road is ours, as never theirs;
Is not one thing on us alone bestowed?
For us the master-joy, oh, pioneers—
We shall not travel, but we make the road!

      —V. H. FRIEDLAENDER

Some have narrowed their minds, and so fettered them with the chains of antiquity that not only do they refuse to speak save as the ancients spake, but they refuse to think save as the ancients thought. God speaks to us, too, and the best thoughts are those now being vouchsafed to us. We will excel the ancients!

      —SAVONAROLA

THE QUEST

There is a Quest that calls me
  In night when I'm alone,
The need to ride where the ways divide
  The unknown from the known.
I mount what thought is near me
  And soon I reach the place,
The tenuous rim where the Seen grows dim
  And the Sightless hides its face.

I have ridden the wind,
I have ridden the sea,
I have ridden the moon and stars,
I have set my feet in the stirrup seat
Of a comet coursing Mars.
And everywhere
Thro' earth and air
My thought speeds, lightning-shod,
It comes to a place, where checking pace
It cries, "Beyond lies God."

      —CALE YOUNG RICE

Tho' world on world in myriad myriads roll
Round us, each with different powers,
And other forms of life than ours,
What know we greater than the soul?
On God and Godlike men we build our trust.

      —ALFRED TENNYSON

BETWEEN MIDNIGHT AND MORNING

You that have faith to look with fearless eyes
  Beyond the tragedy of a world at strife,
And trust that out of night and death
    shall rise
  The dawn of ampler life;
Rejoice, whatever anguish rend your heart,
  That God has given you, for a priceless
    dower,
To live in these great times and have your
    part
  In Freedom's crowning hour;
That you may tell your sons who see the light
  High in the heaven—their heritage to
    take—
"I saw the powers of darkness put to flight!
  I saw the morning break!"

      —OWEN SEAMAN

BIGOT

Though you be scholarly, beware
  The bigotry of doubt.
Some people take a strange delight
  In blowing candles out.

      —ELEANOR SLATER

STRUGGLES

Trials are medicines which our gracious and wise physician prescribes, because we need them; and he proportions the frequency and weight of them to what the case requires. Let us trust his skill and thank him for his prescription.

—ISAAC NEWTON

Life is mostly froth and bubble;
Two things stand like stone:—
Kindness in another's trouble,
Courage in our own.

—GORDON

EXAGGERATION

We overstate the ills of life, and take
Imagination, given us to bring down
The choirs of singing angels overshone
By God's clear glory,—down our earth
   to rake
The dismal snows instead;
   flake following flake,
To cover all the corn. We walk upon
The shadow of hills across a level thrown,
And pant like climbers. Near the alder-brake
We sigh so loud, the nightingale within
Refuses to sing loud, as else she would.
O brothers! let us leave the shame and sin
Of taking vainly, in a plaintive mood,
The holy name of Grief!—holy herein,
That, by the grief of One, came all our good.

—ELIZABETH BARRETT BROWNING

Go to your friend for sympathy; that is natural. Go to your books for comfort, for counsel. But the time will come when no book, no friend, can decide your problem for you; when nothing can help you, nothing can save you, but yourself. Begin now to stand alone.

—ANGELA MORGAN

There is a purity which only suffering can impart; the stream of life becomes snow-white when it dashes against the rocks.

—JEAN PAUL RICHTER

COMFORT

Say! You've struck a heap of trouble—
   Bust in business, lost your wife;
No one cares a cent about you,
   You don't care a cent for life;
Hard luck has of hope bereft you,
   Health is failing, wish you'd die—
Why, you've still the sunshine left you
   And the big, blue sky.

Sky so blue it make you wonder
   If it's heaven shining through;
Earth so smiling 'way out yonder,
   Sun so bright it dazzles you;
Birds a'singing, flowers a-flinging
   All their fragrance on the breeze;
Dancing shadows, green, still meadows—
   Don't you mope, you've still got these.

These, and none can take them from you;
   These, and none can weigh their worth.
What! You're tired and broke and beaten?
   Why, you're rich—you've got the earth!
Yes, if you're a tramp in tatters,
   While the blue sky bends above
You've got nearly all that matters—
   You've got God, and God is love.

—ROBERT W. SERVICE

It is by my fetters that I can fly; it is by my sorrows that I can soar; it is by reverses that I can run; it is by my tears that I can travel; it is by my cross that I can climb into the heart of humanity. Let me magnify my cross, O Lord!

—GEORGE MATHESON

True fortitude I take to be the quiet posession of a man's self, and an undisturbed doing his duty, whatever evil besets or danger lies in his way.

—JOHN LOCKE

In the deep, unwritten wisdom of life there are many things to be learned that cannot be taught. We never know them by hearing them spoken, but we grow into them by experience and recognize them through understanding. Understanding is a great experience in itself, but it does not come through instruction.

—ANTHONY HOPE

TELL ME ABOUT THE MASTER

Tell me about the Master!
  I am weary and worn tonight.
The day lies behind me in shadow,
  And only the evening is light.
Light with a radiant glory
  That lingers about the west,
My poor heart is aweary, aweary,
  And longs like a child for rest.

Tell me about the Master!
  Of the wrong He freely forgave,
Of His love and tender compassion,
  Of His love that is mighty to save.
For my heart is aweary, aweary,
  Of His woes and temptations of life,
Of the error that stalks in the noonday,
  Of falsehoods and malice and strife.

Yet, I know that whatever of sorrow,
  Or pain or temptation befall,
The Infinite Master has suffered,
  And knoweth and pitieth all.
So tell me the old, old story
  That falls on each wound like a balm,
And my heart that was burdened and broken
  Shall grow patient, and calm, and strong.

THE SHIP THAT SAILS

I'd rather be the ship that sails
  And rides the billows wild and free;
Than to be the ship that always fails
  To leave its port and go to sea.

I'd rather feel the sting of strife,
  Where gales are born and tempests roar;
Than to settle down to useless life
  And rot in dry dock on the shore.

I'd rather fight some mighty wave
  With honor in supreme command;
And fill at last a well-earned grave,
  Then die in ease upon the sand.

I'd rather drive where sea storms blow,
  And be the ship that always failed.
To make the ports where it would go,
  Than be the ship that never sailed.

In a sinless and painless world the moral element would be lacking; the goodness would have no more significance in our conscious life than that load of atmosphere which we are always carrying about with us.

We are thus brought to a striking conclusion, the essential soundness of which can not be gainsaid. In a happy world there must be pain and sorrow, and in a moral world the knowledge of evil is indispensable. The stern necessity for this has been proved to inhere in the inner-most constitution of the human soul. It is part and parcel of the universe.

We do not find that evil has been interpolated into the universe from without; we find that, on the contrary, it is an indispensable part of the dramatic whole. God is the creator of evil, and from the eternal scheme of things diabolism is forever excluded.

From our present standpoint we may fairly ask, what would have been the worth of that primitive innocence portrayed in the myth of the Garden of Eden, had it ever been realized in the life of men? What would have been the moral value or significance of a race of human beings ignorant of sin, and doing beneficent acts with no more consciousness or volition than the deftly contrived machine that picks up raw material at one end, and turns out some finished product at the other? Clearly, for strong and resolute men and women, an Eden would be but a fool's paradise.

—JOHN FISKE

THE LAST MINSTREL

The way was long, the wind was cold,
The Minstrel was infirm and old;
His withered cheek, and tresses grey,

Seemed to have known a better day;
The harp, his sole remaining joy,
Was carried by an orphan boy.
The last of all the Bards was he,
Who sung of Border chivalry;
For, welladay! their date was fled,
His tuneful brethren all were dead;
And he, neglected and oppressed,
Wished to be with them, and at rest,
No more on prancing palfrey borne,
He carolled, light as lark at morn;
No longer courted and caressed,
High placed in hall, a welcome guest,
He poured to lord and lady gay
The unpremeditated lay:
Old times were changed, old manners gone;
A stranger filled the Stuarts' throne;
The bigots of the iron time
Had called his harmless art a crime.
A wandering Harper, scorned and poor,
He begged his bread from door to door,
And tuned, to please a peasant's ear,
The harp a king had loved to hear.

—WALTER SCOTT

ENDURANCE

If some great angel came to me to-night,
   Bearing two fatal cups, and bade me sip
The sweet contentment or the bitter fight,
   I know full well which draught would
      kiss my lip.
Give me the suffering. Let me taste the dregs
   Of life's full cup of bitterness, and share
The tortured hour of silent night that begs
   Oblivion from the pale eyes of Despair.
Then, and then only, shall my love be free
   From earth-born shackles. Gladness
      never clears
The heart of selfish dross, or yields the key
    Which opens the flood-gates of
      enhallowed tears.
Give me the suffering! But I would be
    strong,
   To meet the hours bravely, with a song!

When sickness comes and bids us rest awhile
In some calm pool, beside life's too swift
   stream,

Why rail at Fate, and count ourselves ill
   used?
'Tis then one's soul awakes, weaves dream
   on dream.

THEIR FINEST HOUR

The whole fury and might of the enemy must very soon be turned on us. Hitler knows that he will have to break us in this island or lose the war. If we can stand up to him, all Europe may be free and the life of the world may move forward into broad, sunlit uplands. . . . Let us therefore brace ourselves to our duties, and so bear ourselves that, if the British Empire and its Commonwealth last for a thousand years, men will say, "This was their finest hour."

—WINSTON CHURCHILL

THE HARD JOB

It's good to do the hard job, for it's good
   to play the man,
For the hard job strengthens courage
   which the easy never can.
And the hard job, when it's over,
   gives the man a broader smile—
For it brings the joy of knowing that's he's
   done a thing worth while.

Oh, stand you to your hard job with the
   will to see it through,
Be glad that you can face it and be glad
   it's yours to do;
It is when the task is mighty and the
   outcome deep in doubt,
The richest joys are waiting for the man
   who'll work it out.

Beyond the gloom of failure lies the glory
   to be won,
When the hard job is accomplished and
   the doubtful task is done;
For it's manhood in the making and its
   courage put to test—
So buckle to the hard job—it's your chance
   to do your best.

—EDGAR A. GUEST

GIVE ME THE HEART OF A MAN

More than half beaten, but fearless,
  Facing the storm and the night;
Breathless and reeling, but tearless,
  Here in the lull of the fight,
I who bow not but before Thee,
  God of the Fighting Clan,
Lifting my fists I implore Thee,
  Give me the heart of a Man!

What though I live with the winners,
  Or perish with those who fall?
Only the cowards are sinners,
  Fighting the fight is all.
Strong is my Foe—he advances!
  Snapt is my blade, O Lord!
See the proud banners and lances!
  Oh, spare me this stub of a sword!

Give me no pity, nor spare me;
  Calm not the wrath of my Foe.
See where he beckons to dare me!
  Bleeding, half beaten—I go.
Not for the glory of winning,
  Not for the fear of the night;
Shunning the battle is sinning—
  Oh, spare me the heart to fight!

Red is the mist about me;
  Deep is the wound in my side;
"Coward" thou criest to flout me?
  O terrible Foe, thou hast lied!
Here with my battle before me,
  God of the Fighting Clan,
Grant that the woman who bore me
  Suffered to suckle a Man!

—JOHN G. NEIHARDT

THE TIRED HEART

Dear Lord, I bear a tired heart tonight
And need that Thou shouldst come and
  comfort me,
For well I know what rest and peace will
  come
Upon the weary soul which turns to Thee.

Take Thou my lifted hands within Thine
  own,
And let me know that prayer will bring
  Thee near.

And that no cry of pain or sigh for help
Will fail to reach Thine ever-listening ear.

So though I bear a tired heart tonight,
I know that Thou wilt come and comfort me,
And with the morn the heaviness will pass,
And joy will come because of trust in Thee.

I have recently become aware that in the history of human endeavor physical and material force has determined success or failure only in a proportion of thirty per cent, while spiritual force has amounted to seventy per cent of the total strength exerted.

With men and women it is the same. If their faith is firm, their spirit robust and their hearts inspired with high resolve they can, despite bodily weakness, support whatever suffering they are called upon to endure and actually profit by their weakness. If on the other hand their spirit falters and their will is weak the best physique will not enable them to recover from setbacks and face dangers and difficulties.

—MADAME CHIANG KAI-SHEK

GRACE TO DO WITHOUT

My heart rejoices in God's will,
  'Tis ever best—I do not doubt;
He may not give me what I ask,
  But gives me grace to do without.

I blindly ask for what I crave,
  With haughty heart and will so stout;
He oft denies me what I seek,
  But gives me grace to do without.

He makes me love the way He leads,
  And every fear is put to rout;
When, with my fondest wish denied,
  He gives me grace to do without.

O blessed, hallowed will of God,
  To it I bow with heart devout;
I will abide in all God's will,
  His will is best, I do not doubt;
He may not give me what I ask,
  But gives me grace to do without.

MY TRIUMPH

Others shall sing the song,
Others shall right the wrong,—
Finish what I begin,
And all I fail to win.

What matter, I or they?
Mine or another's day,
So the right word be said,
And life the sweeter made?

Ring, bells in unreared steeples,
The joy of unborn peoples!
Sound, trumpets far-off blown,
Your triumph is my own!

—JOHN GREENLEAF WHITTIER

PAIN

Why must I be hurt?
Suffering and despair,
Cowardice and cruelty,
Envy and injustice,
All of these hurt.
Grief and terror,
Loneliness and betrayal
And the agony of loss or death—
All these things hurt.
Why? Why must life hurt?
Why must those who love generously,
Live honorably, feel deeply
All that is good—and beautiful
Be so hurt,
While selfish creatues
Go unscathed?
That is why—
Because they can feel.
Hurt is the price to pay for feeling.
Pain is not accident,
Nor punishment, nor mockery
By some savage god.
Pain is part of growth.
The more we grow
The more we feel—
The more we feel—the more we suffer,
For if we are able to feel beauty,
We must also feel the lack of it—
Those who glimpse heaven

Are bound to sight hell.
To have felt deeply is worth
Anything it cost.
To have felt Love and Honor,
Courage and Ecstasy
Is worth—any price.
And so—since hurt is the price
Of Larger living, I will not
Hate pain, nor try to escape it.
Instead I will try to meet it.
Bravely, bear it proudly:
Not as a cross, or a misfortune, but an
Opportunity, a privilege, a challenge—
to the God that gropes within me.

—ELSIE ROBINSON

Though you be scholarly, beware
The bigotry of doubt.
Some people take a strange delight
In blowing candles out.

—ELEANOR SLATER

HUNGERING HEARTS

Some hearts go hungering thro' the world
And never find the love they seek.
Some lips with pride or scorn are curled
To hide the pain they may not speak.
The eyes may flash, the mouth may smile—
And yet beneath them all the while
The hungering heart is pining still.

For them does life's dull desert hold
No fountain's shade, no gardens fair,
Nor gush of waters clear and cold,
But sandy reaches wide and bare.
The foot may fail, the soul may faint,
And weigh to earth the weary frame,
Yet still they make no weak complaint
And speak no word of grief or blame.

O eager eyes, which gaze afar,
O arms which clasp the empty air,
Not all unmarked your sorrows are,
Not all unpitied your despair.
Smile, patient lips, so proudly dumb—
HAVE FAITH! Before life's tent is furled
Your recompense shall come,
O hearts that hunger through the world!

WORSHIP

We worship Thee whose will hath laid
Thy sovereign rule on all things made;
The faithful stars, the fruitful earth,
Obey Thy laws that gave them birth.

We turn aside and tread the ways
That lead through wonder up to praise;
Wherever Thou by man art found
The homely earth is holy ground.

—HENRY VAN DYKE

All the way to heaven is heaven.
—CANON FARRAR

An old hymn says,
"Brethren, we have met to worship,
And adore the Lord our God;
Will you pray with all your power,
While we try to preach the word?
All is vain unless the Spirit
Of the Holy One comes down;
Brethren, pray, and holy manna
Will be showered all around."

The kingdom of God is a society of the best men, working for the best ends, according to the best methods. Its law is one word—loyalty; its gospel one message—love. If you know anything better, live for it; if not, in the name of God and of humanity, carry out Christ's plan.

—HENRY DRUMMOND

Christians are supposed not merely to endure change, nor even to profit by it, but to cause it.

—HARRY EMERSON FOSDICK

This, then, is Christianity: to smash the barriers and get next to your fellowman.

—JOHN T. FARIS

Take the Sunday with you through the week,
And sweeten with it all the other days.

—HENRY WADSWORTH LONGFELLOW

Acquaint thyself with God, if thou wouldst taste His works.

—WILLIAM COWPER

Those who know the path to God, can find it in the dark.

—IAN MACLAREN

THY PRESENCE

Thy calmness bends serene above
My restlessness to still;
Around me flows Thy quickening life,
To nerve my faltering will;
Thy presence fills my solitude;
Thy providence turns all to good.

—SAMUEL LONGFELLOW

Worship is the highest act of which man is capable. It not only stretches him beyond all the limits of his finite self to affirm the divine depth of mystery and holiness in the living and eternal God, but it opens him at the deepest level of his being to an act which unites him most realistically with his fellow man.

—SAMUEL H. MILLER

My God, my Father, while I stray,
Far from my home in life's dark way,
O teach me from my heart to say,
"Thy will be done!"

—CHARLOTTE ELLIOTT

The life of every moment is a phenomenon of God's heart. Every task is the combustion of the flame of God. He greets us in the kitchen. He gazes intently upon us at the well-curb. In the bustle and hustle of the factory or when hanging on the strap in the crowded car we breathe God. When we lift the iron sledge and are hammering out the steel we are in God's bosom.

This is the mood of the true soul. To be drunk, not with liquor, but with God. To feast to one's heart's content, not on food, but on God. In dreaming and in waking hours, in sorrow and in laughter, to walk in a world flooded with light, this is a phenomenon experienced only by those who truly know the soul's art.

In the castle of my soul
Is a little postern gate,
Whereat, when I enter,
I am in the presence of God.
In a moment, in the turning of a thought,
I am where God is.
This is a fact.

When I enter into God,
All life has a meaning.
Without asking, I know;
My desires are even now fulfilled,
My fever is gone
In the great quiet of God.
My troubles are but pebbles on the road,
My joys are like the everlasting hills.

So it is when my soul steps through the
*   postern gate*
Into the presence of God.
Big things become small, and small things
*   become great.*
The near becomes far, and the future is near.
The lowly and despised is shot through
*   with glory.*

God is the substance of all revolutions;
When I am in him, I am in the Kingdom
*   of God*
And in the Fatherland of my Soul.

DESIGN

This is a piece too fair
To be the child of Chance, and not of Care.
No Atoms casually together hurl'd
Could e'er produce so beautifull a world.

JOHN DRYDEN

Who taught the raven in a drought to throw pebbles into a hollow tree where she espied water, that the water might rise so as she might come to it? Who taught the bee to sail through such a vast sea of air, and to find the way from a flower in a field to her hive? Who taught the ant to bite every grain of corn that she burieth in her hill, lest it should take root and grow?

—FRANCIS BACON

WALK WITH GOD

Is it possible for any of us in these modern days to so live that we may walk with God? Can we walk with God in the shop, in the office, in the household, and on the street? When men exasperate us, and work wearies us, and the children fret, and the servants annoy, and our best-laid plans fall to pieces, and our castles in the air are dissipated like bubbles that break at a breath, then can we walk with God? That religion which fails us in the every-day trials and experiences of life has somewhere in it a flaw. It should be more than a plank to sustain us in the rushing tide, and land us exhausted and dripping on the other side. It ought, if it come from above, to be always, day by day, to our souls as the wings of a bird, bearing us away from and beyond the impediments which seek to hold us down. If the Divine Love be a conscious presence, an indwelling force with us, it will do this.

He who believes in God is not careful for the morrow, but labors joyfully and with a great heart. "For He giveth His beloved, as in sleep." They must work and watch, yet never be careful or anxious, but commit all to Him, and live in serene tranquillity; with a quiet heart, as one who sleeps safely and quietly.

—MARTIN LUTHER

God often visits us, but most of the time we are not at home.

—JOSEPH ROUX

WORSHIP

*It is a good thing to give thanks unto the
Lord, and to sing praises unto thy name,
O most High: To shew forth thy
loving-kindness in the morning, and thy
faithfulness every night.
Upon an instrument of ten strings, and
upon the psaltery; upon the harp with a
solemn sound.
For thou, Lord, hast made me glad through
thy work;
I will triumph in the works of thy hands.
O Lord, how great are thy works! and thy
thoughts are very deep.*

—PSALMS 92:1-5

TRIUMPH OF HIS GRACE

*O, for a thousand tongues to sing
  My dear Redeemer's praise!
The glories of my God and King,
  The triumphs of His grace!*

*My gracious Master and my God!
  Assist me to proclaim,
To spread thro' all the earth abroad,
  The honors of Thy name.*

*Jesus—the name that calms my fears,
  That bids my sorrows cease;
'Tis music to my ravished ears;
  'Tis life, and health, and peace.*

*He breaks the power of canceled sin,
  He sets the prisoner free;
His blood can make the foulest clean;
  His blood availed for me.*

—CHARLES WESLEY

NOR EYE HAS SEEN

*Nor eye has seen, nor ear has heard,
  Nor sense nor reason known
What joys the Father has prepar'd
  For those that love the Son.*

*But the good Spirit of the Lord
  Reveals a heaven to come:
The beams of glory in His Word
  Allure and guide us home.*

*Those holy gates forever bar
  Pollution, sin and shame;
None shall obtain admittance there
  But followers of the Lamb.*

*He keeps the Father's book of life,
  There all their names are found;
The hypocrite in vain shall strive
  To tread the heavenly ground.*

—ISAAC WATTS

THROUGH HIS NAME

*I look at the sun, and I think of the power
  And majesty of God;
I look on the earth where the flowers bloom,
  And I think of the path he trod.
I look at the trees, and think of the wood
  Which made his cross of shame;
Then I look in my heart, and see my sin,
  And believing, I've life through his name.*

SACRIFICE

*The keynote of life's harmony is sacrifice.
  Not twice nor thrice
Of will, or time, or pleasure-giving treat,
But many times
  that life's chord may be sweet.*

* Who sacrifices most
Drinks deepest life's rich strain,
  counting no cost,
But giving self on every side,
Daily and hourly sanctified,
  But in the giving
    Living
Is but the straining of the strings,
The growth of harmony's pure wings.
Life is the tuning time, complete
Alone when every chord is sweet
Through sacrifice. No untried string
  Can music bring.
    True living
Is learning all about the giving.*

GIVE ME HARD TASKS

*Give me hard tasks,
  with strength that shall not fail;*

Conflict, with courage that shall never die!
Better the hill-path, climbing toward the sky,
Than languid air and smooth
sward of the vale!

Better to dare the wild wrath of the gale
Than with furled sails in port forever lie!
Give me hard tasks,
with strength that shall not fail;
Conflict with courage that shall never die!

Not for a light load fitting shoulders frail,
Not for an unearned victory I sigh;
Strong is the struggle that wins triumph high,
Not without loss the hero shall prevail;
Give me hard tasks,
with strength that shall not fail!

It takes no brains to be an atheist. Any stupid person can deny the existence of a supernatural power because man's physical senses cannot detect it. But there cannot be ignored the influence of conscience, the respect we feel for moral law, the mystery of first life on what once must have been a molten mass, or the marvelous order in which the universe moves about us on this earth. All of these evidence the handiwork of a beneficent Deity. For my part, that Deity is the God of the Bible and of Christ, his Son.

—DWIGHT D. EISENHOWER

Some persons think God must be dead or asleep or on a journey. They see such stalking evils, such collapses of civilization, such ugly shadows over the fair world, that they cannot hold their thin clew of faith any longer. It has snapped and left them standing alone in their dark cave.

But He is there all the same, though they see Him not nor know Him. He does not vanish in the dark or in the storm. There is much love working still in these hard, dark days.

—RUFUS M. JONES

CALL FOR REDEEMERS

Think not there is one Calvary alone.
Nor say the soul of truth but once can
die.
In every age the mob cries, "Crucify!"
In every age the Pharisees are known.
Who speaks for truth must plead to hearts
of stone.
Who fights for truth must face the
cynic lie,
Must know the martyr's fiery agony
In every age, till wrong is overthrown.

There is a Lincoln statue down the way,
And men beside it gather, old and gray,
Seeing forgotten years, as old men can.
"In every age," one says,
"God finds his man."
"God's man," another answers.
"Man's man too,
Yet how men hated him—
before they knew!"

Count me o'er earth's chosen heroes—
they were souls that stood alone,
While the men they agonized for
hurled the contumelious stone,
Stood serene, and down the future
saw the golden beam incline
To the side of perfect justice,
mastered by their faith divine,
By one man's plain truth to manhood
and to God's supreme design.
Then to side with Truth is noble
when we share her wretched crust,
Ere her cause bring fame and profit,
and 'tis prosperous to be just;
Then it is the brave man chooses,
while the coward stands aside,
Doubting in his abject spirit,
till his Lord is crucified,
And the multitude make virtue
of the faith they had denied.

—JAMES RUSSELL LOWELL

Every morning lean thine arms awhile
Upon the window-sill of heaven
And gaze upon thy Lord,
Then, with the vision in thy heart,
Turn strong to meet thy day.

CAPTURED

Hast thou heard Him, seen Him,
   known Him,
   Is not thine a captured heart?
Chief among ten thousands own Him,
   Joyful choose the better part.

What has stripped the seeming beauty
   From the idols of the earth?
Not a sense of right or duty,
   But the sight of peerless worth.

Not the crushing of those idols,
   With its bitter void and smart;
But the beaming of His beauty,
   The unveiling of His heart!

'Tis that look that melted Peter,
   'Tis that Face that Stephen saw,
'Tis that Heart that wept with Mary
   Can alone from idols draw.

Draw and win and fill completely,
   Till the cup o'erflow the brim;
What have we to do with idols
   Who have companied with Him?

DELAY

I loved Thee late
   Too late I loved Thee, Lord,
Yet not so late
   But Thou dost still afford
The proof that Thou wilt bear
   With winning art,
One sinner more
   Upon Thy loving heart.
And may I prove,
   When all my warfare's past,
Though late I loved Thee,
   I loved Thee to the last.

—St. Augustine

NEVER

There is never a day so dreary
But God can make it bright
And to the soul that trusts Him
He giveth songs in the night.

There is never a path so hidden
But God will lead the way
If we seek for His loving guidance
And patiently wait and pray.

There is never a cross so heavy
But the nail-scarred hands are there
Outstretched in tender compassion
The burden to help us bear.

There is never a heart so broken
But the loving Lord can heal
For the heart that was pierced on the hill top
Doth still for the sorrowing feel.

There is never a life so darkened
So hopeless and so unblest
But may be filled with the light of God
And enter His promised rest.

There is never a sin or sorrow
There is never a care or loss
But that we may bring it to Jesus
And leave at the foot of His cross.

—Lilla M. Alexander

HOLD FAST YOUR DREAMS

Hold fast your dreams!
Within your heart
Keep one still, secret spot
Where dreams may go,
And, sheltered so,
May thrive and grow
Where doubt and fear are not.
O keep a place apart,
Within your heart,
For little dreams to go!

MY GOD AND I

The stars shine over the mountains,
   the stars shine over the sea,
The stars look up to the mighty God,
   the stars look down on me;
The stars shall last for a million years,
   a million years and a day,
But God and I will live and love when
   the stars have passed away.

—Robert Louis Stevenson

❖ YOUTH ❖

The important thing is that children should grow up with parents who believe that there are some ways of life which for us today are better than others and that these ways are worth defending with every ounce of our strength.

—ANNA W. M. WOLF

OF ANCIENT SHACKLES

I am among those unregenerates
Who do not seek "New Freedom,"
   who enjoy
The ancient shackles of old-fashioned love,
Of faith and duty, and would not destroy
All moorings of the spirit that are old.
I like old-fashioned, peaceful firesides,
The steadfastness old homes and
   gardens knew;
I hold the old belief that love abides,
The old sustaining credences of men
That God must be the nurture of the soul,
That He will lean and listen to a prayer
And watches every man move toward his
   goal.
I am an unemancipated one
Who wears such fetters with a full content;
I see New Freedom's tortured restlessness
And of my bonds am deeply reverent.

—ADELAIDE LOVE

Nothing is impossible to a valiant heart.

THE BAREFOOT BOY

Blessings on thee, little man,
Barefoot boy, with cheek of tan!
With thy turned-up pantaloons,
And thy merry whistled tunes;
With thy red lip, redder still,
Kissed by strawberries on the hill;

With the sunshine on thy face,
Through thy torn brim's jaunty grace,
From my heart I give thee joy,—
I was once a barefoot boy.
Prince thou art,—and grown-up man
Only is republican,
Let the million-dollared ride!
Barefoot, trudging at his side,
Thou hast more than he can buy,
In the reach of ear and eye—
Outward sunshine, inward joy;
Blessings on thee, barefoot boy!
Oh, for boyhood's painless play,
Sleep that wakes in laughing day,
Health that mocks the doctor's rules,
Knowledge never learned of schools,
Of the wild bee's morning chase,
Of the wild flower's time and place,
Flight of fowl and habitude
Of the tenants of the wood;
How the tortoise bears his shell,
How the woodchuck digs his cell,
And the groundmole sinks his well;
How the robin feeds her young,
How the oriole's nest is hung,
Where the whitest lilies grow,
Where the freshest berries grow,
Where the ground-nut trails its vine,
Where the wood-grape's clusters shine,
Of the black wasp's cunning way,—
Mason of his walls of clay,—
And the architectural plans
Of gray-hornet artisans!—
For, eschewing books and tasks,
Nature answers all he asks,
Hand in hand with her he walks,
Face to face with her he talks,
Part and parcel of her joy,—
Blessings on the barefoot boy!

Oh, for boyhood's time of June,
Crowding years in one brief moon,
When all things I heard or saw,
Me, their master, waited for.
I was rich in flowers and trees,
Humming-birds and honeybees,
For my sport the squirrel played,
Plied the snouted mole his spade;
For my task the blackberry cone
Purpled over hedge and stone;
Laughed the brook for my delight

Through the day and through the night,—
Whispering at the garden wall,
Talked with me from fall to fall;
Mine the sand-rimmed pickerel pond,
Mine the walnut slopes beyond,
Mine, on bending orchard trees,
Apples of Hesperides!
Still, as my horizon grew,
Larger grew my riches too;
All the world I saw or knew
Seemed a complex Chinese toy
Fashioned for a barefoot boy.

Oh, for festal dainties spread,
Like my bowl of milk and bread,—
Pewter spoon and bowl of wood,
On the doorstone, gray and rude!
O'er me, like a regal tent,
Cloudy-ribbed, the sunset bent,
Purple-curtained, fringed with gold,
Looped in many a wind-swung fold.
While for music came the play
Of the pied frog's orchestra,
And, to light the noisy choir,
Lit the fly his lamp of fire.
I was monarch: pomp and joy
Waited on thee, barefoot boy!

Cheerily, then, my little man,
Live and laugh as boyhood can!
Though the flinty slopes be hard,
Stubble-speared the new-mown sward,
Every morn shall lead thee through
Fresh baptisms of the dew;
Every evening from thy feet
Shall the cool wind kiss the heat;
All too soon these feet must hide
In the prison cells of pride,
Lose the freedom of the sod,
Like a colt's for work, be shod,
Made to tread the mills of toil,
Up and down in ceaseless moil;
Happy if their track be found
Never on forbidden ground;
Happy if they sink not in
Quick and treacherous sands of sin,
Ah! that thou couldst know the joy,
Ere it passes, barefoot boy!

—John Greenleaf Whittier

Love and desire are the spirit's wings to great deeds.
—Goethe

YOUTH

Alfred Tennyson wrote his first volume at eighteen.

Alexander was a mere youth when he rolled back the Asiatic hordes that threatened to overwhelm European civilization almost at its birth.

Napoleon had conquered Italy at twenty-five.

Byron, Raphael and Poe died at thirty-seven after writing their names among the world's immortals.

Newton made some of his greatest discoveries before he was twenty-five.

It is said that no English poet ever equaled Chatterton at twenty-one.

Victor Hugo wrote a tragedy at fifteen. Many of the world's greatest geniuses never saw forty years.

ON YOUTH

The whole secret of remaining young in spite of years, and even of gray hairs, is to cherish enthusiasm in oneself, by poetry, by contemplation, by charity,—that is, in fewer words, by the maintenance of harmony in the soul. When everything is in its right place within us, we ourselves are in equilibrium with the whole work of God. Deep and grave enthusiasm for the eternal beauty and the eternal order, reason touched with emotion and a serene tenderness of heart—these surely are the foundations of wisdom.

—Henri Frederic Amiel

HEAR, O YOUTH

Young men, you are the architects of your own fortunes. Rely upon your own strength of body and soul. Take for your star, self-reliance. Don't take too much advice—keep at your helm and steer your own ship, and remember that the great art of commanding is to take a fair share of the work. Think well of yourself. Strike out. Be in earnest. Be self-reliant. Be generous. Be civil. Read the papers. Advertise your business. Make money, and do good with it. Love your God and fellow men. Love truth and virtue. Love your country and obey its laws.

—Porter

THANK GOD FOR YOUTH

Youth—heir of the sufferings, ministries, achievements of past generations; whose lifeblood is the very lifeblood of those who give them birth; whose intellectual grasp is the product of patient tutelage at home and at school; whose spiritual ideals root in the great souls of yesterday and today—youth, heir of all the past.

Youth—come into a wanton world created by the sin and stupidity of its elders; handicapped by the mistakes of well-meaning but blind generations; burdened but not overwhelmed by the immensity of the problems of the hour—youth, creature of the past but creator of the future.

Youth—energetic and dissatisfied, sometimes moved by a reckless restlessness and again by a divine discontent; misguided and uncontrolled, at times, wasting its substance in riotous living; divinely motivated and sublimely purposed, at times, daring to attempt a perfection which seems, to cautious older minds, to be idealistic folly—youth, unwilling to accept the world as it is.

Youth—suffering deep pent-up sorrows, enduring well-nigh crushing defeats, hoping against tremendous odds, fighting cruel inner battles, winning unheralded but glorious triumphs—youth, victim and victor.

Christian youth—captured by the dream of the young Idealist of Nazareth, impelled by the lofty concerns which led him to Calvary; Christian youth, seeking to know and follow the will of God, embracing all human kind within the family circle; determined to rid the world of its besetting sins and unnecessary sorrow—Christian youth, with whom the name "Christian" takes on a new and yet its oldest, meaning.

O CHILD OF TODAY

O Child, had I thy lease of time!
*   such unimagined things*
Are waiting for that soul of thine
*   to spread its untried wings!*

Shalt thou not speak the stars,
*   and go on journeys through the sky?*
And read the soul of man as clear
*   as now we read the eye?*

Who knows if science may not find
*   some art to make thee new,—*
To mend the garments of thy flesh
*   when thou has worn them through.*

'Tis fearful, aye, and beautiful,
*   thy future that may be.*
How strange;—perhaps death's conqueror
*   sits smiling on my knee!*

—JAMES BUCKHAM

I AM JUST A YOUNG MAN

Scores say this: "I am just a young man." In other words, what thousands of men today would like to be! A potentiality with his face to the East! A lifetime stretching ahead! The Book of Life with clean pages to be written on as he may elect! "Just a young man" in a time like this: in a land like this: in a world like this! Then he deprecates himself! In a land of opportunity where every chance beckons and every road invites! A road straight and clear, and the high peaks of achievement beyond—and oh! so few on them! To carve out of Life what one wills! How many men there are who would gladly give all they possess to have that chance once more!

—EDWARD W. BOK

He wears the rose of youth upon him.

—SHAKESPEARE

POETRY INDEX

Authors, Titles, and First Lines

195

❧PROSE INDEX❧

Authors and Titles